Female

Talha Fadaak

Female Poverty in Saudi Arabia

A study of poor female headed households, social policies and programmes in Jeddah City

LAP LAMBERT Academic Publishing

Impressum / Imprint

Bibliografische Information der Deutschen Nationalbibliothek: Die Deutsche Nationalbibliothek verzeichnet diese Publikation in der Deutschen Nationalbibliografie; detaillierte bibliografische Daten sind im Internet über http://dnb.d-nb.de abrufbar.
Alle in diesem Buch genannten Marken und Produktnamen unterliegen warenzeichen-, marken- oder patentrechtlichem Schutz bzw. sind Warenzeichen oder eingetragene Warenzeichen der jeweiligen Inhaber. Die Wiedergabe von Marken, Produktnamen, Gebrauchsnamen, Handelsnamen, Warenbezeichnungen u.s.w. in diesem Werk berechtigt auch ohne besondere Kennzeichnung nicht zu der Annahme, dass solche Namen im Sinne der Warenzeichen- und Markenschutzgesetzgebung als frei zu betrachten wären und daher von jedermann benutzt werden dürften.

Bibliographic information published by the Deutsche Nationalbibliothek: The Deutsche Nationalbibliothek lists this publication in the Deutsche Nationalbibliografie; detailed bibliographic data are available in the Internet at http://dnb.d-nb.de.
Any brand names and product names mentioned in this book are subject to trademark, brand or patent protection and are trademarks or registered trademarks of their respective holders. The use of brand names, product names, common names, trade names, product descriptions etc. even without a particular marking in this works is in no way to be construed to mean that such names may be regarded as unrestricted in respect of trademark and brand protection legislation and could thus be used by anyone.

Coverbild / Cover image: www.ingimage.com

Verlag / Publisher:
LAP LAMBERT Academic Publishing
ist ein Imprint der / is a trademark of
AV Akademikerverlag GmbH & Co. KG
Heinrich-Böcking-Str. 6-8, 66121 Saarbrücken, Deutschland / Germany
Email: info@lap-publishing.com

Herstellung: siehe letzte Seite /
Printed at: see last page
ISBN: 978-3-659-22643-4

Zugl. / Approved by: Liverpool, University of Liverpool, Diss., 2011

Copyright © 2012 AV Akademikerverlag GmbH & Co. KG
Alle Rechte vorbehalten. / All rights reserved. Saarbrücken 2012

Abstract

Combating poverty in Saudi Arabia has become an important national target; this study researches poverty in Saudi Society and in particular, female poverty, focusing on poor female-headed households (FHHs) in Jeddah City. This is an exploratory study to highlight the social reality of the FHHs and their female heads, with a focus on the details of their everyday lives and their relationships with social support institutions, namely: the Social Security Department (SSD) and the Charitable Women's Associations. The main aim of this study is to explore the social reality of these families and how, during their struggles to obtain or maintain a standard of living, they interact with these social support institutions. The study investigated a main sample of 112 FHHs represented by their female heads who were selected purposefully according to a matrix designed to ensure adequate representation across the main sample according to marital status, age group and place of residence (south or north) in Jeddah City. They were also selected by their marital status according to five sub-groups: widows' families, divorced women's families, abandoned women's families, prisoners' wives' families and finally married women's families. A further sample was 18 informants (called 'elites') who were selected purposefully from a range of experts, officials and decision makers from different governmental and non-governmental departments to explore and interpret issues raised during the women's interviews. The interviews with the female heads were based on questions designed to achieve four main goals: 1- to study and identify the social, cultural and demographic characteristics of poor FHHs in Jeddah City. 2- to study and present the poor FHHs' experiences and how they interacted with their social reality. 3- to study social policies in practice and highlight the relationship between the FHHs and the social support institutions. 4- to make recommendations for formulating an effective social policy for combating poverty among women and poor FHHs in Saudi society. The data and information was collected via different methods such as interviews, document searches, observations, field notes and digital recordings. The data was organized and analysed using a thematic approach to reduce the data, present it and provide conclusive statements. The main findings are organized in chapters 5, 6 and 7 and cover the study goals. The main findings are as follows:

The typical poor FHHs were mostly large families and the male head tended to be missing from family life, thus the family was headed by the female. The women had suffered divorce, widowhood, imprisonment of their husbands, abandonment, or their husbands suffered sickness, old age or unemployment. These female heads were mostly uneducated or had a low or basic level of education. The families typically had no regular earned income because the head of the family was not in employment. The majority of the FHHs were tenants and lived in small flats. A significant number of FHHs was deprived of both official support from the SSD and from the women's associations for various reasons. Some of the women were regarded legally and socially as minority groups because of their ethnicity, family backgrounds and/or nationality. These details provided an honest and clear picture of the lives of the poor FHHs and showed the inter-penetrated realms of these families and their heads that were: 1- public realms (society, culture, state, welfare systems and social support institutions); 2- private realms (women's worlds, specific stories and experiences that had led the women to head their families such as divorce, widowhood, abandonment or the imprisonment of the head of the family). The details of everyday life showed how the sub-categories and their female heads had a similar experience in some aspects of the public realm but they experienced quite different private realms. The study concludes with some important strategic, public and specialized recommendations aimed at improving and reforming the current welfare system and social policies and suggests integrated social policies to eradicate poverty in general and among FHHs in particular.

Acknowledgments

I would like to take this opportunity to express my sincere gratitude to the people who have been very supportive throughout my journey in completing this thesis; without them, it would not have been possible for me to fulfil my research.

My supervisor, Professor Ken Roberts, who has always been ready to give me steady encouragement, constructive feedback and honest opinions and guidance throughout the work.

All the staff and postgraduate students at the School of Sociology and Social Policy at the University of Liverpool, for their generous assistance.

All the female heads of households connected with the SSD and the Charitable Women's Associations (FWS and KWS) and other charitable residences (CH) whose stories and experiences form the core of this research and who allowed me access to their lives and shared their sadness, happiness, dreams and also their food.

All the staff of the social security department (SSD) at the main office in Riyadh and the main office at Jeddah and in particular, the General Manager of the SSD Jeddah office, Mr Abduallah Al–Tawee for all his assistance and his facilitation of the difficulties faced in a male work environment.

All staff of the Ministry of Social Affairs (MSA) who helped me and provided me with data, information and case studies, especially Mr Muhammed Al-Okla, Undersecretary of the Ministry of Social Affairs. Also Dr Abdullah Bin S. Muaigel, General Secretary of the National Poverty Reduction Strategy (NPRS) and the National Charity Fund (NCF).

All the managers, staff and social work departments in all the three Charitable Women's Associations at Jeddah City, especially KWS and FWS. Also my special thanks to Lyla

Gamal, the Director of Dar Al-Ramah (charitable housing) who provided me with useful discussions on female poverty in Saudi society and with some significant case studies.

Special thanks to my colleague, Dr Mishan Al-Otaibi, the Dean of Distance Learning, University of Taibah, Saudi Arabia, who provided me with help and support during this study to clarify and understand a lot of things relevant to the conceptual work on poverty and research methodologies and who continued to read and revise my work and provided me with wonderful insights.

My special thanks to Ms Alice Bennett, who read my work many times and provided me with a lot of support and comments regarding the language and writing style and also her encouragement to keep me going.

Lastly, I offer my regard and blessing to all those who supported me in many ways during the completion of this research.

This research is dedicated to:

My husband Salim.

My parents Fatimah and Hussein.

My daughter Amal.

All the poor people of Saudi Arabia and in particular, poor women and female-headed households who suffer and struggle in silence and who asked me to deliver their voices to the decision makers to create the necessary and fair changes in their lives in line with social justice. They are strong women but they deserve immediate and rational solutions for improved and fair life conditions.

The thinkers, scholars, philosophers and activists who inspire us to dream and fight for a better, fairer world.

Publication arising from this research

Fadaak, T. (2010), Poverty in the Kingdom of Saudi Arabia: An Exploratory Study of Poverty and Female-headed Households in Jeddah City. Social Policy & Administration, 44: 689–707.
 doi: 10.1111/j.1467-9515.2010.00738.x

Table of Contents

Abstract	I
Acknowledgments	III
Dedication	V
Publication arising from this research	VI
Table of content	VII
List of Tables	X
List of figures	XII
Abbreviations	XIII
Preface	XIV

Introduction	1
Chapter one : Theoretical background and literature review	8
Introduction…………………………………………………………………..	8
1.1 Poverty: concepts and definitions………………………………………….	9
1.2 Poverty measurement………………………………………………………	11
1.3 Poverty and gender issues: global perspectives…………………………..	14
Conclusion……………………………………………………………………..	24

Chapter two : Poverty in Islam and the Islamic world	26
Introduction…………………………………………………………………..	26
2.1. Poverty in the Islamic context…………………………………………….	27
2.1.1 Conceptual framework………………………………………………….	28
2.1.2 Islamic perspective and policy framework for eradication of poverty	39
2.2 Poverty in contemporary Islamic countries: the dilemma of theory and practice……………………………………………………………………….	52
2.3.Women and poverty in Islam…………………………………………….	57
Conclusion……………………………………………………………………..	61

Chapter three: Poverty within the Arabic and Saudi Contexts	65
Introduction ……………………………………………………………………	65
3.1 Poverty in the Arabic Context…………………………………………….	65
3.2 Poverty in the Saudi Context……………………………………………...	76
3.3 Welfare System and Social Policies for the Eradication of Poverty in KSA	85

3.4 Finances..	91
3.5 Projects and programmes for alleviation and eradication of poverty in KSA...	94
3.6 Female poverty in Saudi Arabia...	101
Conclusion...	106

Chapter four: The Research Problem and Research Methodology   108

Introduction	108
4.1 Research problem...	109
The importance of research...	109
Statement of the research problem: the main research goals, operational objectives, and research questions	112
Research limitations...	113
Operational definitions of the main research concepts...................................	116
Difficulties...	118
4.2 Research methodology..	120
The research design / approach...	120
Three main methods (key strategies) for gaining study goals.........................	121
1. Comprehensive reading...	122
2. Meeting the experts and officials...	122
3. In-depth qualitative study of FHHs..	124
Data collections tools...	140
Data treatment (data management and data analysis)....................................	146
Language and translation..	148
Ethical considerations..	150

Chapter five: The socio-cultural and demographic characteristics of poor female headed households in Jeddah City (poverty profile)   153

Introduction...	153
5.1 The study site: Jeddah City, the place, the culture and the people.............	153
5.2 Number of poor in Jeddah City at the time of the field study (2009)..........	156
5.3 Description of social, cultural and demographic characteristics of the sample.	157
Conclusion: typical poor FHHs...	167

Chapter six: The social reality of the everyday lives of poor female-headed households   169

Introduction...	169
6.1 The definition of some terms...	169
6.2 Interviews with the study sample...	170
6.2.1 The case of widow's families' category: home without pillars...............	170
6.2. 2 The case of divorced women's families...	191

6.2.3 The case of abandoned women's families (a horny life/ or complexity of life)... 213
6.2.4 The case of the prisoners' wives families (families in the wind).............. 231
6.2.5 The case of the married women's families (shadow of a man is better than a shadow of the wall).. 243
Conclusion 259

Chapter seven : Social Policy in Practice   261

Introduction... 261
7.1 Analysis of the interviews with FHHs to explore social policy in practice...... 261
7.2 Analysis and results of the interviews with elite informants........................ 269
7.3 Recommendations for reforming, improving and formulating effective social policies for the eradication of poverty among FHHs...................................... 278

Chapter eight: Conclusions   298

Introduction... 298
8.1 Summary of thesis content... 299
8.2 Summary of the main findings in the light of the objectives and the research questions.. 300
8.3 Implications for policy... 307
8.4 Recommendations for further studies.. 307

Bibliography   311

Appendices   325

Appendix A: Plan and timetable of the stages of the field work........................ 326
Appendix B: Interview questions for the female heads of households............... 327
Appendix C: Socio-cultural and demographic characteristics of FHHs (profile)... 329
Appendix D: Interview schedule for the elite informants and decision-makers.... 330
Appendix E: Coding cases.. 331
Appendix F: List of elite informants and decision makers who were interviewed.. 332
Appendix G: List of consulted policy documents... 334

List of Tables

Title	Page
Table 3.1 Population of KSA 1425 H (2004)	76
Table 3.2 Population of Mecca province 1425 (2004)	76
Table 3.3 Housing Units (Occupied with Households), Households, and Individuals, in all the provinces of Saudi Arabia (total population, Saudi and non-Saudi)	77
Table 3.4 Housing Units (Occupied with Households), Households, and Individuals, in Mecca province (total population, Saudi and non-Saudi)	77
Table 3.5 Number of the poor (beneficiaries) in KSA on the income support system of SSD (SSP) (2004/2005) according their categories	84
Table 3.6 Numbers of the poor (beneficiaries) in Mecca province on the income support system for (SSP) and (SSUB) 1425H-1426H (2004/2005).	85
Table 3.7 Numbers of charities and women's associations in the KSA (2004-2005).	90
Table 3.8 Budget and financial allocations of SSD paid to the beneficiaries as SSP and SSUB 1426-1425 (2004-2005)	91
Table 3.9 Budget and financial allocations of charitable associations paid to beneficiaries as social assistance 1427 (2006)	92
Table 3.10 Increases in SSP compensations for individuals and families from 1963 to 2005	93
Table 3.11 unemployment rate by sex and nationality	103
Table 3.12 Numbers of beneficiaries on SSP & SSUB in all kingdoms 2006/2007	104
Table 3.13: Numbers of beneficiaries on SSP in Mecca province 2006/2007	105
Table 4.1: the procedures and methods of the in-depth qualitative study via the three research visits	125
Table 4.2: Number of poor FHHS in Jeddah 1429-1428 (2007-2008)	128
Table 4.3: The matrix shows the distribution of a purposive sample for 60 FHHs according to the area of the city, age and marital status.	130

Table 4.4: The numbers of FHHs who were interviewed during fieldwork — 137

Table 4.5: the distribution of FHHs / women who were interviewed according to the institution from which they were drawn — 137

Table 4.6: topics and themes of the in-depth interview schedule (guide). — 141

Table 4.7: Elite informants who were interviewed during the fieldwork — 144

Table 5.1: Total number of poor in Jeddah City 2008- 2009 according to the organizations from where the sample was selected — 156

Table 5.2: Distribution of FHHs according to the educational level of the female heads — 157

Table 5.3: Distribution of FHHs according to the job of the female head — 158

Table 5.4: Distribution of FHHs according to the main source of income — 159

Table 5.5: Distribution of FHHs according to their living area — 160

Table 5.6: Distribution of FHHs according to the number of family members — 160

Table 5.7: Distribution of FHHs according to the type of their houses — 161

Table 5.8: Distribution of FHHs according to ownership of their houses — 161

Table 5.9: Distribution the FHHs according to the places from where they were selected — 162

Table 5.10: Distribution of FHHs according to receipt of SSD — 162

Table 5.11: Distribution of FHHs according to being supported by charitable associations — 163

Table 5.12: Distribution the FHHs according to the female head's nationality — 163

Table 5.13: Distribution of the FHHs according to their tribal backgrounds — 164

Table 5.14: Distribution of the FHHs according to the female head's ethnicity — 164

Table 5.15: Distribution the FHHs according to the places of residence of their families — 165

Table 5.16: Distribution of FHHs according to their husband's or ex-husband's nationality — 166

Table 5.17: Distribution the FHHs according to origin of the female heads — 167

Table 6.1 Summary of the special features and needs of widows' families — 189

XI

List of figures

Title	Page
Figure 3.1 The structural organization of Ministry of Social Affairs Ministry of Social Affairs	87
Figure 3.2: Increases in SSP compensations for individuals and families from 1963 to 2005	93
Figure 3.3: Unemployment rate by males and females for Saudis citizens from 2001 to 2007	103
Figure 5.1: Map of Saudi Arabia and the geographical location of Jeddah City	154

Abbreviations

BWS: Al Bir Welfare Society.
CCPF: Care Committee for Prisoners' Families.
DMSS: Deputy Minister of Social Security.
EK: Ektefaa association.
FHHs: Female-Headed Households.
FWS: Al Fasylaya Women's Welfare Society.
GDI: Gender-related Development Index.
GDP: Gross Domestic Product.
GCC: Gulf Cooperative Countries.
HPI: Human Poverty Index.
HDI: Human Development Index.
HDR: Human Development Report.
AHDR: Arab Human Development Report.
JUO: Jeddah Urban Observatory.
KWS: First Welfare Society.
KSA: Kingdom of Saudi Arabia.
MSA: Ministry of Social Affairs.
MEP: Ministry of Economy and Planning.
ML: Ministry of Labour.
MFA: Ministry of Foreign Affair.
MHHs: Male-Headed Households.
MDGs: Millennium Development Goals.
NPRS: National Poverty Reduction Strategy.
NCF: National Charity Fund.
OWSMP: Office of Women's Supervision in Mecca Province.
PPP: Purchasing Power Parity.
SSD: Social Security Department.
SSP: Social Security Pension.
SSUB: Social Security Subsidy.
SSOs: Social Security Offices.
UNDP: United Nation Development Programme.
UN-ESCWA: United Nations Economic and Social Commission for Western Asia.

Preface

The terms 'poverty' and 'women' in Saudi Arabia are at once complex and loaded with controversy. They are the source of a great deal of discussion, whether they are dealt with as separate subjects or treated as a pair (as in "women's or female poverty"). Many socio-cultural and political factors overlap and interact to create what we can call the "Saudi scene" in which certain issues can be difficult or unusual to discuss in public – and among these issues are "poverty" and also "women".

Saudi Arabia is an oil-rich country with the world's largest oil reserves, and yet it has remained for decades very conservative in dealing with poverty as a serious problem. The major turning point occurred when the Crown Prince Abdullah bin-Abdul-Aziz visited slum areas in the capital Riyadh in 2002. The problem of poverty was thus officially recognized and from then on was discussed openly in public as a serious issue, with the eradication of poverty being formally set as a national target. However, women's issues were (and remain) shrouded by the veils of a mainstream traditional culture that is well-known for its strict and conservative attitude towards women in general.

Considering these contextual issues regarding the terms "women" and "poverty", I arrived at a line of research that would enable me to address the core problem by investigating "Social policy for the eradication of poverty among FHHs" as the subject for my PhD thesis.

As a sociologist, women's issues were at the core of my interest. Therefore my critical thinking centred on the social reality of women, both indoors and outdoors, and also on the conflict and contradiction between a traditional culture (that narrows women's participation and space in the public arena) and the typical image of women in Islam (in which the space is wider and women's position is more significant). Put simply, I concentrated on the socio-cultural context of women within the public and private spheres in Saudi Arabia. My previous postgraduate research experience had expanded my cultural knowledge and enabled me to gain greater access into Saudi women's realms. In particular, I had investigated family support and kinship relations in contemporary Saudi society by means of a socio-anthropological study that was undertaken in 2003 with a focus on a sample of families in Jeddah City. One of the significant results of this study was to reveal how FHHs suffer as a result of the lack of family support in a transitional society such as Saudi. Consequently, FHHs and single mothers appear on the margins of society as noticeably vulnerable categories, and this is the result of many variables that influence family structural and kinship relations within a changing Saudi society. This is because family responsibilities and moral obligations within contemporary Saudi families have been subject to many changes and have been influenced by modernity. However, civil society institutions, that in other 21st century societies would play a crucial role in supporting vulnerable groups, are not found in the same form in Saudi Arabia. This is because of the transitional nature of contemporary Saudi society that is located part-way between tradition and modernity, and all social systems remain influenced by this state of flux, pulled by the opposing tides of tradition and modernity. So what can women do in a society where there is no family support and no clarity about the role of civil institutions?

In 2004, I took a post as an academic lecturer in the Department of Social Work in Umm-Alqura University, Mecca. At that time, in addition to my teaching duties, I took part in the supervision and practical training of female undergraduate students. This training would usually take place within various governmental or non-governmental institutions serving various categories of vulnerable people such as elderly care homes, institutions caring for orphans, charities and women's associations where the beneficiaries are predominantly poor women and FHHs. With regard to this latter group, since I was close to the environment of poor women and FHHs, I was well aware of how the system could often be blind to issues relating to female poverty. In addition, I realised how wide was the gap between the theoretical side in these institutions (the rules and regulations) and the practical side (how the regulations were being applied). Therefore, when preparing a proposal for a PhD, the combined issues of social policy and female poverty were at the top of my subject list.

Something that had encouraged me to think deeply about social policy is that "Social Policy" as an academic subject does not exist in Saudi universities, nor is the role of social policy in promoting well-being clearly understood in Saudi society. Accordingly, there is an urgent need in Saudi Arabia for this specialization to take root, to enable social policy specialists to play a future role in supporting policy-makers with evidence-based research. My own choice of investigating "social policy and female poverty" makes me the first such researcher in this area. Also, my gender, as a woman choosing to work in this field in Saudi society, gives me an especially significant position

All the preceding factors influenced my selection of this subject, in which my primary intentions were twofold. First, I wanted to shed light on the real lives of poor females who head Saudi families, and especially to show their struggles, hopes, and dreams for their families, as well as their relationships with the social welfare system (both formal and informal). Second, I hoped that my thesis would not become one of those relics on a university bookshelf, but rather that the results of this research would reach decision-makers in Saudi governmental bodies, informing them as they develop social welfare policies particularly with respect to poor women and FHHs.

In the meantime, after four years of having researched this subject, I can say that although it has undoubtedly proved a correct selection for me, it was not without its difficulties. This was because of many challenges, including the following:

The complexity and overlap between poverty, social policy and gender issues;

The cultural considerations that surround the women's arena in Saudi society, restricting access to the world of women in general and poor women in particular;

The special nature of Saudi society has certain methodological implications for matters such as the selection and application of research methods, data collection, data analysis and interpretation, as well as ethical issues, obstacles, the implications of being a female researcher, and so on.

In terms of the first challenge, as mentioned above, the themes of poverty, social policy and gender have interlocked dimensions. In Saudi society, it is never easy for a researcher to gain access to official data or information, nor to make a direct arrangement to meet relevant decision-makers or policy-makers. In my case, I was obliged to depend on my personal relationships to enable me to access various gatekeepers (members of the same communities being researched) who in turn were able to operate as access points. In addition, personal contacts enabled me to make contact with some decision-makers and senior figures in various ministries and official departments. These in turn helped me to gain access to the world of poor women via the Department of Social Security – which is staffed exclusively by male employees - and women's associations.

The second challenge – of gaining access to the women's arena in Saudi Arabia – was a context in which the idea of being an 'insider' was more useful than being an 'outsider'. In my own case, as an indigenous researcher (researching within my own society), I was able to understand the positions of the local women and the cultural implications of my own society more closely than if I had been a non-indigenous researcher. On the other hand, this closeness might also have had some disadvantages – for example, being an insider implies subscribing to the cultural norms and values of the group and to the sanctions that follow a breach of valued behaviours, which means applying the same moral judgment. This placed more obligations on my mission, especially when I was required to meet some male decision-makers in their own (exclusively masculine) work environment, as well as to meet many FHHs within the Social Security Department - which is also an exclusively male environment. In all these situations, I had to pay particular attention to my appearance (including the wearing of hijab) and to be careful about my interactions with men (by leaving the necessary distance, by not speaking loudly or laughing, and by not shaking hands, nor looking directly into their eyes). I needed to reflect what was expected from me as a Saudi woman even though I had studied (and was continuing to study) abroad. I did not forget, on making my first visit to these institutions, to take my brother with me, since this gave me more respect. If I had broken any of these cultural rules, I would have been subjected to a negative moral judgment, which might have had a damaging effect on my research mission.

The methodological considerations presented another challenge, to the extent that the preparation and justification of the research tools took around one year. During that period, three stages (exploratory, pilot testing and main fieldwork) were applied to the examination, development and application of the research methods and data collection tools. The interview guide was developed progressively and the focus group technique was eventually omitted due its non-effectiveness as a method within the Saudi context. Another challenge was presented by the overlapping variables of 'class' and 'gender': Saudi women cannot be treated as a single category because the classification process within Saudi society itself involves women as part of their communities and social groups. This classification considers several determinants including social and economic status (whether wealthy, middle class, or poor), race and ethnicity (whether black or white, with or without Arab blood), and family origins (whether Bedouin/rural or urban, tribal or non-tribal, Saudi by origin or by naturalization). Thus, women in each category face specific issues and problems, and yet they are also surrounded by the dominant sub-cultural values and norms. However, all women's categories are subject to the impact of the general traditional cultural framework which monitors women's practice and behaviour in their daily lives, and organizes their relationships within the private and public spheres. Accordingly, to set and formulate my research problem, two essential variables were carefully combined: those of 'class' and 'gender'. Class in this context means how poor women and FHHs can be considered because of their status to be part of the 'Saudi poor' in general, since these women participate with other poor people in the same living conditions and social circumstances, but in addition they have a special position as women. The 'gender dimension' has a particular impact on the lives of poor women and FHHs in Saudi Arabia, since such women are living in a society that enhances gender differences and gender segregation, and women's issues are treated within a traditional cultural framework. This means that poor women participate alongside other (non-poor) women in the general socio-cultural context, but they also experience this differently by virtue of being women in poverty.

In this context, poor women would be expected to suffer more than other poor categories and would also suffer more than non-poor women. So the fact of being a 'poor female' means having to face two types of condition: the condition of their class (of being part of the poor class) and the condition of their gender (being women). In general, their position as poor women in poor FHHs gives them another 'poverty gender classification'.

In terms of data analysis and interpretation, I combined the manual method and NVivo8 software for reducing, coding and recoding the qualitative data. Also I used SPSS to organize the socio-cultural and demographic characteristics of cases. The data analysis and interpretations are based on the Arabic, Islamic and Saudi perspectives on poverty in general and female poverty in particular, with a view to examining the role of society and the state in relation to female poverty.

Introduction

Poverty is considered a big problem that precludes the continuous socio-economic development process of society; moreover, this problem may lead to an increase in the crime rate and bring about social and political instability (UN-ESCWA, 2003: 1). However, poverty seems to be a global phenomenon that is not exclusive to developing countries or the Third World but is also seen in developed and industrial countries that have issues such as social injustice and social inequality (1).

Exclusion and inclusion are universal features of social interaction, and institutions serve to structure these processes through the state, market, communities, and voluntary associations (Jordan, 1996: 39). Therefore, poverty involves several dimensions that are related to how individuals interact with society, culture, and modern life requirements within a certain social and cultural context. In addition, it is important to consider how the state and civil institutions deal with the needs of the poor.

According to the Combat Poverty Agency and Equality Authority (2003), people are living in poverty if their income and resources do not allow them to have a socially acceptable standard of living. Consequently, they may be marginalised and excluded from participation in activities that are available to other people in that society.

As statistics show, one in five of the world's population - two thirds of them women - live in abject poverty (Short, 2000:6). Furthermore, almost half of the population of the Last Development Countries (LDCs) lives in extreme poverty (Poverty Forum 2006). In the Middle East and North Africa, the proportion of the population living on less than $1 per day in 2004, adjusted to take PPP (Purchasing Power Parity) into consideration, was 3.4%. However, when the international poverty line was defined as $2 per day per person, estimates suggested a ratio of 31.5% (UN, 2005).

---

[1] - For instance, look at the implication of this problem in Western countries in: Gordon, David and Peter Townsend (2000).

The United Nations is an important global organisation that has made considerable efforts to combat poverty around the world. In December 1995, the general assembly proclaimed the first United Nations resolution for the eradication of poverty (1997-2006); the assembly declared the theme for the decade as a whole to be "Eradicating poverty is an ethical, social, political and economic imperative of humankind" (UN, 2006). However, the Department of Economic and Social Affairs organised a forum on 15-16 November 2006 at the United Nations headquarters in New York to mark the end of the first UN decade for the eradication of poverty (1997-2006) (UN, 2006). Economists, civil society leaders, and representatives from governments, academia, the private sector and international organisations met to discuss the main challenges and novel ways to reduce poverty (UN-Department of Public Information, 2006).

In the Arab world, many local and regional (territorial) organizations are interested in poverty such as ESCWA (Economic and Social Commission for Western Asia) and AGFUND (Arabic Gulf Programme for United Nations Development Organisation). Many studies have been conducted by the ESCWA into the social and economic development of Arab countries, which are related to issues such as poverty, social policy, women empowerment, and democratic and political reform.

In addition to this, AGFUND is a non-profit regional development institution, established in 1980 by the initiative of Prince Talal Bin Abdul Aziz Al Saud, with the support of the leaders of the Arab Gulf States that constitute its membership and contribute to its budget. AGFUND is concerned with the support of sustainable human development efforts targeting the neediest in developing countries (AGFUND, 2006).

In the Kingdom of Saudi Arabia, poverty used to be a sensitive issue and difficult to talk about, but after the visit of Prince Abdullah Ben Abdul-Aziz (2) to the slum areas in the capital Riyadh in 2003, poverty has been highlighted and has revealed a category of Saudi people living in extreme poverty in a country that is supposed to be rich. Prince Abdullah adopted a new vision to deal with this problem by declaring that poverty is a serious problem, and that an anti-poverty strategy should be formulated to overcome

---

[2] - Currently King of Saudi Arabia.

this problem. Therefore, the eradication of poverty has become a national target and the Poverty Fund Programme (3) has been established to support the government anti-poverty strategy.

Many studies have been conducted to identify the extent and type of poverty in Saudi Arabia; these are necessary for establishing an effective anti-poverty strategy. However, although a massive budget has been spent, the results so far have been unsatisfactory. One of the barriers to be faced is the lack of statistics monitoring the poverty situation in Saudi Arabia. A journalist's report published online showed that some unofficial reports indicate that more than 1/2 million people live in poverty in Saudi Arabia; another report from the Saudi Department of Statistics claimed the rate of unemployment among the Saudi workforce to be 8.5%; some international statistics raise that to 12% while other sources cite an unemployment rate of 15%-20% (Islam Online, 2005).

A report published in Alriyadh newspaper on 24 May 2005 presented the results of a survey conducted by the Ministry of Public Works and Housing. The results showed that 51% of Saudi households did not have a stable income; 40% had an income of less than 6000 Riyal monthly (4) whereas 9% had unlimited income (Islam online, 2005).

The problem of poverty has a special implication among poor women, which is relevant to the gender dimension. Although there have not been any serious studies showing gender differences in poverty in Saudi society, many official reports by the Social Security Division and by charitable women's associations have indicated that the numbers of poor women and poor female-headed households (FHHs) who are entitled to social benefits and social support, are greater than the numbers of poor men and poor households headed by males (Al-Shubiki, n.d, p 12). Therefore, poverty in Saudi Arabia, particularly among women who are heads of households, is a complicated issue that needs to be investigated and that highlights the multi-dimensions of poverty in respect of women, family, society and state.

---

[3] - Poverty fund: This programme aims to alleviate poverty and investigate poor people's problems.
[4] - One sterling Pound equals nearly (7) Riyals.

Therefore, this research attempts to investigate the social policies and programmes for the eradication of poverty among poor FHHs in Saudi society. It investigates the social, cultural and demographic characteristics of FHHs. The research then discusses how poor female heads of household understand the meaning of their poverty, and how these women conduct and deal with everyday life. In addition, we will look at what sort of relationships have been developed between these women, and state and civil society organisations (private sector organisations and women's charitable associations) in terms of the sort of benefits and social support to which they are entitled. The researcher will indicate the extent to which the social policies and programmes for the alleviation and eradication of poverty are compatible or incompatible with the real life requirements of the FHHs.

My thesis is presented in three main parts: theoretical background and literature review; methodology; and analysis.

The theoretical background and literature review provides the basis from which the discussion is considered. This is included in Chapters One, Two and Three.

Chapter One discusses the theoretical background and a global literature review. This includes poverty definitions, measurements, and poverty and gender issues. This chapter aims to build a fundamental understanding of poverty concepts and their implications. It also explores the overlap and interpenetration of poverty and gender issues, and how these are mirrored in international studies.

Chapter Two is concerned with Poverty within Islam and Islamic world. This chapter provides an essential theoretical framework for data analysis. It addresses the following three issues:

We consider how poverty is conceptualised in an Islamic perspective, where discussion will be based upon the "normative system" or "value system" of Islam, as reflected in the scriptures of the Qur'an and Sunnah (Hadith). Accordingly, the section seeks to present an interpretation of the social meaning of Islamic religious texts relating to poverty and related concepts. The main themes of this section include poverty definitions and the Islamic policy framework for the eradication of poverty.

A second issue is how poverty as a social problem has existed as a result of weaknesses in the social structure of contemporary Islamic societies. The discussion here involves the system of practice that mirrors the social reality of these societies; it also illustrates how poverty has multiple dimensions (in the political, economic, social, religious and cultural spheres).

A third issue is the situation of women and poverty from an Islamic perspective. This section aims to provide some evidence on Islam's position towards the gender dimensions of poverty. In particular, we raise the question of how gender and poverty have been approached from an Islamic perspective, and we raise the question of whether Islam is able, through its value system, to present a distinctive social vision of this particular problem.

Chapter Three discusses poverty in both pan-Arab and Saudi contexts. It is divided into seven sections mainly focusing on two issues. The first is poverty in the Arabic context, and the second is poverty in the Saudi context. Poverty in the Arabic context discusses and reviews some poverty studies in the Arabic world, and how the Arabic region has been presented in UNDP reports. Poverty in the Saudi context starts with background information on the KSA and presents evidence on poverty in Saudi society through reviewing existing studies and reports. The chapter also discusses the welfare system and social policies for the eradication of poverty in Saudi as well as mentioning female poverty via some government statistics on female unemployment and female poverty according to the SSD statistics.

Chapter four is on methodology, and provides in-depth details about where and how the research was conducted. The methodological rich details are presented through two linked elements in this chapter: the 'research problem' and 'research methodology'. It is evident that these are strongly connected. The research problem is presented and the chapter identifies the key concepts of the research, goals, and questions. The methodology is explained in detail: how the research goals were to be achieved and how the research questions would be answered. This involves the research design (approach), the data collection tools, the strategy for data analysis and the interpretation of the results.

Chapters five to seven provide the main themes of data analysis. Chapter five explores the socio-cultural and demographic characteristics of the poor female headed households in Jeddah City (poverty profile) by considering two questions: who are these poor households, and who are these female breadwinners? Then the chapter presents aspects of their socio-cultural and demographic characteristics. At the beginning of this chapter, there is some background information on Jeddah City, the study site.

Chapter six is the core analysis of this study which offers a deep discussion of the everyday lives of five sub-groups in the sample of FHHs. It. discusses rich details of the daily lives of the poor female heads that were reflected in their interviews. The chapter is divided according to the five categories of FHHs who are widows, divorced women, abandoned women, prisoners' wives, and finally the married women's families. Each category presents stories followed by a discussion of the stories in that category. More consideration is given to issues such as: 1- The social reality of that category of FHHs and how the family became poor as well as how the woman became the breadwinner and head of the family. 2- The barriers and problems that are faced by heads of FHHs. 3- Finally the requirements and needs of that category. In this chapter we shall see that the female heads talked and reflected through their words on their struggles with poverty and their needs within their unseen or hidden world.

Chapter seven is about social policies and how they work in practice. There are important policy implications which are reached through discussing the results of the interviews with the female heads on the one side and with the key informants on the other. The chapter proceeds as follows. 1- Analysis of the interviews with the FHHs to explore the social policy applications in practice, drawing on the women's experiences with the social support institutions. 2- Analysis of the interviews with the elite informants to reveal their views on issues relevant to the poor FHHs. 3- On the basis of the foregoing, suggestions and recommendations to improve and formulate effective social policies for poverty reduction. These recommendations are arranged by level: strategic, general, and detailed recommendations. The recommendations are to be forwarded to the decision makers in several official bodies in the political system, local authorities and social support organizations.

The last chapter is chapter eight and presents a brief conclusion addressing the following. 1- Thesis summary. 2- Summary of the main findings in the light of the research objectives and research questions. 3- Implications for policy, and finally 4- Recommendations for further studies.

Chapter one
Theoretical background and literature review

Introduction

This chapter aims to dissect the concept of poverty as presented in the global poverty literature. There are limitations as to what can be included: firstly, there is an abundance of literature and theoretical debates on poverty, which vary according to the different contexts of developed and developing countries (see for example Vecchio & Roy 1998). Secondly, this review is restricted by word limit so choices had to be made about the most relevant topics to focus upon. Finally, the aim of this chapter is to give an introductory account on the most important poverty concepts relevant to this research, therefore the focus is on poverty definitions, poverty measurement and poverty and gender issues.

This chapter provides analysis of the global viewpoint of poverty based on poverty literature that provides essential poverty concepts. A fundamental methodological point to make at this stage is that this research in its investigation, data analysis, and findings and their interpretation will rely on a specific framework with a focus on the Saudi, Arabic, and Islamic perspectives on poverty and female-headed households (FHHs). Thus the review of the global literature on poverty in this chapter will benefit the analysis when the researcher compares the findings of her study with implications that might arise from the global literature on poverty, specifically in respect of female poverty and FHHs.

This chapter is divided into three main sections: poverty definitions that provide different concepts and definitions of poverty; poverty measurement, which shows how poverty is measured in accordance with different perspectives and finally, poverty and gender issues, where revised studies in this section focus on female poverty, FHHs, social policy and welfare reform in developed and developing countries.

1.1 Poverty: concepts and definitions

There is no singular agreed definition of poverty because the term has multi-dimensions. Yet attitudes to this term are shaped on the basis of social, economic and political visions of society. Poverty definitions indicate various types of poverty and where it is shaped and exists according to particular standards and indicators. The most common distinction is made between 'absolute' and 'relative' poverty.

'Absolute poverty' is one model of poverty in which the definition is based on the minimum standard needed for subsistence. Classic studies of poverty with this meaning were conducted in the UK by Charles Booth and Seebohm Rowntree (see Booth 1902, Rowntree 1901) where Booth studied poverty in London using income as a measurement and presented the concept of a ' poverty line' which was defined as a level below which families were unable to meet their needs for subsistence. In his study of poverty in York, Rowntree also used the subsistence definition (see Rowntree, 1901).

In March 1995 in Copenhagen, the World Summit for Social Development was convened by the United Nations, where 117 heads of state declared that the governments had to set a goal for eradicating absolute poverty and the alleviation of overall poverty in the world during the 21st century (UN, 1995). In this summit, a developed definition for poverty was adopted and two concepts were considered: absolute and overall poverty. Absolute poverty is defined as:

> a condition characterised by severe deprivation of basic human needs including food, safe drinking water, sanitation facilities, health, shelter and information. It depends not only on income but also on access to services (UN, 1995: 75).

Another model of poverty is 'relative poverty', based on comparisons of poor people with others in the same society. One of the classic definitions of poverty with this meaning is by Townsend (1979: 31):

> Individuals, families and groups can be said to be in poverty when they lack the resources to obtain the type of diet, participate in the activities and have the living conditions and amenities which are customary, or at least widely encouraged or

approved, in the society to which they belong. They are, in effect, excluded from ordinary living patterns, customs and activities.

The Copenhagen Summit pointed to a similar meaning in its definition of 'overall poverty' where overall poverty was defined as follows:

> Poverty has various manifestations, including lack of income and productive resources sufficient to ensure sustainable livelihoods; hunger and malnutrition; ill health; limited or lack of access to education and other basic services; increased morbidity and mortality from illness; homelessness and inadequate housing; unsafe environments; and social discrimination and exclusion. It is also characterised by a lack of participation in decision-making and in civil, social and cultural life... (UN 1995, cited in Gordon and Townsend, 2000: 49, 50).

Thus, overall poverty, according to the preceding point of view, means not being able to obtain or access those things that society and other people deem to be basic necessities, as well as not being able to do things that most people take for granted because they either cannot afford to participate in the usual activities, or because they are discriminated against in other ways. Thus, overall poverty seems similar in many aspects to the 'relative' and 'consensual' definitions of poverty that have been used in poverty surveys in Europe for many decades (Gordon and Spicker, 1999, cited in Gordon and Townsend 2000: 52).

The United Nation Development Programme (UNDP, 1997) introduced a concept of 'Human Poverty' in its report entitled 'Human Development to Eradicate Poverty'. This report mentioned poverty from the perspective of human development, which means more than income poverty; it is the denial of choice and opportunities for living a tolerable life. This report outlined the Human Poverty Index (HPI) that measures deprivation in basic human development using the same dimensions as the Human Development Index (HDI): longevity, knowledge and a decent standard of living. The variables used in HPI are the percentage of people expected to die before the age of 40, the percentage of adults who are illiterate, and overall economic provision in terms of the percentage of people without access to health services and safe water, and the percentage of under-weight children under five (UNDP, 1997).

The World Bank has defined poverty as 'the inability to attain a minimal standard of living' (WB, 1990: 26, 27). In this definition, the World Bank is concerned with the world's poorest but with little interest in the wider social conditions of the people in the poorest countries. However, the World Bank has adopted a poverty line of $1 per day income per person which has been designed as a "universal poverty line which is needed to permit cross-country comparison and aggregation" (Gordon and Townsend, 2000: 83; Spicker *et al.*, 2007: 227). The World Bank (WB, 1996) established a set of country-specific poverty assessments that bring together quantitative and qualitative data based on different indicators such as household surveys; poverty profiles; participatory studies; beneficiary assessments; public expenditure reviews; country-economic memoranda and sector reviews. Consequently, the WB could identify key poverty issues for each country and bring together different definitions of poverty (cited in Spicker *et al.*, 2007: 228).

In a joint report on social protection and social inclusion presented by the European Commission (2006a), poverty and social exclusion are defined as complex and multi-dimensional forms related to income and living standards, access to good quality health services, education and work opportunities. The report outlines how the European Union has adopted a multi-dimensional perspective based on a set of indicators agreed at EU level to monitor progress in this area. These indicators are in three dimensions: the income dimension of poverty and social exclusion, the labour market dimension of poverty and social exclusion, and the skills and health dimensions.

It is clear that each definition of poverty has its implications within specific contexts.

1.2 Poverty measurement

Poverty definition is important in order to develop poverty measures. Hence, the definition of poverty necessarily implies indicators that show what poverty is and who suffers from it. Definitions should highlight how poverty should be measured and which indicators are the most adequate for measuring particular types of poverty. For instance, some studies and statistics mention a "poverty line" as a measurement of 'income poverty', whereas some organizations such as the World Bank and the UN indicate different methods. The UNDP considers an 'index of human development' as a measurement of 'human poverty', while the World Bank adopts some elements in addition to the poverty line to measure poverty. The EU reports multi-dimensional indicators for poverty measurement. Some bodies such as the Poverty and Social Exclusion Survey of Britain (PSE) have used particular measurements that combine subjective and objective indicators of absolute and overall poverty. A brief discussion of the methods of poverty measurement is presented below.

- **World Bank and poverty measures**

The World Bank uses consumption or an income-based measure of poverty, in addition to the non-income dimension of poverty. According to the World Bank report on poverty reduction in 1990 (cited in Gordon and Townsend, 2000: 84) there are two elements which are consumption-based: 'the expenditure needed to buy a minimum standard of nutrition and other basic necessities and a further amount that varies from country to country reflecting the cost of participating in the everyday life of society'. 'Poverty line' is the most commonly applied technique used to measure income poverty and this may embody either a relative concept or absolute concept (Gordon and Townsend, 2000: 30). The World Bank has used a 'poverty line' to measure poverty income where a person is considered poor if his or her income level falls below the poverty line, which is supposed to be the minimum level necessary to meet basic needs. Therefore, the poverty line varies in time and place and each country uses lines that are appropriate to its level of development and social norms and values. As mentioned earlier, the World Bank uses reference lines set at $1 and $2 per day (more precisely $1.08 and $2.15 in 1993 Purchasing Power Parity terms).

- **The Poverty and Social Exclusion Survey of Britain (PSE)**

According to Gordon and Townsend (2000), the PSE survey relied on a scientific approach to measuring poverty that combines two things: firstly, it incorporates the views of members of society, not just judgements of social scientists, about what the necessities of life are that all adults and children should have. Secondly, it calculates the level of deprivation that constitutes poverty by using a scientific method rather than arbitrary decisions. Gordon and Townsend (*ibid.*) refer to an operational measurement designed by British scientists that the PSE used to estimate the extent and nature of absolute and overall poverty. This method combined an objective and subjective measure. The method was applied in three stages:

1- Show the respondent the definition of absolute and overall poverty adopted by the United Nations World Summit of Social Development (see the definitions above).
2- Ask the respondent his/her views on the level of income that is needed to keep people above the poverty line.
3- Ask the respondent how far above or below that level his/her household is.

In their study, Gordon and Townsend (2000) present many tables and indicators that show how to use the objective and subjective measurements of absolute and overall poverty, and how this method is applicable, after suitable modification, for other European countries.

- **Measuring Poverty in Europe**

Many studies have measured poverty in Europe. A notable one is that carried out by the European Panel Analysis Group (EPAG) and supported by the European Commission (Berthoud, 2004) on 'patterns of poverty across Europe'. The study aimed to investigate the geographical distribution of income poverty among European countries and was based on data from the European Community Household Panel survey (ECHP) which was launched in 1994 with a final wave of interviews in 2001. The study chose two basic variables: 'current income' and 'annual income'. The 'inequality index' is a useful tool to help summarize the distribution of income poverty in Europe. The study has significant implications related to the methodology of poverty study.

In the 'Joint Report on Social Protection and Social Inclusion 2006' (European Commission, 2006b) another method of measuring poverty and social exclusion was utilized. This method is concerned with multi-dimensional indicators covering three main aspects of poverty and social exclusion: the income dimension, the labour market dimension, and the skills and health dimensions. This approach advocates (or supports) the idea of overlapping notions of poverty and social exclusion. In addition, it introduced some operational indicators for measuring the multi-dimensional aspects of poverty and social exclusion.

Another argument on measuring poverty in Europe is presented by Gordon, Panazis and Townsend (see Gordon and Townsend, 2000, Chapter 5) who discuss the idea that if Europe wishes to abolish the problem of poverty and social exclusion effectively, there needs to be a valid and reliable success measurement, yet at the current time, there are insufficient statistics available on low incomes. They propose that two sets of statistics are required to measure effectively the success of anti-poverty and social exclusion policies: firstly, Europe needs low income statistics that are relevant to a known, measurable and socially approved standard of living. Secondly, the standard of living that people have needs to be directly measured. To deal with the first requirement, they suggested obtaining a modified low-income series from the European Household Panel Survey or national Households Budget Surveys by abandoning arbitrary equivalence methods and income thresholds and instead, using a standard budget approach. They suggest some methods for dealing with the second requirement such as 'the consensual method', which would reveal how many people currently have too few resources to allow them to avoid material and social deprivation. This method would also distinguish between those who are excluded by their own choice and action from those who are excluded due to a lack of income, services and other resources (for more details about this method, see Gordon and Townsend, 2000: 101; Mack and Lansley, 1985, cited in Gordon and Townsend, 2000: 98).

The conclusion is that a scientific operational measurement of poverty is essential for developing an efficient anti-poverty strategy. To obtain that, it is necessary, as previous studies demonstrate, to obtain adequate income statistics. Accordingly, industrial countries, the World Bank and the UN organizations are paying more attention to this idea and have endeavoured to build scientific operational measurements of poverty which are adjustable according to the social conditions of every country (for example see Coudouel *et al.*, 2002).

1.3 Poverty and gender issues: global perspectives

In both developed and developing countries, women are more likely than men to suffer from poverty (see Scott 1984; George 1988; Daly 1989; Payne, 1991 cited in Spicker *et Al.,* 2007: 81). This section deals with female poverty and FHHs based on a review of some global studies from both developed and developing countries, in order to highlight some evidence, indicators and factors relevant to this issue.

Female poverty is not an easy subject to deal with as many complicated issues overlap. The aim of this section is to provide a review of relevant studies and to highlight issues. The researcher reviewed many studies on female poverty, FHHs, the feminization of poverty, the gender poverty gap, poverty and gender inequality, methodological issues relevant to female poverty measurement, female poverty, social policy and welfare reform. The studies have been grouped according to the following:

- Female poverty, FHHs and the feminization of poverty;
- Female poverty and some related factors;
- Women, poverty and welfare reform in developed countries;
- Women and poverty in developing countries.

Female poverty, FHHs and the feminization of poverty

Many studies have indicated that a relationship exists between family structure and the incidence of poverty, especially in the case of FHHs where they are at a much higher risk of falling below the poverty line. Family size can also affect poverty where households with more members have a higher probability of experiencing poverty than those with fewer members (see Cramer 1974, cited in Kimenyi and Mbaku, 1995).

However, FHHs are related to the concept of the "feminization of poverty". This term was first used by Diana Pearce who observed in 1976 that almost two-thirds of poor people over 16 years of age were women and almost half of poor families were headed by females (Pearce, 1978). Some studies have developed this concept in terms of its definition and how it can be measured. In their study, Medeiros and Costa (2008a and 2008b) defined the feminization of poverty as "a change in poverty levels that is biased against women and FHHs" They argued that because the feminization of poverty involved change, so this concept should be not confused with the more widespread or the higher level of poverty among women or FHHs. They clarified an important methodological point when they identified the feminization of poverty as being a process whereas the "higher level of poverty" was a state .They stated that the feminization of poverty is a relative concept based on a comparison of men and women along with the households headed by them, focusing on the differences between men and women at each stage. Thus, the study mirrored important methodological insights such as: the feminization of poverty as a process not merely reliant on the evidence of the higher number of poor women and FHHs; the feminization of poverty is reliant on the comparison between men and women and their household structures during each stage.

In terms of measuring 'female poverty', in a paper entitled "What does feminization of poverty mean? It isn't just lack of income", Fukuda-Parr (1999) argued that poverty income measurement is not appropriate to measure poverty among FHHs. The alternative approach is to use the Human Poverty Index (HPI) that the Human Development Report (1997) devised. Based on these terms, survival, knowledge, a decent standard of living and social participation are more appropriate for measuring the "feminization of poverty".

A report published by the European Commission (2006) entitled " Gender Inequality in the Risks of Poverty and Social Exclusion for Disadvantaged Groups in Thirty European Countries" highlighted the importance of using 'gender-based analysis' to understand the extent and form of poverty and social exclusion among vulnerable or disadvantaged groups within the population. One of the important reasons for using this approach is exposure to different dimensions of poverty and social exclusion that put women in a situation of 'double disadvantage', where women may face the additional burden of racism as well as gender discrimination. The report focused on a range of disadvantaged groups identified in social inclusion policies (the elderly, young people, disabled people, homeless people, immigrants/immigrant women, minority groups, lone parents and FHHs) to demonstrate how gender mainstreaming - supported by gender impact analysis - is a necessary tool for analyzing the causes and dimensions of poverty and social exclusion. In terms of lone-parents and FHHs, the report stated that in all European countries (except Denmark, Finland and Sweden) the risk of poverty is significantly higher among these types of households. The report suggested a range of policies and priorities to aid lone parents such as: increasing the lone-parent employment rate and increasing their income through employment and training initiatives.

Some studies have discussed in more detail how the feminization of poverty can be explained. For example, Pressman (2003) in a study entitled 'Feminist Explanation for the Feminization of Poverty' argued that three inter-related factors could explain the gender poverty gap for non-elderly households. Firstly, there can be differences in labour force participation, where the FHHs seemed likely to participate at a lower level than other households. This means reduced income for FHHs and increases the chance for them to be poor. This factor has a great influence on female poverty and seems to be the major cause of the gender poverty gap. Secondly, there exists gender-based occupational segregation, where women are systematically excluded from higher-paying occupations, thus their wages and incomes will be lower than those of men. Thirdly, as a result of the fluctuations of the labour market, FHHs rely on state support to stay out of poverty; but to access the support system, FHHs are required to satisfy many conditions in order to negotiate through state tax and spending regulations. The consequences are the increase of poverty among women and FHHs along with expanded gender poverty gaps.

In terms of the gender poverty gap in developed countries, a study was conducted by Passman (2002) called 'Explaining the Gender Poverty Gap in Developed and Transitional Economies'. The study used data from the Luxembourg Income Study (LIS) to compare the poverty rates for FHHs with the poverty rates for other households in a number of developed and transitional economies. The results showed different 'gender poverty gaps' across countries and that neither age nor education could explain such gender poverty gaps. Fiscal policy is only able to explain a proportion of gap. The analysis of data highlighted two policy conclusions: firstly, endeavours to improve the economic conditions of FHHs by developing their skills and improving education are not likely to be effective because human capital factors have very little effect on the gender poverty gap. Secondly, fiscal policy is very important and must focus more on the problems facing FHHs with spending directed more to low income FHHs.

The results of this study supported other previous studies that found that the type of welfare state and the characteristics of social policy and spending programmes influenced the poverty rate for single mothers (for example see Duncan and Edward 1997; Lewise 1997, cited in Pressman, 2002).

Female poverty and some related factors

Some studies looked at factors that could affect women and increase their chances of poverty such as widowhood, old age and ill health.

Research conducted in the UK by Corden *et al*. (2008) entitled 'Financial Implications of Death of Partner' aimed to investigate the economic and financial consequences of bereavement for a surviving partner and the household. The research used mixed methods and involved in-depth interviews with 44 people from different life stages who had recently been bereaved with a longitudinal analysis of data from the British Household Panel Survey from over 750 households that had suffered the loss of a partner. The findings showed the following: the death of a partner is mainly the experience of older women. One in five women were bereaved under the pension age. Decline in income following the death was greatest among people under the pension age as result of the loss of a partner's earning or their withdrawal from paid work. Among people bereaved over the pension age, women's income generally dropped but men's increased, reflecting gender differences in pension entitlements. Elderly women faced the increased risk of persistent or recurrent poverty for two or three years after the death of their partner. Bereaved people faced immediate financial demands such as paying for the funeral, dealing with debt and housing costs including changes in home ownership and tenancy.

The study highlighted some financial difficulties that bereaved women (widows) could face and how the implications of this status could increase the risk of poverty among those women.

A study by O'Grady-LeShane (1990) on 'Old Women and Poverty' investigated the status of older women in the US and their relationship with the Social Security System. The results suggested that old women's economic position depended largely on their marital status where the women who were widowed and other women living alone were among the most poor. In addition, the findings show that decreasing the social security benefit, viewed by some policy makers as a solution to the problem of the federal budget deficit, would increase the poverty of older women who relied on it as a main source of income.

Thus, the marital status of women in old age has a significant relation to women and poverty where the widows and lone women constitute the most poor. The study proposed that the reform of the social security system could increase poverty among old women, especially if it affected their benefits.

Another study by Vartanian and McNamara (2002) investigated how some factors have a significant effect on older women's economic well-being. The study used data from the Panel Study of Income Dynamic (PSID 1968-1997) and selected a sample of women between the ages of 66-70 and 71-85. The findings showed that the midlife characteristics of these women such as work participation, income and rural residence were strongly related to the economic status of women in old age. Thus being poor in middle age was strongly related to poor economic outcomes in old age. On the other hand, late life events and characteristics, such as widowhood or living alone, also affected significantly old women's economic outcomes. Both midlife and late-life characteristics contributed to the persistence of poverty in old age with many groups of poor women.

Thus, the events and characteristics associated with the midlife and late-life of women have a significant impact on the economic situation of these women.

In their study 'Women and Poverty in Scotland', Brown *et al* (2002) (cited in the Scottish Information Unit, 2003) discuss the relationship between women, poverty, and health. They argue that, although the UK has moved towards gender equality, women remain at greater risk of poverty than men and are at greater risk of ill health. Women often have limited access to incomes of their own and on average, their incomes are significantly lower than men's. In addition, their caring role (mother / carer of elderly or ill relatives) places them in a vulnerable economic and personal position. They remain one of the largest groups who experience poverty.

Women, poverty, and welfare reform in developed countries

Many studies (for example Orloff 2002; Kimenyi and Mbaku, 1995; Meucci, 1992; Hoynes, 1995; Abramovitz, 2006 and Davies *et al.*, 2001) discuss the process of poverty and welfare reform, particularly in the USA, and to what extent this process affects social policies relevant to social support, assistance for the poor and how, in particular, poverty and welfare reform impact on women and FHHs. US welfare reform, under the influence of market values and neo-liberalism, aims to minimise the role of the welfare state. This seems to create many conflicts between the circumstances of poor people and the new conditions of the welfare system (see for example Orloff, 2002 and Abramovitz, 2006). This model of welfare reform has been criticized by many researchers, in particular when this is associated with increased suffering of poor people, especially women and FHHs (see for example Kimenyi and Mbaku 1995).

There is a large debate on poverty, women and welfare reform to be found in the western poverty literature. A wide range of studies focus on explanations of welfare reform and how this has influenced the position of poor women and FHHs by affecting social policies and changing the entitlement conditions for those in receipt of social benefits.

A Study conducted by Orloff (2002) on US welfare reform highlighted how this reform included the following changes: the elimination of social rights and care-giving as a basis for making claims for social benefit; an expansion of the role of the market and support for gender 'sameness', meaning mothers and fathers must be employed. The

Earned Income Tax Credit (EITC) reinforces these changes, where parents can only be in receipt if they have been employed.

Social welfare systems and social policies, on the other hand, have been criticized for increasing poverty in some sections of society, such as among lone mothers and FHHs, as a result of some types of benefit. In this respect, Kimenyi and Mbaku (1995) in a study on 'Female Headship, Feminization of Poverty and Welfare' discussed the significant relationships between increasing female headships and social benefits, especially 'Aid to Families with Dependent Children (AFDC)' and the change in the birth rate to unmarried women. The research used weighted measures and suggested that welfare benefit, by increasing female headship, has played a significant role in the feminization of poverty. A similar argument was also made by Meucci (1992), and Hoynes (1995).

Abramovitz (2006) investigated welfare reform in the USA and how this involved issues of gender, race and class. The research studied the US welfare programme for single mothers and how this was associated with the main provisions of welfare reform which are: enforcing work, promoting marriage and limiting the role of the federal state. According to this study, all these provisions affected women and children. Welfare reform, according to the researcher, should be understood in this case as a part of the neo-liberal strategy centralized on five goals: limiting the role of federal government, shrinking the welfare state, lower labour costs, family values, race neutral social policy and reducing the power of social movements.

Welfare reform issues seem to be more related to developed countries where welfare issues are linked with other trends in political and economic development associated with the neo-liberal regime. Also, welfare reform appears to involve some disadvantages especially for poor women and FHHs.

In a study investigating social policy, gender inequality and poverty as applied to Canadian women, Davies *et al.* (2001) suggested that a mother's choices about work and family, shaped and re-shaped by broader gender arrangements, prioritize motherhood and marriage over economic independence. The study suggested that it is important for social policy to address systematic gender inequality because neither marriage nor employment (alone or in combination) will be enough to significantly reduce women's economic insecurity.

Women and poverty in developing countries

Female poverty in developing countries (sometimes referred to as third world countries) is associated with specific issues arising from their socio-economic and cultural contexts. Poor women in the third world live in specific socio-cultural contexts where development does not occur so the benefits of development do not reach women. There is also no cash economy, no education or healthcare system and women's labour is often exploited. Thus third world women have become marginalized and they are deprived of access to resources (Vecchio & Roy 1998: 5). Within this context, most poor women in the developing world merely survive, therefore the issues that are associated with their poverty are different from those of poor women in the developed world.

Women and gender issues did not impact on the Poverty Reduction Strategy Papers (PRSPs) that were formulated according to the approach of the World Bank (WB) and the International Monetary Fund (IMF) to help developing countries to promote the growth of their economies and reduce poverty. Whitehead (2003), in a report entitled 'Falling Women, Sustaining Poverty: Gender in Poverty Reduction Strategy Papers' which has introduced to the UK Gender and Development Network, presented a critical viewpoint on the PRSPs in four developing countries: Tanzania, Bolivia, Malawi, and Yemen. The report examined the form of gender issues in the PRSPs of these countries. The analysis, based on telephone interviews, reviews the primary and secondary documents. The results showed that the national dialogue of governments on poverty seemed uncommitted to participation in policy-making and were simply fulfilling the conditions of a Heavily Indebted Poor Country (HIPC) to access the debt relief fund. The findings showed that poverty analysis in these PRSPs was limited and that there was inadequate integration between the poverty diagnosis and the policy section of PRSPs. Gender issues seemed fragmented. Some women's needs were raised in the sections on health and education, but overall, gender was not integrated. Despite being recommended by the PRSPs, Source Book, the separate chapters on gender were missing in half of the PRSPs reviewed. There was limited analysis of women's issues and resources relevant to their well-being and there was no recognition that macroeconomic policy and national states would be gendered. Therefore the associations or links between all the general objectives for the improvement of women's positions and eradicating women's poverty were unclear and inaccurate.

Vecchio and Roy (1998) in 'Poverty, FHHs, and Sustainable Economic Development' studied poverty in two Indian villages. One of them represented an example of unsuccessful development and the other represented successful development. The study combined quantitative and qualitative methods to investigate characteristics of FHHs, income, and aspects of the dimensions of their poverty. The findings showed that female heads constituted over 50% of these households, and the major reason for poverty was widowhood. The study also highlighted the fact that the benefits of government development programmes had not yet reached remote areas. The study recommended that for development to be successful and sustainable, it was fundamental to raise the socioeconomic status of FHHs. Poverty in FHHs must be eradicated on several levels: income generation, health, education, community attitude and culture, environment and village power structures, with a special emphasis on women's development.

Some researchers like Akinsola & Popovich (2002) have investigated the quality of life of FHHs in urban and rural areas of Botswana. They selected 7 FHHs and used observation, open-ended interviews and secondary analysis to describe the quality of life of members of FHHs according to their ability to meet basic human needs (food, water, shelter, safety, and health). The findings showed that FHHs ranged in age from 40-91 years. With family sizes from 1-11 members, they were living in crowded conditions with a monthly income of approximately $30, thus at high risk of illness. The study suggested that the governments in developing countries need to address FHHs in their programmes for poverty alleviation.

Conclusion

The chapter has introduced notions of poverty in the global literature on poverty. Some important concepts of poverty, relevant to this research, have been discussed. The chapter was divided into three sections: poverty definition, poverty measurement, and poverty and gender issues.

In the poverty definition sections, some fundamental definitions of poverty such as 'absolute poverty'; 'relative poverty'; and 'overall poverty' were explained. There were also definitions adopted by international organizations such as UNDP, WB, and European Commission. These various definitions operate within certain contexts and vary according to the different perspectives and views of organizations that have adopted these definitions.

Poverty measurements vary in accordance with poverty definitions and related indicators. Each definition should involve specific indicators that form a basis on which poverty measurement can be designed. Therefore, it is necessary to obtain a clear and accurate poverty definition to enable an effective poverty measurement. The chapter pointed to some poverty measurements such as 'poverty line' as adopted by the WB; 'HPI' as adopted by the UNHD, 'multi-dimensional indicators measurement' as adopted by the European Commission, and the combining between objective and subjective indicators as adopted by the PSE.

In the respect of poverty and gender issues, some international studies have been reviewed concerned with aspects of female poverty and FHHs worldwide. The review of these studies demonstrated how female poverty within both developed and developing countries is associated with and affected by many socio-cultural, economic and political factors and determinants. These factors and determinants were grouped and discussed within four categories: female poverty, FHHs and the feminization of poverty, women, poverty and welfare reform in developed societies, and finally, women and poverty in developing countries.

To conclude, this chapter has aimed to clarify the idea of poverty and its related concepts and to show how these concepts operate in global contexts. This will benefit this research, in particular in the data analysis and findings discussion where the researcher will compare her findings in the Saudi context with poverty in its global contexts.

Chapter two
Poverty in Islam and in the Islamic world

Introduction

The religious texts of Islam in the 'Qur'an' and 'Sunnah'[5] introduce two types of frameworks: 'theoretical framework' and 'practical framework'. The first one is a normative framework which represented the 'Islamic theory'; or the 'Islamic ideal type of belief and act' as represented in the religious texts (the verses of Qur'an and Hadith of Prophet Muhammad). This operates as a framework of meaning that involves the Islamic belief system, also the ideal types of Islamic ways of life. The second one is the 'practical framework' that is represented by Islamic law (Shari'a law) which is mainly derived from religious texts and where the *Fiqh*[6] plays an important role in formulating this law. This 'practical framework' operates as a 'guideline' and 'organizer' for the practice of everyday life.

This chapter aims to present theoretical discussion on poverty and relevant concepts according to the previous two types of framework. The 'Islamic theory' in this context means the religious texts of Islam that reflect the ideal types of thought and action which revolve around poverty and the 'practical level' that shows the social reality of Muslim countries and how much this social reality is changeable, reflecting various dimensions of poverty. Therefore, this chapter presents the previous theoretical

---

[5] *Qur'an* is the Holy Book of Muslim, consisting of the revelation made by God to the Prophet Muhammad (peace be upon him). The *Qur'an* lays down the fundamentals of the Islamic faith including beliefs and all aspects of the Islamic way of life (Iqbal 2002:xvii). *Sunnah* is the way of the Prophet Muhammad comprising what he did or said or tacitly approved (Ahmad, 1991: 100).

[6] *Fiqh* refers to the whole corpus of Islamic jurisprudence. In contrast with conventional law, *fiqh* covers all aspect of life: religious, political, social, commercial and economic. The whole corpus of *fiqh* is based primarily on interpretation of the *Qur'an* and *Sunnah* and secondarily on *ijma* (consensus) and *ijtihad* (individual judgment). While the *Qur'an* and *Sunnah* are immutable, *fiqh* verdicts may change due to changing circumstances (Iqbal, 2002: xii).

discussion through three sections: poverty in the Islamic context, poverty in contemporary Islamic countries, and women and poverty from the Islamic viewpoint.

Poverty in the Islamic context shows the 'Islamic theory' of poverty, where the conceptual framework of poverty in Islam is presented in the first part of this section. The second part is concerned with how Islam established a policy framework for the eradication of poverty. This section is supported by many religious texts that reflect an Islamic theory on poverty.

Poverty in contemporary Islamic countries mirrors how poverty is understood within contemporary Muslim societies. This section presents a review of some studies on poverty in Muslim societies and shows various dimensions of poverty that exist in contemporary Islamic society as a result of changeable social realities. This section, therefore, reflects the level of social reality as lived out in the daily practices of Islamic society (referred to forthwith as practice systems).

Women and poverty is an essential issue in this research, so this section offers an overview on how women and the gender dimension of poverty have been understood in Islam (Islamic theory) and how it is explained and interpreted in the reality of current Muslim societies.

2.1 Poverty in the Islamic context

Poverty has existed in Muslim society since the period of the Prophet Muhammad, where the Muslim community in that time involved poor people and dependent categories such as women, slaves and immigrant groups of the Muhajirun, who emigrated from Mecca to Madinah to keep their faith and religious beliefs safe. Immigration produced impoverished people who left their possessions behind in Mecca. In Madinah, the Muhajirun found support from the Ansar, the other Muslim group living in Medina at the time. Some of the poor people were forced to inhabit the mosque in Madinah and thus were called 'people of the portico' (ahl la-suffa). Those poor introduced a model to the later Muslims who adopted voluntary poverty as a fundamental doctrine of Sufism (Sabra et al., 2006: 490). Thus, the poor comprise an important category of early Muslim society. Poverty became (and remains) a subject for many religious rituals that revolved around Islamic charitable institutions.

Poverty in the Islamic context provides a framework of terms and definitions of poverty, as well as explanation and discussion on the Islamic perspective of poverty eradication that comprises a specific policy framework.

2.1.1 Conceptual framework

The conceptual framework is concerned with three issues: terms and concepts relevant to poverty in Islam; how the term poverty is defined in Islam and how this definition developed and reflects the social context of that concept, and misconceptions relevant to poverty where this concept became a religious ideal in part of historical Islam, Sufism, which affected beliefs and practice systems in Muslim societies.

2.1.1.1 Terms and concepts relevant to poverty in Islam

There are many terms and concepts relating to poverty and charitable institutions in Islam. Some of these terms are outlined below but some are explained in more detail later in the chapter.

Zakah (Mandatory Alms)
"Zakah is the third of the five pillars of Islam and hence is obligatory for every Muslim who fulfils the stipulated conditions of pay. Being a pillar of Islam, it has to be paid and collected whether the destitute and the poor exist in society or not. As such it is indeed a permanent source of revenue for the alleviation of the destitute and the poor" (Alhabshi, n.d: 7)

Waqif / Awqaf pl. (Charitable Trusts or Endowments)
"Charitable trusts transfer wealth from private ownership to beneficial, social, and collective ownership. Islam does not make this practice obligatory but has strongly encouraged it and left it to voluntary initiatives of individuals. The Muslims accepted that and created charitable trusts, since the period of the Prophet for important social and economic functions. Such trusts that were created in different countries and ages have successfully brought about tremendous changes in the welfare of the needy" (Ibid.)

Al Maniha (Gifts)

"Al Minha and Al Maniha are special kinds of gifts. The Prophet Muhammad in his various traditions used this method to assist the early Muslim migrants from Mecca to Madinah who were in real need of some help. Al Maniha means the granting of the usufruct of a productive asset to a needy person for a specific period. These gifts as mentioned in the various Prophetic traditions include money (cash), riding animals, dairy animals, agricultural land, fruit bearing trees, houses, kitchen utensils, tools, etc" (Ibid.)

Al Fay' (Booty)

"Al Fay' is the wealth that Muslims acquire from the enemy without actual fighting. The recipients of fay' are the Prophet, his family, the orphans, the needy and the wayfarer" (Ibid. 8)

This is explained in the Qur'an as follows:

"What Allâh gave as booty (Fai') to His Messenger (Muhammad) from the people of the townships - it is for Allâh, His Messenger the kindred (of Messenger Muhammad), the orphans, Al-Masâkin (the poor), and the wayfarer, in order that it may not become a fortune used by the rich among you. And whatsoever the Messenger gives you, take it; and whatsoever he forbids you, abstain (from it). And fear Allâh; verily, Allâh is Severe in punishment. (And there is also a share in this booty) for the poor emigrants, who were expelled from their homes and their property, seeking Bounties from Allâh and to please Him, and helping Allâh (i.e. helping His religion) and His Messenger (Muhammad). Such are indeed the truthful (to what they say) "
(Qur'an 59: 7-8).

Al Ghanimah (Spoils of War)

"Al Ghanimah is the wealth acquired from the enemy by force during war. One-fifth of the Al Ghanimah is to be distributed to all the recipients of the fay' and the remaining four-fifths go to the soldiers who participated
in the war" (Ibid.)

Rikaz (Treasure)

"Rikaz is buried wealth found in land which has no owner. The finder will have to pay 20 per cent or one-fifth of the wealth. The opinions of the jurists on the recipients of this one-fifth of the wealth are divided. Some are of the opinion that it should be distributed to the recipients of the fay'. Some others opine that it should be distributed as zakah. Whichever way it is distributed, it is still an important source for the needy" (Ibid.)

Nafaqah (Obligatory Maintenance by Relatives)

"The Islamic system makes it obligatory on each wealthy person to provide sufficient maintenance for his poor relative who is unable to earn a living. The juristic opinion that seems to be most appropriate is that it is based upon inheritance rights. The maintenance of the incapacitated poor man is obligatory on his rich relative(s) who will inherit from this poor man if this poor man leaves any inheritance. If there are a number of such rich relatives, the amount of maintenance is distributed amongst them according to the share of their inheritance from him." (Ibid.)

Sadaqah (Charity)

"Sadaqah or Charity is 'voluntary action for the public good' and this action includes an individual giving money or material goods or rendering services in the form of donated time and expertise as well as the formation of association that both collect and disburse these same commodities" (Singer, 2008: 8)

The above terms and concepts constitute important sources for the 'Public Treasury' of the Islamic state. In addition, these terms revolve around poverty and are defined from the Islamic perspective in the next section.

2.1.1.2 Islamic definition of poverty

The Islamic perspective on poverty is based on two basic concepts: how Islam identifies human needs and how Islam classifies and prioritizes those needs in accordance with the human needs or hierarchy of satisfaction.

Fundamental Human Needs

According to Alhabshi, (n.d: 3, 4) there are five basic groups of activities and things that constitute the fundamental human needs in Islam, they are: religion, physical self, intellectual knowledge, offspring and wealth.

- 1- Religion: this is a basic need from the Islamic perspective for everyone. The person has freedom to choose, believe, and practice his religion without compulsion. Islam sees religion as a fundamental need to achieve peace and also to work as guidance in a person's life

2. Physical self: this involves keeping a healthy body and keeping all things necessary for life such as food, water, clothes, health care, shelter, etc.
3. Intellect or knowledge: this means all knowledge that is necessary to secure a person's daily life. There are two types of knowledge in Islamic: the basic knowledge that is necessary to learn and deal with all aspects of life (for all people) and specialized knowledge that is not essential for everyone, but necessary for society to develop and progress, for example medicine, physics, mathematics, etc.
4. Offspring: Islam places emphasis on the human race, so it considers sex not merely as a need in itself but as a means of reproduction and increasing the human race; this process in Islam is organized and surrounded with strong rules, responsibilities and ethics.
5. Wealth: this means the basic need for human life where wealth can be cash, a property, or employment that brings income.

According to the relationship with people and the wider society, human needs can be classified as:
- Personal needs of the individual such as food, housing, clothes, furniture, and daily life requirement.
- Social services that are provided by society such as health care, education, social services, water supplies etc.

Referring to Alhabshi (n.d: 5) the human needs are categorized into three levels, namely: necessities (dharuriyyat); convenience (hajiat); and refinements (kamaliat).

Necessities (dharuriyyat): this involves all activities and things that keep the five essential needs at the lowest level, in other words to achieve the minimum level of satisfaction for these needs. In Islam, this level means the minimum to enable a person to do his religious activities as well as keeping his life secure by the provision of basic food, clothes, and shelter. Also included are obtaining a suitable education and having the ability to work and gain income for a living. Thus the level of necessities means having the minimum on which to live.

Conveniences (hajiat): This level involves all activities and things that meet the five basic human needs but with additional comforts that make those basic needs easier to endure such as transportation to work.

Refinements (kamaliat): This level involves all activities and things that aim to satisfy human needs above necessities and conveniences in ways that improve the comfort of life and provide aspects of luxury.

The definition of Poverty in Islam

Islam defines poverty according to two main concepts: the necessities and nisab. Poverty in Islam is defined in accordance with its association with the concept of necessities. According to the Islamic perspective of human needs, the person who does not have 'sufficient necessities' to achieve or cover all basic human needs is considered poor. Therefore all individual and social needs must be achieved but if one of the needs is not met, the person is regarded as poor (Ibid.).

Poverty can also be defined in Islam according to its association with the concept of 'nisab'. Nisab is a term relevant to zakah and means "to get a minimum quantum of any goods or wealth that makes a person eligible to pay zakah". Thus a person who does not possess nisab would not be liable to pay zakah; accordingly, they will be considered poor and therefore eligible to receive zakah (Ibid.).

Islam identifies two categories of poor, namely the poor and needy or destitute. The poor are those who do not possess the necessities, whilst the needy are those whose level of necessities does not reach half of that of the poor (Ibid.). The differences between 'poor' and 'needy' are controversial and are discussed in more detail below.

Concept of Poverty as Identified by the Linguistics Framework

Arabic is generally known as 'the official language of the Qur'an' where the terminology and rules (grammar) of the Arabic language is highly reliant on the linguistic structure of the holy Qur'an. However, over the course of Islamic history, many terms and concepts of poverty have been created and developed as a result of implications within specific social and historical contexts. Some language definitions will be presented here and will demonstrate how poverty has dynamic concepts according to its social conditions.

One of the definitions found in *Lisan al-Arab*, written by Ibn_Mandhour (d.c. 1311 CE) - the standard Arabic dictionary:

'Inability of individual to satisfy his own basic needs and the needs of his dependents'.

(ESCWA, 1994 cited in Spicker et al., 2007)

Another definition cited in *Fiqh al-Lugha*, written by Tha'aliby (d.c. 1037 CE) referred to eight different levels of poverty, assigning to each a specific term:

- Loss of savings;
- Loss of assets or property due to drought or natural disaster (this type of poverty is temerity);
- An individual is forced to sell the decorative items on his sword (the equivalent in today's standards would be to sell non-essential material belongings);
- The individual/household can only afford to eat bread made of millet, which is cheaper than the usual wheat-flour bread;
- The individual/household has no food available;
- The individual/household has no belongings left which he can sell to purchase food;
- The individual/household has become humiliated or degraded due to poverty;
- The individual/household is reduced to ultimate poverty.

(Ibid.: 10)

The definitions above outline many types of poverty and identify many categories of poor and needy according to the degree of their need. The descriptions fall between the meaning of extreme poverty (for example, the loss of a basic need such as food) to the relative meaning of poverty (where a person might have the necessities, but on other hand they are unable to reach the standard for their society). The above definition also refers to social exclusion, where the poor are humiliated and marginalized due to their poverty.

Sabra (2000) highlights another definition of poverty where involves a social and religious meaning:

> The Arabic language contains number of words which evoke the concepts of poverty. First and foremost among them is the term *faqir* which has two meanings: poverty and need. Being in need is considered by Muslim thinkers to be a characteristic of humanity as a whole. All creatures are in need of their creator; hence, any believer may style himself *al-faqir ila llah* or *al-faqir ila rabbih* (the one in need of God, the one in need of his Lord). Thus, poverty can be a specific attribute of a person lacking material passion or a general attribute of humanity as a whole, just as wealth (*ghina*) can refer to an individual's possession or God's having no need for his creation (p 9).

The term need in Islamic culture, as the above definition describes, takes two meanings: the need for decent life conditions, or the need for God as an expression to the spiritual dimension of need or poverty.

In the lexicographic tradition, *faqir* is always accompanied by *miskin* and both refer to the person who suffers from material deprivation but with different degrees (Ibn Manzur 1988: 15, cited in Sabra 2000: 9). The distinction between the use of these two terms is important where it is used in the Qur'an to give guidance about who deserves to be given alms *(sadaqah and zakah)* where the *faqir* and *miskin* are put against the top of the eight categories of people who deserve zakah (Sabra 2000:9).

Muslim jurists[7] disagree about the exact meaning of these two terms, wherein some of them identify the *faqir* as destitute, while the *miskin* is identified as possessing

---

[7] Also called 'Islamic Fiqh schools' or 'Islamic schools of law' or 'the four Sunni madhabs' that mention Hanafi, Maliki, Shafi'i, Hanbali.

some property. In contrast, some argue the opposite, that the *miskin* possess nothing whereas the *faqir* have some few things (Sabra et al., 2006: 491). In the legal context, however, both *faqir* and *miskin* continue to be used as a reference to those sufficiently poor to receive alms (zakah) (Sabra 2000:10).

To conclude, as previous definitions demonstrate, poverty as a social phenomenon is not isolated from other aspects of its contexts. Thus the concept of poverty in the Islamic context is associated with the human needs of individuals, where those individuals are basically social creatures, therefore they will not be able to live or satisfy their needs outside of their social frame (i.e. of society and family). Moreover, the previous definitions of poverty indicate the social status and social category of the poor where the poor are not a homogenous group, even though they experience the same conditions of poverty, their degrees of need differ greatly. Accordingly, the categories of the poor and poverty vary according to many variables relevant to their social context. However, the classification and categorizing of the poor has a significant impact on Islamic religious rituals where charity and alms distribution in Islam, especially regarding mandatory alms (zakah), is based on several conditions of eligibility and entitlement, so the beneficiaries have to satisfy these conditions.

However, poverty in Islamic history takes a religious meaning where it is sometimes indicative of a type of piety, which especially occurred in medieval times.

2.1.1.3. Poverty as religious ideal

As mentioned above, poverty takes an important religious and ideological dimension in medieval Islam, especially with Sufism' as a trend that affected many aspects of Muslim life and where poverty became an indication of 'extreme piety'. The development of Sufism passed through a number of stages and by the late eleventh century, the principle of poverty as key to renouncing the world reached the peak of its intellectual development as can be seen in the writings of Abu-Hamid Muhammad **al-Ghazzali** (450-505/1058-1111). **al-Ghazzali**'s view was fully explained in his famous book *Ihya ulum al-din* 'The Revival of the Religious Sciences' in a chapter entitled 'The book of poverty as Asceticism'. This book was unrivaled in popularity in medieval Muslim thought (Sabra, 2000 17,172).

Sabra (2000) analyzed **al-Ghazzali** significant work on 'poverty and charity in Medieval Islam' where poverty is viewed as the 'religious ideal' in the medieval Islamic age. He analyzed in more detail **al-Ghazzali**'s notions of poverty as piety and virtue and how poverty achieved ideological and spiritual dimensions where the choice of poverty became an indication of a high spiritual status and the poor were regarded as pious people. According to Sabra:

> **al-Ghazzali** defined poverty as 'the absence of what is needed' according to this definition, all being other than God are poor (or needy), since they all depend on Him for the continuation of their existence. God on other hand is 'the Absolute Wealthy One', since He does not depend on any other being for His existence. Although the state of human beings can be describe as 'absolute poverty' since they rely on God for their continued existence, al-Ghazzali prefers to speak of relative poverty that is the lack of sufficient property to obtain all of one's needs. Since man's needs are potentially limitless, different levels of need correspond to different levels of poverty.
>
> (Sabra, 2000: 20)

al-Ghazzali, a Sufi philosopher, was regarded as exaggerated when he turned it towards a deep philosophical discussion where poverty was centralized as a positive sign of piety. He believed that 'extreme poverty' was about the neediness of God, and that 'relative poverty' was about the neediness of other life requirements. This is representative of strict asceticism of the Sufi doctrine, in contrast with the original Islamic beliefs which emphasize a moderated style of life.

al-Ghazzali identified five different states of poverty, which are:

1. Where one hates wealth so much, and suffers from it so much, that one flees from it. This state is called 'asceticism' (zuhd); its practitioner is an 'ascetic' (zahid).
2. Where one neither desires wealth when one lacks it, nor hates it when it is present. If one receives wealth, one spends it sparingly (yazhudu fihi). The practitioner of this state is called 'content' (radin).

3. Where one prefers the presence of wealth to its absence, due to one's desire for it. Despite this desire, however, one does not seek it out. If one receives wealth easily, without intending it, one is joyful; but if obtaining it requires effort, one does not concern oneself with it. The practitioner of this state is called 'satisfied' (qani), since he is satisfied with what he has such that he abandons seeking out wealth due to weak desire for it.
4. When one abandons seeking out wealth due to one's 'inability' (li-ajzihi) although one desires wealth and would seek it out, even by expending considerable effort, if one could find a way to do so. The practitioner of this is called 'avaricious' (haris).
5. Where one lacks the wealth that one needs, such as the hungry man who lacks bread or the naked man who lacks clothes. The practitioner of this state is called 'needy' (mudtarr). His desire for wealth may be weak or strong.

(Ibid. 20, 21).

al-Ghazzali cited many states of poverty, the fifth of which explains the state of being poor in a sociological sense. The other four categories involve different degrees of poverty. The central point in **al-Ghazzali's** thinking on poverty is the person's stand point towards wealth as a sign or indicator of temptation generally. The emphasis is on rejection of the material world and admission of the dependence on God, according to the ascetic does not need wealth because he believes his God will provide all that he needs (Ibid. 21).

Another controversial idea of **al-Ghazzali** is his statement that 'the poor are more virtuous than the wealthy'. He describes the 'manner of the pious pauper' as follows:

> The pauper should be content with his lot, not complain of, or publicize, his poverty. In addition, the pauper should not humiliate himself before a wealthy man because of the latter's wealth. Indeed, he should recognize that his station is higher than that of a wealthy man, and avoid even being in the latter's company. He should speak the truth before the wealthy, even at the risk of losing their patronage.
> (**al-Ghazzali**, cited in Sabra, 2002: 22).

al-Ghazzali recommends keeping a person's state as a pauper by not accumulating wealth, and clarified three levels of permitted wealth accumulation, as follows:

1. To accumulate enough for no more than one day and night. This is the rank of the righteous (darajat al-siddiqin).
2. To accumulate enough for forty days. This is the rank of the pious (darajat al-muttaqin)
3. To accumulate enough for one year, this is the rank of the devout (darajat al-salihin). (Ibid. 22).

Thus it can be inferred that **al-Ghazzali** disagreed with saving money or accumulating wealth due to the main principle in the life being extreme asceticism. al-Ghazzali was subjected to criticism from other medieval Muslim thinkers and scholars such as Ibn al-Jawzi (510-597/1116-1200), Ibn Taymiyya (661-728/1263), and Ibn Qayyim al-Jawzyya (691-751/1292-1356). They rejected al-Ghazzali's views on poverty as piety and clarified how the value of 'asceticism' in Islam did not involve a radical rejection of the material world (Ibid. 23-24). In this respect, Islamic thought regarding poverty was divided into two groups. The first group placed emphasis on the importance of renouncing the material world so they rejected wealth; the second group believed that the person is tested by God in different ways, so the pious person is he who realizes how to act his social reality correctly. This group did not reject wealth, but recognized the risk that came with it and believed that risk to be no more than the risk of poverty (Ibid.: 25).

Thus, the idea of poverty as a 'religious ideal', especially in medieval Islam, occurred within specific social and historical contexts. In that context, poverty developed and took an ideological meaning when this concept linked to religious trends such as 'Sufism'. As a result, this made a great impact on the social life and charity system in the Muslim society of that time, especially on the role of the 'pious endowment' where the waqif was used to establish housing, hospitals, Qur'an schools for orphans, and endow food and water, which provided to the poor occasionally or according to a specific timetable (Sabra, 2000).

As discussed, Sufism played a significant role in promoting poverty as a religious ideal. While the root of Sufism dated back to early Islam, it developed into a great and influential institution in the late twelfth century. The trend took a direction towards 'self organization' where Sufism in the Islamic world promoted fund raising and getting benefit from patronage, in particular from the military elite. In that period, two types of Sufi organizations emerged as a result of that development: the *zawiya,* usually dominated by a specific *shaykh* and his followers, and the *khanqah* which was established by the elite patronage for the benefit of foreign and travelling mystics (Ibid.: 25, 172).

To conclude, as this section illustrated, poverty has been a concept from the early stages of Islamic history. According to the historical evidence, the meaning and implications of poverty developed within its social and historical context. Based on that, poverty took a social meaning by indicating the sort of need associated with specific categories of poor. Another direction emerged when poverty developed to become a 'religious ideal', when poverty was associated with 'Sufism' and marked as the route to piety. Accordingly, all these developments influenced the social reality of Muslim society, as reflected in medieval Islam when 'charity systems' were promoted, in particular the waqif, and became great institutions that focused on the benefit of the poor. Thus, in Islam, the concept of poverty is inextricably linked with a munificent institution. This institution is surrounded and supported by religious texts of the Qur'an and Sunnah, which organized the systems of belief and practice regarding charity and alms giving. Many of these texts formulated a policy framework for the eradication of poverty, as discussed in the next section.

2.1.2 Islamic perspective and policy framework for eradication of poverty

The policy framework for the eradication of poverty, as found in the Islamic texts of the Qur'an and Sunnah is constructed on rules and legislations that organize a Muslim's relationship with family, state and society. The characteristics of that policy framework are explained below.

2.1.2.1 Human rights in Islamic law (Shari'a law)
The Qur'an, which is the main source of Islamic law, and the Sunnah, which is the second source of Islamic law, both outlined the core elements of human rights. That framework of human rights was the basis of the moral and legal system of Muslim

society. Human rights in Islam are situated within a comprehensive framework that shaped all aspects of human life politically, economically, socially, legally and religiously. Referring to Ahmad (1991):

> All human rights granted by Islam are based on the principle of 'general good' (*al-maslaha al-ammah*). Some human rights in Islam are listed as follows:
> 1. Right to life. Human life is sacred and inviolable, and every effort should be made to protect it.
> 2. Freedom of profession and work where there should be free entry into all professions and work that are permitted in Islam.
> 3. All persons are equal before the law and entitled to redress their grievance in accordance with shari'a.
> 4. Every person is entitled to own property individually or in association with others. State ownership of certain economic resources in the public interest is legitimate.
> 5. The poor have a right in the wealth of the rich to the extent that the basic needs of everyone in society are met.
> 6. Human exploitation at any level in any shape under any circumstances is anti-Islamic and must be ended.
>
> (Ahmad, 1991: p. 15)

The Holy texts of the Qur'an and Sunnah assert these rights and place emphasis on the elimination of all aspects and forms of exploitation, oppression and injustice for both the individual and society.

2.1.2.2 Encouragement of productive work and emphasis on work ethic

> "It is We Who have placed you with authority on earth, and provided you therein with means for the fulfillment of your life: small are the thanks that ye give!" (Qur'an 7:10).

> "And made your sleep for rest. And made the night as a covering. And made the day as a means of subsistence?" (Qur'an 78: 9-11)

> Narrated Az-Zubair bin Al'Awwam: The Prophet (p.b.u.h) said, "It is better for anyone of you to take a rope (and cut) and bring a bundle of wood (from the forest) over his back and sell it and Allah will save his face (from the Hell-Fire) because of that, rather than to ask the people who may give him or not."

(Hadith : Bukari, Volume 2, Book 24, Number 550)

Narrated Ibn 'Umar: I heard Allah's Apostle (p.b.u.h) while he was on the pulpit speaking about charity, to abstain from asking others for some financial help and about begging others, saying, "The upper hand is better than the lower hand. The upper hand is that of the giver and the lower (hand) is that of the beggar."
(Hadith : Bukari, Volume 2, Book 24, Number 509).

Islam emphasizes productive work as a crucial aim for human beings, no matter what the work is: whether physical, such as agricultural, industrial, commercial or manual work; or intellectual work, such as invention and creation, ideas and knowledge. Islamic teachings (as the Qur'an and Sunnah indicate) make a strong association between two sides: beliefs and practice, so Muslims have to adopt both sides and translate their beliefs into behaviours in everyday life. One of the essential beliefs is related to 'work and work ethic' where work in Islam is sacred and considered as having a religious value. Thus, every Muslim has a duty to invest in his environment in a correct and acceptable way, not merely to benefit him but also to benefit his family, community and the wider society. This idea is opposite to what Sufis understood (see the previous discussion on al-Ghazzali). In this respect, Islam looks at poverty within the framework of unemployment, a lack of production and a lack of skills and abilities.

Many religious texts of the Qur'an and Sunnah (as mentioned above) support this orientation and encourage the able-bodied to earn their living and abstain from seeking assistance from others except in urgent circumstances and desperate need (Ahmad, 1991: 26). Work and self-dependence and expenditure of own earnings take a significant symbolic meaning in Islam where the expression 'the upper hand is better than the lower hand' establishes an ethic in Muslim social life. According to that expression, dependency on charity is not acceptable; charity should be for those who are unable to work according to their vulnerability and circumstances.

2.1.2.3 Islamic vision for organization work environments and business practices

Islam is against laziness, dependency and begging. Islam encourages productive work and organizes work practice by many guiding principles, as outlined below:
1. All types of work are acceptable, agricultural, trade, manufacture, and manual work, if they are compatible and consistent with Islamic law.
2. All able-bodies have to work and seeking work is their responsibility. The state has another responsibility, which is to provide society with job opportunities.
3. Islam keeps the rights of workers and employees within their work environment. Accordingly, they have salaries and must work in suitable conditions in terms of place, time and safety.
4. Islam forbids adopting 'begging' as a job or income resource. According to Hadith the Prophet said: "when a man is always begging from people, he would meet Allah (in a state) that there would be no flesh on his face" (Sahih Muslim: book 5, Number 2262). This is a reference to the loss of self-esteem and human dignity through the act of begging.
5. Islamic principles prescribe comprehensive codes of business ethic that organize work practices and prevent all types of exploitative practice for the enrichment of a few; thus that which causes inequality of income and wealth. Therefore Islam organizes the production process on the basis of Islamic law that asserts the following : equal opportunity should be available for all; some market transactions such as monopoly as a form of business organization are forbidden; adulteration; short weight and short measurement, usury (Riba), and interest .
6. Islam places emphasis on equality in basic economic rights where individuals should have the opportunity to choose and develop their business; they should also have the freedom to access natural resources and to be free of any discrimination. On the other hand, it does not mean that Islam seeks to obliterate all inequalities of income and wealth because some income differences, according to the Islamic view, are necessary for the economy and market dynamics, especially if these differences were produced as a consequence of permissible economic activities. However,

Islam is strongly against social stratification caused by opportunities only being available for elite groups. Such exploitative practices are forbidden in Islam because this would raise inequalities in income and reinforce social injustice, thereby leading to many social problems (Ahmad1991: 19, 20, 32).

7. Justice of distribution is the one important element in the Islamic vision of a just socio-economic order where the Islamic scheme places emphasis on securing basic needs of all, irrespective of the stage of development of a country. This involves the eradication of what is known as 'absolute poverty' in the current poverty literature. Thus Islam gives the state the role of ensuring at least a basic minimum standard of living for all citizens. Because of this, it is compulsory for the state to establish a social security system in which the religious levy of zakah (poor due) plays an essential role for funding this system. If the revenue of zakah is not sufficient, the state has to supplement it from a general budget (Ibid.: 16, 97).

2.1.2.4 Social solidarity and social cohesions

"Worship Allâh and join none with Him (in worship); and do good to parents, kinsfolk, orphans, Al-Masâkîn (the poor), the neighbour who is near of kin, the neighbour who is a stranger, the companion by your side, the wayfarer (you meet), and those (slaves) whom your right hands possess. Verily, Allâh does not like such as are proud and boastful"
Qur'an 4:36

Social solidarity in Islam is essential in order to achieve the social cohesion of Muslim society. It means that society has to look after all vulnerable people who are unable to achieve their standard of living. Islamic teachings articulate individual and social responsibilities towards people such as the elderly, orphans, widows, disabled people and people who are incapable of working. Social responsibility for vulnerable people is a basic element in Islamic thinking and starts with the responsibility of the individual towards securing his living through the act of 'work'. The next level of responsibility rest with the individual's family and relations network, who would support that individual by 'Nafaqah' if he could not earn a living by his own means. The next level of responsibility lies with the local community, who will support those who have no family or relatives through mechanisms such as 'sadaqah', 'Neighborhood right' and 'waqif' which play significant roles in funding local communities. Finally, the state has an essential role to motivate people to undertake their responsibility. The state also has a role to establish the Social Security System (funded mainly by zakah) to support and maintain those who do not have work or family support.

Thus, social responsibility in such cases means there are many financial and non financial obligations towards different categories of vulnerable people. Those obligations are fulfilled through various mechanisms such as nafaqah, sadaqah, zakah, waqif which all work as 'social glue' to strength the social boundaries and achieve social cohesion. Some of these tools and mechanisms are explained below.

- **Nafaqah (Obligation maintenance by relative)**

    Narrated Abu Mas'ud Al-Ansari: The Prophet said, "When a Muslim spends something on his family intending to receive Allah's reward it is regarded as Sadaqah for him."
    (Bukhari, Volume 7, Book 64, Number 263)

    The Prophet said: Sadaqah given to a poor man is just Sadaqah, but when given to a relative it serves a double purpose, being both Sadaqah and a connecting link.
    (Ahmad, Tirmidhi, Nasai, Ibn Majah,).

Islam identified particular responsibilities for all better off members to help their close relatives through an institutional mechanism called 'nafaqah', which means obligation maintenance by relatives (Ahmad, 1991: 33). The Shari'a law promotes the rights of close relatives who need maintenance support (nafaqah) from those who are in a good position to help. Islam encourages individuals to support their relatives voluntarily, but in case they cannot or do not, the alternative way is to enforce maintenance support from individuals to their needy relatives (Ibid.: 96).

Ahmad (1991), referring to some the Islamic jurists, cited that:

> Legal compulsion is used for the provision of maintenance support in the following positions:
> 1. For a wife from her husband irrespective of her own financial position.
> 2. For poor and needy parents from their son.
> 3. For minor sons and daughters, unmarried or widows or divorced adult daughters in need of assistance, and adult son incapable of earning his living, from their father.
> (p. 59)

Ahmad discussed Islamic jurists having different opinions towards the use of legal compulsion in case of other relatives. Legal compulsion could be used to force rich individuals, under the inheritance scheme of Islam, to pay maintenance to their poor relatives. Therefore, based on this view, brothers, sisters, grandfathers, grandmothers, grandsons, granddaughters, and specific other relatives are also entitled to maintenance support (Ibid.: 59).

- **Sadaqah (voluntary alms)**

> The likeness of those who spend their wealth in the Way of Allâh, is as the likeness of a grain (of corn); it grows seven ears, and each ear has a hundred grains. Allâh gives manifold increase to whom He wills. And Allâh is All-Sufficient for His creatures' needs, All-Knower. (Qur'an 2:261)

Sadaqah is a large concept that involves many forms of charitable acts and almsgiving, but in general this term is associated with 'voluntary alms'. In the literary sense, the word of sadaqah could be interpreted in many ways. For instance, there is an obligation to sadaqa called 'zakah'. Also, there are pious endowments called waqif or sadaqah jariya. Another is the voluntary spending for the welfare of the poor called infaq. All these forms of charitable acts are called, literally, sadaqah in the Islamic context. The difference between the types of almsgiving is whether or not there is a type of mandatory obligation to give alms to create a type of 'right' for the poor. This is combined with moral and religious rules that organize the relationships between the needy and the almsgiver. For example, in the case of zakah, there is a religious obligation on the rich to give the poor their rights in the wealth of the rich. In contrast, voluntary alms is centred on a generous act of the almsgiver and their feeling of responsibility towards the poor and needy (Singer, 2008; Ahmad, 1991; Sabra, 2000)

The Qur'an and Sunnah emphasize some important ethics of sadaqah or almsgiving, for example, Muslims have to give sadaqah secretly, without show; also sadaqah should not be followed by any action that might hurt the feelings of the poor. A Muslim has to give sadaqah to the real needy people; not, for example, to people who adopt begging as a job.

> O you who believe! Do not render in vain your sadaqah (charity) by reminders of your generosity or by injury, like him who spends his wealth to be seen of men, and he does not believe in Allâh, nor in the Last Day. His likeness is the likeness of a smooth rock on which is a little dust; on it falls heavy rain which leaves it bare. They are not able to do anything with what they have earned. And Allâh does not guide the disbelieving people. (Qur'an 2: 264)

2.1.2.5 Social Security System: zakah (mandatory alms)

> The Mosques of Allâh shall be maintained only by those who believe in Allâh and the Last Day, perform As-Salât (Iqâmat-as-Salât), and give Zakât and fear none but Allâh. It is they who are on true guidance.
> Qur'an 9:18

> Hadith Narrated by Ibn 'Umar:
> "Allah's Apostle said: Islam is based on (the following) five (principles):
> 1. To testify that none has the right to be worshipped but Allah and Muhammad is Allah's Apostle.
> 2. To offer the (compulsory congregational) prayers dutifully and perfectly.
> 3. To pay zakah (i.e. obligatory charity).
> 4. To perform Hajj (i.e. Pilgrimage to Mecca)
> 5. To observe fast during the month of Ramadan."
> (Bukhari, Volume 1, Book 2, Number 7)

The term zakah has two meanings: 'to purify' and 'to increase' (Singer, 2008, Ba-Gader, 2004, MAIA, 1992). Legitimately, zakah can be defined as a "poor due or poor tax on the wealth of well-to-do Muslims in accordance with the provision of Shari'a" (Ahmad, 1991: 100). Zakah can also be defined as "the amount payable by a Muslim on his net worth as part of his religious obligation, mainly for the benefit of the poor and needy" (Iqbal, 2002: xix).

Sunnah classified zakah as the third base of Islam, as mentioned in the Hadith (above); whereas the Qur'an describes the good Muslim as the one who persists in doing Salah (prayer) and giving zakah. Accordingly, the typical Muslim (or real Muslim) is not just a believer, but one who translates his 'beliefs' and 'faiths' into practices in his everyday life. In this respect, zakah is a great test for the generous act of a person and how he can overcome the nature of greed and selfishness.

According to Islamic law, zakah is not a voluntary action but a mandatory one and an obligation of a Muslim to God; so zakah is not a 'grant' or 'donation' from the rich motivated by their feeling of pity or mercy towards the poor, but zakah is the right of the poor. Based on that, if a better off Muslim rejects paying zakah, this will be considered as breaking one of the Islamic bases.

> Hadith: "Tell them that there is a charity due upon them to be taken from their rich and to be given back to their poor" (al-Tirmidhi, al-Jami as-Sahih, cited in Ahmad, 1991: 60).

The state or central authority has a responsibility to ensure the application of this basis; accordingly the state can enforce people who refuse to pay zakah to take responsibility. This is what the prophet Muhammad and his followers did in the early period of Islam (Bonner, 2003).

The state has the responsibility to collect and distribute zakah. There are eight categories of people who are entitled to zakah, where the poor and needy are placed at the top of the list. The following verses show that:

> " Alms are for the poor and the needy, and those employed to administer the (funds); for those whose hearts have been (recently) reconciled (to the truth); for those in bondage and in debt; in the cause of Allah; and for the wayfarer: (thus is it) ordained by Allah, and Allah is full of knowledge and wisdom."

(Qur'an 9:60)

Although the preceding verse restricted the entitlement of zakah to those eight categories, some Islamic scholars and jurists (Ulama) expanded the categories to include other types of needy who suffer from the hard demands of modern life. According to Al-Gyzani (2007), the following categories can also be entitled to zakah:

- Households who are in needy conditions but are ashamed to seek support (their self-esteem prevents them from asking for support)
- Those whose earnings or income is insufficient for their needs or their family's needs.
- Those who work but their income is deemed a 'fixed income' or 'limited income'.
- Workers and employees with low productive capacity.
- Widows, orphans, elderly and divorced women who do not have a sponsor or breadwinner.
- Students in all age categories who do not have sponsored support for them.

The types of property on which zakah is due are: livestock, agricultural products, minerals, gold, silver, treasure and merchandise. Jurists agree that in modern times there are many items on which zakah should be paid, for example the holding of currency, the different types of financial assets such as bank deposits, shares and securities. Items of personal use are not subject to zakah (Ahmad, 1991).

There are many conditions for which zakah must be due including: full possession of an item which fulfills the *nisab* (the minimum quantity or amount which makes it liable to zakah) and the lapse of a full year (MAIA, 1992). The *nisab* for gold is 85 grams, for silver it is 595 grams and the *nisab* for cash and other financial assets and merchandise is similar to that for gold and silver. The *Nisab* for agricultural products is 5 *wasaq* (950 kg). The rate of *zakah* on the different items was clarified in *hadiths* where the lowest rate applicable in the case of gold, silver, cash, financial assets and merchandise is 2.5%, 10-15 % for agricultural products and 20% in the case of a treasure trove (Ahmad, 1991).

- **Zakat- al-fitr**

There is another type of obligation alms called 'zakat al-fitr' which has to be given to the poor by the end of the holy month of Ramadan (the fasting month). Zakat al-fitr is mandatory on all Muslim regardless of their gender, age or social status, as Hadith mentions:

> Narrated Ibn Umar:
> Allah's Apostle enjoined the payment of one Sa' of dates or one Sa' of barley as Zakat al-fitr on every Muslim slave or free, male or female, young or old, and he ordered that it be paid before the people went out to offer the 'Id prayer. (One Sa' = 3 Kilograms approx.)
> (Volume 2, Book 25, Number 579)

Zakat al-fitr is due on the individual himself rather than on his possessions as per the previous zakah). Zakat al-fitr aims to support the poor by providing them with food and enabling them to share and celebrate in the festival of Eid al-fitr (that comes after Ramadan). All able Muslims have to pay this zakat and usually the head of family is responsible for paying on behalf of himself and for each member of his dependent family. Usually zakat al-fitr can be paid in cash or any type of basic food such as barley, dates, wheat and raisins.

From the information above, it is clear that the institution of zakah plays a crucial role in the re-distribution of wealth and in the eradication of poverty. Zakah as a social security system in Islam can be regarded as political and economic tools. As a political tool, zakah enables the state to fulfill social justice and social stability. As an economic tool, zakah has a strong effect that would enable the state and society to eliminate and eradicate poverty, particularly when considering the huge amount of money paid annually as zakah and the amount of food given by Muslims as zakat al-fitr, enabling the poor to have food and overcome their hunger during the Eid festival.

2.1.2.6 Encouragement spending for welfare of poor (Waqif or pious endowment)

> The Prophet said: "When a person dies, his achievement expires, except with regarding to their things- ongoing charity (sadaqah jariya) or knowledge from which people benefit or a son who prays for him"
> (Sahih Muslim)

Waqif means endowment for general or specific purposes under Islamic Law (Ahmad, 1991: 100). Another definition, cited in Singer (2008: 92), is "Waqif is the most widespread form of 'ongoing charity' historically in the Islamic societies and it aimed to establish and sustain beneficent endeavors over time". According to some Islamic jurists, waqif is "the alienation of revenues - generating property with the principle remaining inalienable, while its revenues are disbursed for a pious purpose in order to seek God's favor" (Sabra, 2000: 70).

The key point in 'waqif' is the alienation of specific property where its revenues should be spent on charitable purposes, and would continue over time. Therefore waqif is one of the important charitable sources in Islam. Historical evidence showed that although waqif has existed since the early stages of Islam, it became widespread and influenced institutions in Islamic societies from the early 19th century. Waqif has strong influences on the social and cultural life of Muslim societies where it evolved within the Islamic cultural context, taking into account the social requirements of the Muslim communities and the political, economic and social realities of theses societies (Singer, 2008).

Generally, there are two groups of 'waqif' in Islam for public and for private beneficiaries. Firstly, the pious endowments for the public good where the funder aims to endow mosques, education institutions, health care, housing or other societal services. The benefits here could be specified for the poor and the needy or for Muslim rituals, social and cultural institutions (buildings, staff and activities). Secondly, the pious endowment for family members such as sons, daughters and other relatives (Singer, 2003, 2008).

Waqif and zakah play a crucial role in providing welfare for the poor. In addition, waqif is regarded as a form of social solidarity system because it is centred on serving the categories of vulnerable Muslims or supporting family members who are in need. This would, therefore, strengthen the family responsibilities towards the needy in particular, women, disabled people and the elderly.

By spending on public good, waqif plays a significant role in pushing forward the development and poverty eradication process, where waqif works to fund many essential processes of development such as building schools, hospitals, housing developments, water and food supplies, as well as other services such as providing training and job opportunities. In modern Muslim society, waqif is utilized to meet the demands of new necessities of public good spending such as: treatments for illness, the education system, providing scholarships for students, establishing social services, sponsoring research centres, activating the empowerment of the poor through offering education, training and job opportunities and funding the marriage institution by supporting youths in the cost of their marriage. Thus waqif is regarded as a crucial and complementary institution that has its weight not merely in poverty reduction, but also in advancing and pushing forward the development of modern Muslim societies.

Social structure and social function of 'waqif' in the Islamic history: charitable housing for women 'Ribat' as an example

Many studies discuss the importance of waqif in the Islamic context; one was conducted by Sabra (2000) who used a historical approach for studying and analyzing the social history of poverty and charity in the medieval Islam of Mamluk, Egypt. He explained the social roles of 'waqif' and how it became a social institution, providing food, education, housing and medical care to the poor of medieval Egypt, where many of these endowments were established by the elites of that era. The study exposed the social structure and social function of the 'waqif' and its relationship with the social historical context.

One of the most interesting points mentioned by Sabra was the social organization of charitable housing called 'Ribat/Arbita pl'. These types of charitable housing were mostly established for the benefit of poor women; in particular widows and divorced women. Sabra described the function of 'Ribat' as an institution that organized the life of women indoors, when every Ribat had a 'Shekah'[8] who was usually a woman from the local residency. This woman took the responsibility of supervision of the women's behaviour as well as the distribution of charity that was delivered to the Ribat. The Shekah would also educate the women, especially in the instruction of religious issues. The residents of these charitable housing projects were mostly women who had no men or other providers of income, so over time, the role of the Ribat developed to be stricter on women's behavior and many rules emerged to control the movement of the women outside of the residence. The women, therefore, became in a sense 'imprisoned', especially those women who were awaiting the end of their 'waiting periods' (al-oddah)[9]. This control on women's lives was, according Sabra, thought to be motivated by the patriarchy of society that desired control of the sexual behaviour of these women which would therefore guarantee that they were not engaged in any misconduct (see Sabra, 2000, chapter 4).

2.2 Poverty in the contemporary Islamic country: the dilemma of theory and practice

---

[8] - Shekah means in Arabic language a woman who is leader, head, or boss over other women. This label still exists in some Arbita of women such as can be found in Jeddah city. The label of Shekah gives the leader a special position and role as well as status among the residents. Ribat is still the popular name of the charitable residences of the poor, especially that of women.

[9] - The woman who had lost her husband by death or divorce must start 'the waiting period' called al-oddah. A widow has to spend four months and ten days as oddah. The divorced woman has to spend three months only. There are many things forbidden for women to do during this period, particularly remarriage. This time is assumed a sort of right for her ex-husband to ensure whether or not there is a pregnancy that belongs to him.

A global conference held in Malaysia (14 - 15 December 2004) and organized by the International Institution for Muslim Unity (IIMU) discussed the problem of poverty in the Islamic world. Many international papers and studies were presented in order to discuss the rich details of this problem. The discussion took two directions: a presentation of the multidimensional causes of poverty, and the Islamic vision for solutions.

Some studies mentioned the political dimension where the problem of poverty in the Islamic world has a strong relationship with issues such as the political regimes of Islamic countries and the impact of globalization and development (Al-Kalili, 2004, Ab-Lyail and Sultan-Ulma, 2004, Hamaam, 2004). The political regimes of some Islamic countries adopted some western political ideologies such as communism, socialism and capitalism and therefore could not deal with the demands of social reality. In terms of the impact of globalization, these political systems, which were unable to govern within an Islamic framework, failed to balance globalization's effects. However, the discourse of development was one of the controversial issues for some researchers (see Hamaam, 2004), where development in Islamic countries was considered a 'dependent development strategy' based on western models. As a consequence, the development model was not compatible with Muslim nations' demands and social contexts. The western development models were based on different epistemological bases (theories, concepts, and methods) from the Islamic epistemological perspective, thus problems such as poverty, hunger, and human alienation were intensified in Islamic society.

Another argument has been based on the economic dimensions of poverty in the Islamic world. As some studies have pointed out (Mylad and Abu-Gararah, 2004, Ali, 2004, Abu-Yarab, 2004, Al-Refaie, 2004), the main economic problem in the Islamic world is not the scarcity of economic resources but the injustice and inequality in resource distribution. The studies illustrate some economic issues that are the causes of poverty in Islamic countries such as:

- The underdevelopment economy caused by adopting dependent development, based on the western approaches.
- The current fiscal system in Islamic countries that undermines Islamic economic principles such as *Raba* (usury) and interest, both of which are forbidden in Islam.
- Weaknesses of the education system and its inadequacy for the requirements of the labour market.
- Lack of a social solidarity system based on financial worship such as *zakah, sadaqah, nafaqah, and waqif.*
- Weaknesses of investment in the Islamic world also increase debts that restrict the economic system in Islamic countries.

These multidimensional causes highlight many drawbacks and defects at both the micro and macro levels of the socio-economic structures within the Islamic world.

The ideological, spiritual, and moral dimensions of poverty in the Islamic world are another part of the current debate. Studies argue that the lack of production and inequality of resource distribution are in the fact caused by misunderstanding of the Islamic doctrines of work, production and distribution. The original Islamic perspective on work was as a religious duty, but over time, this meaning has changed. Al-Najaar (2004) highlights the following factors:

- The growth of 'Sufism' which made the link between piety, asceticism, and poverty, thus rendering the term 'work' as worthless. This caused the decline of 'work and production' as social values, particularly when notions of work and production seemed negative in meaning and when poverty became better than wealth from a Sufi Perspective.
- Although teachings of Islam advocate the work ethic, a negative perception towards work grew in some Muslim societies. For example, there was distortion for the meaning of 'depending on God' when some Muslims misread the religious text of this concept. Accordingly they believed that the concept meant that a person would not need to work because livelihood is guaranteed by God. Others believed that it was not necessary for a person to work because life was to be based on 'faith and destiny'. Therefore, such

beliefs and practices in some Muslims countries created negative attitudes towards the value and ethic of 'work', thus causing disruption to the economic life of society.

- In some Muslim and Arabic countries, there is a negative viewpoint towards some types of work such as manual labour and handicraft work. This type of work is correlated with low social status. On the other hand, there is widespread preference for intellectual and administrative work. Thus it can be seen how these attitudes and behaviours caused decline in the 'production processes' in Muslim societies.
- There was also a preference towards the human and social science over applied sciences (see for example al-Ghazzalli). This resulted in the decline of scientific production and subsequently a decline in inventions and military products.
- In terms of the distribution of production, the principle in Islam is that production processes in society belong to all its members. Accordingly, distribution must be based on ways that insure the needs of everyone. Social solidarity is a main principle in Islam; therefore, the Muslim community should be supportive and cooperative by using mechanisms such as zakah for the financial maintenance of the poor. However, misunderstanding for such Islamic principles and mechanisms affected negatively the distribution of production in Islamic countries, resulting in the rich having a monopoly on wealth and means of production.

Other studies focus on the moral dimension of poverty arguing that the individual is the main cause of poverty due to what he does, how he does it and how he behaves towards himself, society and the physical world. It is also thought that poverty affects the thinking, practices and morality of society, particularly when a section of that society finds themselves, as result of their circumstances, forced to engage in immoral and illegal actions (Al-Omir, 2004).

The social and cultural dimensions of poverty have been largely discussed by many researchers. Social and cultural factors associated with the lifestyle of Muslim societies are influenced by social and economic changes, thus impacting on Muslim life. One of these factors is when the function of zakah (the social security system in Islam) is made 'disable or inactivate' which has led to the loss of an important financial resource for the eradication of poverty. Another social dimension of poverty relevant to the social characteristics of population is the high percentage of the Muslim population living in rural and Bedouin areas, where many have negative attitudes towards features of urbanization and modernity, thus creating barriers for development plans of the state.

Some studies refer to the lack of social solidarity and family responsibility among relatives as another social dimension causing poverty. Other factors include traditional cultures that again cause obstacles for development, the trend of increased consumption, the impact of globalization and rapid social changes that affected social and economic life, all of which might be considered as primary or secondary factors that result in poverty. There are further factors, including increased populations, widespread illiteracy, disabled women and their participation in the development and public spheres, similarly are factors that have increased poverty rates dramatically in Islamic countries (Al-Rabie, 2004; Al-Daruti, 2004; Karofa, 2004; Ba-Gader, 2004).

So it can be seen that poverty in the Islamic world has different dimensions as result of the interaction between many social, economic, political, cultural, religious, and ethical factors. All these factors work within their social contexts to form a whole representation of the social reality of the Islamic world. This illustrates the gap between the theory (ideal thoughts and acts) and practise (the practical scheme that organizes everyday life) of Islam. The Islamic theory functions (or works) on the notion of the unity of the Islamic world (meaning the Islamic nation or Ummah), and assumes that the practise should be coherent with the theory. In terms of poverty in the Islamic world and according to the previous studies, the social reality of Muslim countries seems not inconsistent with Islamic theory as a result of the 'practise' or the 'practical scheme' expressing different interests and concerns for each part of society.

Thus, to produce an 'anti-poverty discourse' based on the notions of Islam is not an easy task and one that needs to adopt a 'holistic and comprehensive scheme' based on the requirements of Islamic theory whilst taking into account the geographical and cultural differences in application as well as the distribution of the resources of charity institutions (sadaqah, waqif and so on) and the social security system (zakah).

2.3 Women and poverty in Islam

Some studies on poverty and women in the Islamic world are concerned with the idea of the gender dimension of poverty (see for example Sabra et al., 2006). This idea shows how poverty increases among women and female-headed households (FHHs) as a result of gender differences in these societies, where women become subject to social and cultural factors that make them more vulnerable than other categories in society, resulting in poverty. For example, there exists discrimination against women based on their gender resulting in fewer opportunities to access education, employment, health care and social services.

This section aims to clarify the position of women in Islam in terms of gender difference that causes an increase of the incidence of poverty among women and FHHs. In other words, how the Islamic theory (the texts of Qur'an and Sunnah) look at women in the light of their gender, and whether or not this vision would affect women's position and roles in society in ways that lead women to be more vulnerable and needy. As this is such a crucial topic in itself, only the major points relevant to this thesis will be addressed.

As has been previously discussed, Islam has two sides: the 'normative side' which represents the religious texts and the 'practical side' which represents legislation and Islamic law that organized Muslims practice. The normative side is supposed to be 'static' i.e. nobody can change the sacred texts, whereas the practical side is usually 'dynamic' according to the changeable aspects of the social and historical structures of society. The position of women in Islam will be discussed within these two frames.

Women's position and their rights in Islam

According to some studies that used social historical analysis for the study of women and gender in Islam, much evidence illustrated that the religious texts of Islam gave women significant rights within spiritual and ethical dimensions. These rights provide equality between men and women as human beings who have same range of rights and responsibilities. Women's rights in Islam are stated in the Qur'an and Sunnah where these rights could be divided according to women positions – both indoors and outdoors. For example, the positions and roles of women indoors could be as daughter, wife, mother or sister and every position and role is surrounded by a set of general and specific rights. Generally the most important rights are nafaqah (financial sponsorship for the cost of living) and the protection by *wally* (her male guardian) who could be, for example, father, husband or brother. On the economic level, women have the rights to be economically independent so that the man will not be able to intervene on this issue without the woman's permission. Women have the rights to work and administrate their own business. Socially, women have the right to be educated or work (if they so desire); women can share and participate in the public sphere (such as women in the age of the Prophet Muhammad); a woman has the right to choose her husband or even refuse him; she has the right to claim divorce or even divorce her husband in court by the authority of Islamic law; women have the right to get her own dowry (Maher) and can put whatever conditions in the 'marriage contract' where these conditions would be obligatory by Islamic law. A woman has the right of nafaqah and hathanah (fostering and custody of her children) in the case of divorce. She has the rights of inheritance and the right to possess her wealth without the obligation of sharing. A woman is also not obliged to pay for or share the cost of living for her family, even if she is rich and her husband poor (but she can do so on a voluntary basis). Some texts also give women the right to refuse to do house work in her husband's house or even to breast-feed his babies (especially if she was served in her father's house before marriage) because her real position is a 'wife', therefore the husband must bring servants and a nurse; nevertheless the wife can provide those duties as an act of generosity but not as compulsory duty (Nassief, 1997; Wynn, 2008; Sonbol, 1996; Ali, 2008; Abu-Sikah, 1990). Further details of these rights can be found in the *Fikh* books[10]. These rights show that, theoretically, there are no barriers or obstacles in Islam that would force women into a cycle of the 'gender dimension of poverty'. This means that there is no clear reason for women to be discriminated against, oppressed, or prevented access to education, the labour market, or other societal resources. Similarly, the whole theoretical context of the religious texts assumes that women have to be sponsored and protected by men, so the men are obliged to take all social, cultural, and economic responsibilities of family life. Within this context, women have a clear right to be sponsored economically and protected socially by her male relatives at all stages of their lives, thus they do not have to be forced to work to pay costs of living under any condition except for on a voluntary basis. In the case of a woman having no family or other source of income, the state is obliged to support her financially through the social security system.

Theoretically, what the Islamic texts (Qur'an and Sunnah) outlined regarding women and their rights inside and outside the household unit is an ideal framework. However, the practical applications have taken another direction, mostly against (or counter to) women's interests.

Muslim women in the social reality

Many studies (for example, Sonbol, 1996; Abu-Sikah, 1990; Ahmed, 1992) illustrated and argued some historical evidence relevant to the position of women before and after Islam. They discuss how Islam emancipated women from the social

---

[10] Fikh books are where the Islamic Law is written in more detail according to different perceptions and interpretations of the fourth Sunni Madhabs. Those Madhabs almost agree of the beliefs basis issues whereas they have different points of view regarding law and legislation (derived from the texts) and their application in a Muslim's life.

and cultural boundaries that were prevalent in the *Jahilia* era[11] whereby Muslim women enjoyed a unique range of rights and access to participation in public life. In the Prophet's time, interpretation of the religious text was based on spiritual and ethical dimensions that were favourable to women in general. Historical evidence showed that this situation only continued for a short period of time, that period of the Prophet Muhammad and a few decades later. The position of women and their rights declined after that as result of many historical factors, one of which was the restriction on re-reading the religious texts which occurred in the 'Abbasid period'[12]. Consequently, the ethical and spiritual dimensions of the religious texts were ignored, and the political, religious, and legal authorities adopted only the 'andocentric voice of Islam' as these studies described it, whereby authorities used this direction to interpret the religious texts. From that time, all religious institutions and Islamic law and other aspects of Muslim society have adopted the andocentric vision (Ahmed 1992) Based on that, it can be concluded that women's rights and their social conditions underwent different phases of re-reading the 'religious texts' and re-writing 'Islamic law'. This process emerged within specific social and historical contexts that affected negatively the position of women and took into account the demands of social reality where the main players were both the religious and the political authorities.[13]

Generally these studies agreed on the influence of the three historical factors that affected the positions and rights of Muslim women:

1. The re-reading of the religious text that replaced the spiritual and ethical voice of that text by an andocentric voice (Ahmed, 1992).

---

[11] Jahilia in the Arabic language means the period of time that was before the prophet Muhammad, and was described as the dark era.

[12] Al-'Abbāsīyūn or the Islamic Abbasid Caliphate: was the third of the Islamic Caliphates of the Islamic Empire (750–1258).

[13] This is an important point in our argument in this thesis where the situation of women in Saudi society seems not different from other Muslim societies. The women's clam of their rights that secured by Islam will face by another 'andocentric voice' of interpretation the religious texts where the rights and positions of women re-interpreted according to the demands (or general good) of social realty which that serves the prevailing traditional culture.

2. The traditional culture of Islamic societies was influenced by the pre-Islamic patriarchal culture of neighbouring societies (e.g. Arab, Persian, and Indian). Thus patriarchal values were widespread and had a strong impact on Islamic culture, especially when dealing with women's issues. These values became sometimes stronger than the Islamic value itself[14].

3. According to some studies that investigated Arabic and Islamic societies, (see for e.g. Sonbol, 1996) these societies were enjoyed flexibility of the Islamic law until the end of the 19th century. When western modernity entered the Arab world at the beginning of the 20th century, many aspects of Muslim society were changed. Some elements of Islamic law also changed, thus the flexibility of Islamic law replaced the narrow focus on women's issues.

To conclude, this section is concerned with the Islam position regarding gender dimensions of poverty. Islam introduced women within a specific framework which involved ideal roles, rights, and duties to keep women secured against poverty and needy circumstances. On the other hand, the reality of contemporary Muslim societies shows an opposite situation where women's positions have declined and women are being deprived of many of their rights originally given to them by Islam. There were many overlapping and interacting cultural and social factors. This situation also evolved and developed within certain historical and cultural contexts; in addition this was supported by both the political and religious authorities.

Conclusion

This chapter has discussed the three main issues relevant to the subject of this thesis: poverty in the Islamic context; poverty in contemporary Islamic societies and women and poverty from the Islamic perspective.

---

[14] This is an important point in explanation and interpretation many cases through data analysis where the conflict between the Islamic values and the traditional values (patriarchy) in Saudi society.

'Poverty in the Islamic context' aims to present an Islamic theory on poverty where the religious texts of the Qur'an and Sunnah constitute an ideal type of belief and practice that work as a guideline for Muslim society. This section started with a conceptualization of poverty within an Islamic frame where definitions of poverty and related concepts were given. There followed a reflection on how Islam established a policy framework for the eradication of poverty. This framework functions on the level of beliefs and practices where the focus is to set principles and legislations to organize relationships between people. Based on that, many obligations and commitments support the social cohesion within three contexts: family and kinship relations, society and the state. The basic rule in Islam is that the individual is responsible for supporting and sustaining himself and his family through work and earning a living. In the event of this not being possible, this responsibility would transfer to his wider family network. Where there was still no support, the responsibility would be moved to the state to support him and his family. Within this vision, the Islamic texts of the Qur'an and Sunnah established and developed a strong policy framework for the eradication of poverty. This policy framework is promoted and supported by strong charitable institutions that work as a 'social safety net'.

The second section of this chapter, 'poverty in the contemporary Islamic world' highlighted the gap between theory and practice in Islamic societies. The social realities of these societies reflect many social, political, economic, religious and ethical dimensions of poverty, indicating many problems in Islamic society that might be a result of the disconnection between Islamic theory (system of values) and Islamic reality (system of practice).

The final section explored and introduced the Islamic perspective towards women and the gender dimension of poverty. Islamic theory (the religious texts) introduce an ideal framework in which women are located in and surrounded by a system of rights and duties. Within this system, women should be sponsored financially and protected socially by male relatives or by the state. In addition, women have access to other social resources, equal to men. Therefore the linkage between 'poverty' and 'being a woman' is unacceptable in Islamic theory. On the other hand, the Islamic reality offers a different perspective where various social and cultural factors come together to influence the social reality. Within this context, women have become devoid of many of their rights and have become oppressed within a template of deprivation and marginalization. In this way, the social structure of contemporary Muslim society has been re-produced in a form that advocates and supports gender differences and creates female poverty.

This chapter constitutes a basis of this thesis where data will be analysed, explained, and interpreted in the light of the theoretical framework of Islam, Arabic, and Saudi societies. Thus the theoretical discussion is essential for this thesis, where the subject of poverty and FHHs in Saudi society should be understood and conceptualized within an Islamic framework. Thus this chapter has highlighted how the Islamic theory of poverty could be working in Saudi society along with its theoretical implications as well as how the social reality of Saudi society reflects aspects of the practice system and how the space between theory and practice can be judged in terms of poverty, social policy and FHHs.

However, poverty and poor FHHs in Saudi society are subjects rooted and embodied within specific frameworks of meaning where the 'Salafi Islamic discourse'[15] shapes and impacts the social reality of Saudi society. Accordingly, in this research, poverty and poor FHHs will be investigated, understood and interpreted within the Islamic

---

[15] In Saudi Arabia the prevalent religious trend or 'Madhab' is 'Hanbally' in the way of Sihkh Muhammad bin abdul-Wahaab. This trend is the official Madhab of the country and labeled as 'Salafi'. It follows a specific understanding and interpretation of the religious texts; accordingly this trend has shaped and impacted on the whole social reality in Saudi society. Accordingly, Saudi society has its own specific aspects or characteristics of social life that sometimes seem conservative or even restrictive towards some issues such as religious rituals, women, family, social ethics and morality. In Western literature, this trend is usually described as 'Wahabisim' but in fact this description is culturally unacceptable within the Saudi context where the Saudis believe that it is a distortion and misrepresentation of the real meaning of 'Salafi doctrine'. So in this research 'Saudi Salafism' will be used rather than the concept of 'Wahibism' to describe the Saudi understanding and applications of Islam.

context in general and the Saudi context in particular. Therefore, what the Islamic theory introduces as an ideal type and the practical level reflected will both be essential guidelines for the analysis and interpretation of data in this research.

Chapter three
Poverty within the Arabic and Saudi Contexts

Introduction

Investigation of social policy and poor FHHs in Saudi society requires initial contexts wherein this subject can be understood. The contexts are twofold: the Saudi context where the FHHs are located and involved in, and the wider Arabic context that includes the Saudi context. Knowledge of the two contexts is essential for this research wherein data is analysed and findings are interpreted. This chapter offers a discussion on poverty issues within the Arabic and the Saudi contexts.

'Poverty in the Arabic context' will be considered within the Arabic discourse on poverty focused on issues such as poverty characteristics (or profile) of Arabic societies, social and economic development, the problematic social policies, Arab countries as they are portrayed in the UN-HDRs (United Nations Human Development Reports), and female poverty in the Arabic world and how this could reflect structural factors embedded in Arabic societies.

'Poverty in the Saudi context' is central to this research, where the discussion of FHHs must be based on a clear understanding of the Saudi social context. Therefore this chapter is concerned with poverty definition and measurement in Saudi, official statistics on poverty in KSA, images of KSA in the HDRs, the welfare system and social policies, financial issues relevant to the welfare system, programmes and projects for poverty elimination, and finally female poverty in Saudi society.

This chapter provides a picture of poverty in each of the Arabic and Saudi contexts. This will provide a framework for data analysis and interpretation.

3.1 Poverty in the Arabic Context

Many Arabic studies reflect the Arabic social context where the 'rentier state' and 'rentier economy'[16] still prevail despite all the Arabic projects and development

---

[16] - A **rentier state** is a term in political science and international relations theory used to classify those states which derive all or a substantial portion of their national revenues from the rent of indigenous resources to external clients. The term is most frequently applied to states rich in highly valued natural resources such as petroleum (Bisharah, A. , 2007)

programmes in the Arab region that attempt to match the western model of a welfare state (see Bisharah, 2007). This section discuses poverty in the Arab world through four linked concepts: (i) some issues relevant to poverty discourse in the Arabic world such as poverty profile, the dilemma of social and economic development, the institutional dimension of poverty, etc.; (ii) the image of the Arab region as reflected in the UN-HDR reports; (iii) the dilemma of social policies in the Arab world, and finally (iv) female poverty in the Arab region.

3.1.1 Studies on poverty in the Arabic world

One of the classic studies on poverty and income distribution in the Arab world was by Alfaris (2003) who considered the similarities and differences between Arabic countries in terms of poverty and income distribution. The study used a comparative methodology and was based on data that covered three preceding decades. Arabic countries were divided into three groups: high-income countries (oil countries of the Gulf Co-operation Council [six Arab Gulf countries, namely, Saudi Arabia, Kuwait, Bahrain, Qatar, the United Arab Emirates and the sultanate Oman] and Libya), middle-income countries (Egypt, Iraq, Jordan, Syria, Lebanon, Morocco, Algeria, and Tunisia), and the low income countries (Yemen, Sudan, Somalia, Palestine, and Djibouti). The most significant factors helping to reduce poverty in the Arab world were the liberalization of the oil sectors from corporate dominance, attraction of an Arabic work force to oil countries, and inward investments. Negative factors that increased poverty were wars and conflicts. Poverty in all Arab countries is widespread in the rural and agricultural areas. In the oil countries, poverty is widespread among non-citizens, usually the immigrant labour force. Regarding family size, poverty seems to be associated with the larger rather than small families. The result showed a significant reverse (contrary) relationship between poverty, unemployment and education, thus if the educational level is low, the rate of poverty and/or unemployment would be high.

Another area of study was on the idea of 'inequality' and 'income distribution' and their applications in the Arab world. The first concept applies when particular individuals or groups lack the resources necessary for subsistence; the second applies to the standard of living of the entire society where inequality exists in terms of the distribution of wealth, resources and opportunities for social improvement. Inequality in Arab societies reflects many social, economic and political dimensions where resources, income, wealth and opportunities are based on power and the social status of individuals and groups. Alfaris (2003) stated that inequality was most evident in the case of the rich and middle-income countries rather than the poor countries. This could be explained in terms of two sets of differences: structural differences such as geographical locations, natural resources, population size, age, educational structures, size of the agricultural sector, and economic and fiscal policies or internal differences such as the size and structure of families, the size of the rural sector and the phenomenon of rural to urban migration. In the GCC countries (oil countries), inequality was concentrated mainly among non-citizens. In these countries, the majority of the population were middle-income, where government policies tended to support them through, for example, housing, health care, education and job creation in the public sector. However, inequality in other Arabic non-oil countries was concentrated in rural areas that receive less interest and support from the states as opposed to the urban areas.

The institutional dimension of poverty has become part of the Arabic discourse of development and poverty. The eighth annual conference of the Arab Society for Economic Research (ASFER), held in Cairo from 19 to 20 April 2007, placed emphasis on the interactive relationship between poverty, institutions and development in the Arab world. The following studies demonstrate how Arabic countries still suffer many shortcomings and challenges caused by social, economic and political factors.
In a study on macro-policies for poverty reduction in Syria, Abdul-Kaleg (2007) argued that if the state desired the development plan to achieve the United Nation Millennium Development Goals (MDGs), some fundamental requirements would be to: increase interest in the geographical dimension of poverty (equalize the development plan between rural and urban areas); reduce unemployment and income inequality rates; strengthen social security; support agriculture sectors, education, health care and social services.

Mutwali (2007) in a study based in Egypt entitled 'Institutional Framework of Poverty Reduction Programs' demonstrated the significant role of formal institutions (such as health, education and social services) and informal institutions (such as family relationship network, voluntary organizations and informal relationships) in supporting anti-poverty programmes. Mutwali emphasized the importance of cooperation between the two types of institutions. To promote the efficiency of formal institutions, Mutwali suggested that the state should be concerned with three issues: a safety net such as social security and social insurance systems, economic empowerment of the poor through micro-credit projects and micro-finance, and promoting the productive capacities of the poor through the use of the human investment methods that focus on improving health, education and social circumstances.

Another study of Arabic oil countries entitled 'Poverty and Fluctuation in the National Income of the Arabic Oil Countries' by Abdullah (2007) argued the case that Arabic countries have for a long time been subjected to an impoverishment process by western countries in order to exploit Arabic oil. This process brought about the fluctuations of the national income of Arab countries, basically caused by the policies of the oil-consuming countries, as well as the economic fluctuations in these countries (i.e. western countries). This process negatively affected oil exports, its prices and revenue. Abdullah also cited certain internal factors relevant to the Arabic states and political systems, which heightened the situation. The factors were:

- Non-investment of surplus oil revenue by states in industrial or trade sectors, which would lead to a balance of the economic situation in times of fluctuation of oil prices.
- Not establishing an 'Equilibrium Fund' to transfer the surplus oil revenue and use that in times of budget deficit.
- States attempt to appease citizens by distributing a portion of surplus oil revenue in the form of cash or goods and services that will not add much to the productive base.

The fluctuation in individuals' income, inequality and poverty in Arabic countries are not processes that can be explained by studying internal factors; they are governed by external factors as well. The Human Development Report (2009) emphasized Arab economic vulnerability:

'One clear sign of the vulnerability of Arab economic growth is its high volatility tied to capricious oil markets, the region's economic security has been—and remains—hostage to exogenous trends...'(UNDP, 2009: 14)

However, there is a significant relationship between sustainable development and the well-being of society. In a study on 'The Impact of Agricultural Technology on Poverty in the Arab World', Mustafa (2007) outlined the considerable role of agricultural development. The study reflected evidence of the failure of Arab agricultural policies that did not achieve the promotion of agricultural productivity, reduce the food gap, increase national income or achieve a high standard of living for people. The study cited obstacles that hindered Arabic agricultural policies as: the weakness of economic efficiency, mismanagement of the agricultural sector, bureaucracy, giving priority to political objectives over economic ones, under-investment in agricultural research and the scarcity of renewable water resources.

These issues were also recognized by the Food and Agriculture Organization of the United Nations (FAO) and the World Bank in their study 'Farming Systems and Combating Hunger'. The studies argued that combating poverty and hunger should be concentrated on small farmers in their struggles for survival (FAO, 2005 cited in Hassan, 2007: 376). Therefore, the development process in such Arabic countries requires addressing issues such as food security as a basic need and developing appropriate agriculture policies. In this respect, some researchers like Hassan (2007) argue that Arab societies suffer from a 'food gap' caused by factors such as population growth, lack of production of food commodities due to the lack of adequate investments in agriculture, weak incentives for farmers, increasing global prices of food commodities, and political, military, and weather disturbances. The study highlighted the importance for Arabic decision makers to develop an economic policy to deal with poverty through agriculture to raise the income of the poor and to provide food security, which in turn would support social and political security.

3.1.2 Arabic region in the UNDP reports
The Five Arab Human Development Reports (AHDRs) issued from 2002 to 2009, indicated complex problems for social and economic development in the Arab region.

According to the AHDRs, there are many persisting problem areas such as high illiteracy rates, deterioration of education, the slowing down of scientific research and technological development, poor productive bases, increased poverty, raised unemployment rates, freedom and human rights issues and increased discrimination against women (see UNDP, 2002; 2003; 2004; 2005; 2009).

The AHDR (2009) addressed the obstacles to human development in the Arab region, suggesting the cause to be the fragility of the region's political, social, economic and environmental structures, its lack of people-centred development policies and its vulnerability to outside intervention. The report emphasized that human security is a basic condition for human development, and this is a widespread absence in Arab countries, thus holding back progress (UNDP, 2009: 1).

The AHDR (2009) focused on human security as fundamental for development; it analysed the current Arab situation and accordingly gave important recommendations for Arab countries to overcome the obstacles that threaten human security. Referring to the UNDP, human security is defined as "the liberation of human beings from those intense, extensive, prolonged, and comprehensive threats to which their lives and freedom are vulnerable" (*Ibid.*:2).

The report stated seven obstacles that threaten human security in the Arab regions:

1. Pressures on environmental resources
2. The performance of the state in guaranteeing or undermining human security
3. The personal insecurity of vulnerable groups
4. Economic vulnerability, poverty and unemployment
5. Food security and nutrition
6. Health and human security
7. The systemic insecurity of occupation and foreign military intervention
   (*Ibid.*)

The report presented substantial evidence, statistics and examples of the extent to which the problem has spread in Arabic countries. In terms of poverty, in 2005, about 20.3% of the Arab population was living below the two-dollars-a-day international poverty line. Using the international line indicates that, in 2005, about 34.6 million Arabs were living in extreme poverty. In terms of unemployment, data from the Arab Labour Organization (ALO) showed that in 2005, the overall average unemployment rate for Arab countries was about 14.4% of the labour force, compared with 6.3% for the world at large. The unemployment rate among the young in Arab countries is nearly double that compared with the rest of the world. Unemployment often has a female face, where the unemployment rates for Arab women are higher than those for Arab men, and among the highest in the world. According to the report, this reflects more than the failure of Arab economies to create sufficient jobs; it highlights a prevalence of social biases against women (*Ibid.*: 10).

3.1.3 The dilemma of social policy in the ESCWA[17] region

According to the ESCWA studies, the main problems of social and economic development in the Arab region, as also mentioned by the AHDRs, were the 'social policies' which were not integrated into coherent frameworks to support the development process. Accordingly, the programmes and projects of GOs and NGOs in the Arab countries seemed generally disconnected, so these policies were not compatible with the development strategies. The citizens became merely receivers of the services without being involved in the policies in practice or having any type of active roles (see the series of social policies studies: ESCWA, 2005; 2004 and 2009). Another study conducted on 'Security and Social Safety Net' in the Arabic region showed the inefficacy of the safety net policies (see ESCWA, 2008).

The ESCWA approach to implementing the suggestions that made by the AHDRs is through adoption and institutionalization of integrated social policies which should involve:

1. Investigating the social consequences of economic policies throughout the process of economic policy formulation

---

[17] The Economic Social Commission for Western Asia (ESCWA) is one of five regional commissions created by the United Nations in order to fulfil the economic and social goals set out in the United Nations Charter by promoting cooperation and integration between the countries in each region of the world. ESCWA forms part of the United Nations Secretariat, and it comprises 13 Arab countries in Western Asia: Bahrain, Egypt, Iraq, Jordan, Kuwait, Lebanon, Oman, Palestine, Qatar, Saudi Arabia, the Syrian Arab Republic, the United Arab Emirates and Yemen.

2. Informing public policy at every stage with social equity and human rights concerns
3. Bringing people into the centre of policymaking and mainstreaming their needs and voices across sectors and into the development process
4. Demonstrating that sustainable economic development can only be enhanced by the empowerment of all citizens, including the marginalized
5. Reaffirming the key regulatory role of the state and its capacity to translate theoretical and ideological values into concrete and measurable policy frameworks and approaches.

(*Ibid.*: 2).

3.1.4 Female poverty in the Arab region

The Arab Human Development Report of 2005 highlighted the situation of women in the Arabic world as being the result of a number of cultural, social, economic and political factors which interacted to affect levels of human development, as detailed below.

Education: due to a historical lack of opportunities to acquire knowledge, the Arab region has one of the highest rates of female illiteracy (as high as 50% compared with 33% among males).

Health: the maternal mortality rate in Arab countries averages 270 deaths per 100,000 births but in the poorest (i.e. least developed) of the Arab countries, the risk is much higher at over 1,000 deaths per 100,000 births

Economic activities: Arab economic participation remains the lowest in the world with no more than 33.3% of females aged fifteen years and older participating in the formal economy whilst 42% males participate. Both figures are in strong contrast to the world averages of 55.6% (females) and 69% (males).

Women continue to work in the low income economies in primarily traditional roles such as in agriculture and the services sector; in the Arab world, these roles are characterized by low productivity and low salary.

The reasons for Arab women's weak economic participation include:
1. The prevailing male culture, demonstrated by many employers' preference to employ men;
2. The scarcity of jobs in general;
3. Employment and wage discrimination between the sexes;
4. High reproductive rates;
5. Laws that have been designed for the "protection" of women such as personal status and labour legislation, which in reality restrict women's employability freedom because they require a father's or a husband's permission to work, travel or borrow from financial institutions;
6. Women's job opportunities have been undercut by weak support services and structural adjustment programmes.

Each worker in the Arab region typically supports more than two non-working people, thus dependency ratios are high in comparison with less than one in East Asia and the Pacific. The low rate of women's participation in the workforce is the most likely factor. High levels of family support become problematic with no infrastructure that promotes pension plans and work-related insurances and policies such as National Insurance or sick pay. There is a tremendous amount of pressure on females to maintain the family and to care for children and / or sick, elderly or disabled relatives without sufficient financial and social support.

Level of well being: women appear to suffer higher levels of "human poverty" as measured in terms of the deprivation of the three dimensions of the human development index, namely: health, knowledge and income. Women are particularly disadvantaged in terms of their personal liberty.

The spread of poverty and disempowerment of women: the widespread levels of income poverty inevitably lead to women's disenfranchisement from public life: for example, in areas such as politics, professional and technical employment and control of economic resources. Female human poverty is a result of disempowerment and exclusion from upper-level legislative, administrative and organizational roles as well as from the professional and technical arenas.

The impairment of personal liberty

There are specific forms of violence practised against Arab women where it will prove difficult for Arab legislators and governments as well as Arab social movements to achieve change in attitude and more importantly, behaviour. The violence can take the form of honour killings, in which a woman is killed on the pretext of protecting family honour, or domestic violence, condemned in many parts of the world. Additionally, the high incidence of female circumcision in some Arab countries leads to serious health complications for women, which have long term detrimental effects.

Human development – female development

In terms of human development, women would need the following in order to participate equally and fully in society:
1. Full equality of opportunity between women and men so that women can acquire and employ skills, knowledge and labour equal to men;
2. Guaranteed rights of citizenship for all women as equal to men;
3. Acknowledgement of, and respect for, gender differences. Women are different from men, but not relatively deficient. It is not acceptable to use gender differences to support theories of inequality between the sexes or for the purposes of sex discrimination.

Studies such as Ba-gader (2008), Mitualli (2007), and ESCWA (2001) highlight the plight of rural women who suffer increased rates of poverty in comparison with men. According to the studies, rural women tend to be sidelined as a result of family responsibilities, lack of access to the labour market and low representation within society and societal structures. These factors in turn impact on their status, and low status in society often leads to discrimination and is embodied by inequality and deprivation.

ESCWA Centre for Women conducted a study entitled "Female-headed households in selected conflict-stricken ESCWA areas: an exploratory survey for formulating poverty alleviation policies". The study aimed to explore the implications of women's poverty in the ESCWA region by focusing on female heads of households in selected conflict areas: Lebanon, the Palestinian West Bank and Gaza, and Yemen. The study highlighted the link between conflict, gender, and poverty. The findings showed that there was cross-cultural evidence of some similarities and differences between poor female-headed households (FHHs) and other poor females. The study revealed that the women were subject to the same cultural complexities that controlled all women and subjected them to traditional restrictions. In addition, the poor FHHs could be subject to the same debilitating effects of poverty as other poor population groups.

The study pointed out the differences in respect of specific multiple inter-linked burdens such as:

(1)- While female heads of households have taken on the role of sole income provider, they continue to be perceived and treated in terms of their prime responsibility for reproduction and related activities.

(2)- Female heads of households in the three ESCWA areas are not accorded legal recognition, despite their positions as the sole economic supporters of their families.

(3)- The women are faced with legal problems and social marginalization.

(4)- The women are subject to a complexity of factors that limit or even prevent their access to the labour market (which they may have in common with their peers in poor male-headed households).

(5)- Female heads of households live in circumstances where there is no physical male adult presence which in turn provokes some sections of society to monitor the women's behaviour with suspicion in light of their increased physical mobility which is in fact necessary for them to earn a living for their families.

Thus, in the Arab world, female poverty is formed or heightened in certain societal and cultural contexts.

3.2 Poverty in the Saudi context

3.2.1 Background information on the Kingdom of Saudi Arabia

The Kingdom of Saudi Arabia (KSA) is located in the far southwest of Asia. It is the largest country on the Arabian Peninsula, and has an important religious position; it is known as "The Land of The Two Holy Mosques" in reference to Mecca and Madinah, the two holiest places in Islam. Saudi Arabia is the world's leading oil exporter, but although this remains the Kingdom's main source of revenue, there has been a shift to increase and diversify the economy, to reduce dependency on oil.[18]

In terms of the KSA's population, as Table 3.1 shows, according to the census of 2004, Saudi citizens comprise 72.9% of the population whereas non-Saudis comprise 27.1%. Regarding Saudi citizens, males comprise 50.1% while females comprise 49.9%. The KSA consists of 13 administrative provinces; Mecca is one of the biggest and most important provinces and there are a number of large and important cities such as Mecca, Taif and Jeddah. As shown in Table 3.2, the population of Mecca province is 5,797,971; this constitutes 25.6% of the overall population of the Kingdom. The number of Saudi citizens in the province is 3,586,565 (1,793,813 females and 1,792,752 males).

Table 3. 1 Population of KSA 1425 H (2004)

Saudi citizens			Non-Saudi citizens			Total population		
Males	Females	Total	Males	Females	Total	Males	Females	Total
8,285,662	8,243,640	16,529,302	4,271,598	1,872,638	6,144,236	12,557,260	10,116,278	22,673,838

Source: Ministry of Economic and Planning, census of population in KSA 2004

Table 3.2 Population of Mecca province 1425 (2004)

Saudi citizens			Non-Saudi citizens			Total of population		
Males	Females	Total	Males	Females	Total	Males	Females	Total
1,792,752	1,793,813	3,586,565	1,425,273	786,133	2,211,406	3,218,025	2,579,946	5,797,971

Source: Ministry of Economic and Planning, Census of Population in KSA 2004

---

[18] - http://www.saudinf.com/

Number of households in the KSA and Mecca province in 2007

Table 3.3 shows that the number of households in the KSA, both Saudis and non-Saudis, is 4,208,121. Table 3.4 identifies the number of households in Mecca province as 1,245,032, which constitutes 29.6% of the total number of households in the Kingdom.

Both tables identify that the number of Saudi households is 2,922,524. In Mecca province, there are Saudi 727,311 households which constitute 24.8% of the total Saudi households in the Kingdom and 58.4% of all total households in Mecca province. (This means that non-Saudi households constitute 41% of Mecca households).

Table 3.٣ Housing Units (Occupied with Households), Households, and Individuals, in all the provinces of Saudi Arabia (total population, Saudi and non-Saudi)

all 13 provinces of KSA	Saudi	Non-Saudi	Total
Housing Units	2,922,524	1,285,597	4,208,121
Households	2,922,524	1,285,597	4,208,121
Individuals	18,133,570	5,847,264	23,980,834

Source: Ministry of Economics & Planning, Population and Housing Characteristics in The Kingdom of Saudi Arabia: Demographic Survey 1428 H. (2007)

Table 3.٤ Housing Units (Occupied with Households), Households, and Individuals, in Mecca province (total population, Saudi and non-Saudi)

Mecca province	Saudi	Non-Saudi	Total
Housing Units	727,311	517,721	1,245,032
Households	727,311	517,721	1,245,032
Individuals	3,908,363	2,188,714	6,097,077

Source: Ministry of Economics & Planning, Population and Housing Characteristics in the Kingdom of Saudi Arabia: Demographic Survey 1428 H. (2007)

3.2.2 Poverty in the Kingdom of Saudi Arabia

Poverty in Saudi Arabia is considered a neglected research topic given that it is a country rich in exportable oil and one that owns the biggest world petroleum reserve. (Hashim, 2003, cited in Algarib, 2005) undertook a public opinion survey to investigate the reasons and causes of poverty in Saudi society which identified the following:

"...there is a direct positive relationship between poverty and crime. Also there is a direct relationship between poverty and intellectual, moral, social and behavioural deviations. Poverty is deemed a significant factor that leads to social dissolution and vice commission; also poverty contributes in social retardation. Moreover poverty leads to an increase rate of crime, extremism, and maybe terrorism. Poverty plays a significant role in reducing human awareness, and it increases social retardation; violence and riots; thefts; and destroying public property. Poverty also leads to a growth in class hatred and class differences...." (Hashim in Algarib, 2005: 42)

Algarib reflected that as a subject for investigation poverty was a taboo subject in Saudi society, but in 2002 this changed.

In 2002, Prince Abdullah Bin Abdul-Aziz (the current king of KSA) visited the slum areas in the capital Riyadh and there followed an official announcement on the problem of poverty in Saudi. This visit brought about the official announcement of the existence of poverty in Saudi society and the beginning of a qualitative shift in how to deal with the poverty problem. A royal decree was issued in 25/10/1423H (2002) to establish the National Poverty Reduction Strategy (NPRS), a long-term project that aims to tackle and eradicate poverty in Saudi society (see 93 of this thesis for further detail).

There are significant relationships between poverty, unemployment and income inequality, and the state of social policy and the social welfare system. In Saudi society, several studies have outlined important evidence that shows an increase in the problem of poverty. In addition, they have highlighted the drawbacks of the social welfare system in Saudi society. Algarib (2005), in a study entitled "Poverty in Saudi Arabia: readings in the adopted procedures", used an analysis of official documents to identify the important procedures that have been adopted by Saudi society for the alleviation of poverty. He highlighted some procedures such as the establishment of the social security department, the pensions system and the social housing sector. In addition, there are many non-governmental organizations that are a part of the official support system. Although noticeable developments have occurred in these procedures, they remain inadequate and do not cover all the needs of the poor. The study also cited the fact that there is no unemployment benefit.

In a study on welfare programmes Albaaz (2005) investigated poverty in Saudi Arabia in an attempt to introduce a 'poverty measurement'. The study reported some important evidence that showed a noticeable increase in the poverty rate in Saudi society in areas such as the unemployment rate, the proportion of pensioners who depend on a limited pension, and the lack of social benefits that poor people receive from the Social Security Department (SSD). Moreover, there has been a marked decline in purchasing power associated with a high cost of living. Albaaz also distinguished between two categories of people who deserve to be supported by the welfare system; the first category comprises those whose income is classified as "poverty line" and the other is those whose income is classified as "subsistence line." The researcher determined the subsistence line as 1,660 Riyals per person per month and the poverty line as 1,120 Riyals per person per month (poverty line = net income after deducting expected rent for housing) [19]. For this study, Albaaz relied on "income statistics of Saudi Arabia" from the World Development Indicators. He suggested that in order to build an efficient anti-poverty strategy, both personal and societal factors causing poverty should be taken into account. In addition, he recommended that effort to develop 'work values' among poor people should continue.

---

[19] - To determine the poverty line in Saudi Arabia, Albaaz followed a complex mathematical process that relied on the following steps: 1- calculating the median income of the Saudi person, which was found to be 3,320 Riyals per month (39840 per year). 2- If a person has an income of less than half of the median income it means his income is on the poverty line. So, the subsistence line is set at 1,660 Riyals per person per month (19920 per year). 3- The net income after the deduction of the expected rent for housing equals the poverty line, which was found to be 1,120 Riyals per person per month (13,420 per year).

Migration has played a role in the increase in poverty in Saudi cities, as Alneim (2004) mentioned in a study on urban poverty and its relationship to internal migration. She met 400 families and found that the poorest people in Riyadh city came from outside the city and congregated in the slum areas and old districts. In addition, the most important reasons for migrating were transportation difficulties and under-development in the migrants' original areas. As well as mentioning poverty as one aspect of internal migration, the study also revealed the absence of an effective social welfare system, particularly in supporting these people and helping them to live in an appropriate way (Alneim, 2004).

Another statistical study has been conducted by the Saudi Pension Department (cited in Albaaz, 2005) indicating the poor economic situation of military pensioners: 60% of these pensioners have an income of less than 3000 Riyals per month, 40% do not own a property and 58% live in old houses or small flats. Thus the study indicates the significance of improving the pension system as part of an efficient anti-poverty strategy and/or reform the welfare system.

The social security system in the KSA has been the subject of many criticisms. In his critique of the social welfare system, Albaaz (2005) identifies a lack of efficiency in the social security system, and suggested that reform would be necessary in order for the system to achieve poverty reduction more effectively. The questions that arise are whether or not the social security system has achieved its goals of increasing the standard of living of the poor and needy, and whether this system can be adapted to involve all categories of poor. According to Albaaz, the evidence shows many shortcomings on both counts, some related to the administrative processes for social welfare programmes and the fact that the social security system excludes some categories such as unemployed people. The study identifies complex bureaucracy as the most visible barrier facing the poor when dealing with this system. Women and FHHs are believed to suffer particularly from the complexities of the system. Another problem is that the system does not use precise indicators, such as a poverty line, to estimate social benefits and allowances for beneficiaries of SSD.

Al-Shubiki (2005) emphasized in her PhD thesis the importance of poverty line estimates for SSD income support. She suggested an estimated poverty line of RS 9226.63/$2460.4 annually for individuals and SR 64,586.41/$17,223.04 annually for families with seven members. The individual figure is almost identical to the benefit rate in 2005, but for a large family, the prescribed pension was less than half the sum estimated as necessary (see table 3.10). Overall there have been no poverty lines or specific indicators associated with formulating the level of income support for SSD. The earliest estimates of income support, dating back to 1963, did not rely on scientific indicators. Subsequent developments simply increased the amount of income support and allowances according to the size of the state budget.

The studies collectively highlight that there are no clear methods for studying poverty and no clear concepts relevant to poverty definition and measurement. According to the studies, poverty was associated with factors such as migration, unemployment, the lack of social safety nets and the inefficiency of the welfare system and social policies.

3.2.3 Poverty in Saudi Arabia: the problem of definition and measurement

According to the UN report, issued in 2005, entitled 'Progress Towards the Millennium Development Goals in the Arab Region 2005' (UN, 2005: 4), poverty studies and poverty data are hard to locate in the Gulf Cooperation Countries (GCC)[20], with the exception of Bahrain. Regional studies suggest that poverty lines are still vague in GCCs and research on poverty in the region is considered a challenge not merely because of the absence of precise definitions of poverty, but also because of the absence of a clear methodological and conceptual framework that would provide a basis for establishing poverty lines and poverty indicators (Abdul-gafar, 2007). Such a challenge applies more particularly to poverty in Saudi Arabia, where there is no clear picture of poverty, nor even an agreed identification of a national poverty line or poverty indicators (see Algarib, 2005 and Albaaz, 2005).

---

[20] GCC countries consist of six Arab Gulf countries, namely, Saudi Arabia, Kuwait, Bahrain, Qatar, the United Arab Emirates and the sultanate Oman.

3.2.4 KSA in the Human Development Report

Since 1990, the Human Development Report has each year published the Human Development Index (HDI) which looks beyond Gross Domestic Product (GDP) to a broader definition of well-being. The HDI relies on a composite measure of three dimensions of human development: the likelihood of living a long healthy life (measured by life expectancy), of being educated (measured by adult literacy and enrolment at the primary, secondary and tertiary levels) and of having a decent standard of living, measured by purchasing power parity (PPP) and income (see Human Development Report, 2007/2008). The HDI for Saudi Arabia is 0.812, which gives the country a rank of 61st out of 177 countries. Saudi Arabia's human development index is measured as follows: life expectancy at birth is 72.2 years; there is an adult literacy rate of 82.9% for ages 15 and older, with a combined primary, secondary and tertiary gross enrolment ratio of 76%; while GDP per capita is US$15,711. (This data refers to 2005 as reported in the 2007/2008 report). These figures highlight the large gap between GDP per capita and HDI for many countries, and in the particular case of Saudi Arabia there is a clear gap between GDP per capita ($15,711) and HDI (0.812), indicating that the overall levels of human development are still less than might be expected from the GDP of Saudi Arabia. The findings of the report are consistent with those of the United Nations Economic and Social Commission for Western Asia (UN-ESCWA 2003) on poverty in the region, which found that the GDP per capita in these countries is higher than the HDI. This means that the countries have a lower achievement in human development, compared with their GDP.

In terms of building the capability of women, the Human Development Report (1995) introduced the gender-related development index (GDI) as a measurement for inequality in achievement between women and men. Although the GDI uses the same indicators as the HDI, it adjusts the HDI downward for gender inequality. The greater the gender disparity in basic human development, the lower a country's GDI relative to its HDI. Saudi Arabia's GDI value 0.783 should be compared with its HDI value of 0.812: in other words, its GDI value is 96.4% of its HDI value. Out of 156 countries with both HDI and GDI values, 144 countries have a better ratio than Saudi Arabia (UNDP, 2008).

3.2.5 Statistics on poverty in Saudi Arabia

The Social Security Department (SSD) is the government body that deals officially with issues of poverty; people in need apply to this department to access the income support system - Social Security Pension (SSP) and Social Security Subsidy (SSUB). Therefore, the statistics of SSD beneficiaries should indicate the number of poor people in Saudi. These statistics do not include the poor among non-Saudi citizens who number 6.1 million and represent 27% of the Saudi Arabia population. These figures are kept as a separate issue, partly due to the lack of statistics on poverty among non-Saudis. While SSD is a government branch that serves exclusively Saudi citizens, voluntary organizations and women's associations may serve the non-Saudi poor, but with some limitations. However, for more understanding of non-Saudi citizens' status, it is important to note that in accordance with laws and rules of the Ministry of the Interior (the Home Office) and the Ministry of Labour, non-Saudis are unable to stay legally in the country unless they have a work licence and a resident permit (Iqama). The Saudi Labour Law (last version issued by Royal Decree No. M/51 in September 2005) organizes precisely the relationship between employer and employee (or worker). It is in this context that non-Saudis will find themselves in secure conditions. The influx and settlement of non-Saudi residents can be linked to when pilgrims or visitors on Hajj and Umrah visas remain in Saudi, often as illegal immigrants after the end of the religious season. Many of them congregate in slum areas where problems of crime and poverty become prevalent.

Table 3.5 shows the total number of people who relied upon the income support system for the Social Security Pension (SSP) in all provinces of the Kingdom between 2004 and 2005/21. The table is organized according to the categories (groups) who are entitled to income support in accordance with the eligibility criteria. There are three groups: men who are in a situation of complete incapacity, orphans, and single females/FHHs. The table shows that in Mecca province, there were 65,286 poor, which equals 19.4% of the total number of poor in the Kingdom. Within Mecca province, the

---

[21] - Referring to MSA, the annual statistics books of 2004-2005 are the latest issue (version) that can be obtained at the moment.

36,896 single females and FHHs constitute 56.5% of the total number of poor in the KSA. The statistics indicate the importance of studying poverty in the KSA with an emphasis on female poverty. The total number of beneficiaries amounts to only 2% of Saudi citizens, who represent a larger proportion, around 12%, of all Saudi households (see Ministry of Economic and Planning, 2007).

Table 3.° Number of the poor (beneficiaries) in KSA on the income support system of SSD (SSP) (2004/2005) according their categories

	Province	Men with complete incapacity	Orphans	Single females/FHHs	Total
1	Al-Riyadh	13979	1382	32072	47433
2	Mecca	26891	1499	36896	65286
3	Al-Madinah	13254	630	12446	26330
4	Al-Qasim	5334	608	7515	13457
5	Eastern Province	12831	690	19652	33173
6	Asir	27425	1106	24652	53183
7	Ha'il	6829	204	8646	15679
8	Tabuk	4822	274	5779	10875
9	Al-Baha	5682	133	7015	12830
10	Northern Borders Province	1773	155	3096	5024
11	Al-Jouf	2439	297	3867	6603
12	Jizan	18988	1131	14997	35116
13	Najran	4404	228	5515	10147
	Total	144651	8337	182149	335137

Source: Ministry of Social Affairs (MSA) annual statistics book (2004/2005)

Mecca province is one of largest provinces in the KSA. As Table 3.6 shows, Mecca province is divided into 11 cities (of which Jeddah, Mecca and Taif are the three largest), and towns and local areas. The table shows, under various categories, that the number of the poor who were entitled to a Social Security Pension (SSP) and Social Subsidy (SSUB) in cities and towns was 76,001. The majority of the poor, who made up 58.8% of the total number of beneficiaries, were concentrated in Mecca, Jeddah, and Taif. This may be explained by the fact that these cities attract immigrants, whether from inside or outside the Kingdom, because of their commercial and religious positions. It should also be noted that the poor who are on SSP are more numerous than the poor who are on SSUB (see below). In Mecca province, the recipients of SSP represent approximately 9% of all households.

Table 3.˅ Numbers of the poor (beneficiaries) in Mecca province on the income support system for (SSP) and (SSUB) 1425H-1426H (2004/2005).

	Social Security Offices (SSO)	Men complete incapacity	Orphans	Lone female/ FHHs	SSP total	SSUB	Total
1	Mecca	5,413	328	8,970	14,765	2,510	17,274
2	Jeddah	3,436	447	9,154	13,064	2,283	15,347
3	Al Layth	2,790	129	2,031	495	1,161	7,111
4	Taif	4,122	230	6,288	1,0640	1,477	12,117
5	Al Kunfutha	3,555	102	3,340	6,997	1,079	8,076
6	Turba	1,453	57	1,920	3,430	744	4,174
7	Rabig	1,322	19	784	2,125	137	2,262
8	Ranya	801	45	974	1,820	346	2,166
9	Bani Malik	934	19	667	1,620	217	1,837
10	Arada Ashamalyah	1,959	21	1,777	3,757	483	4,240
11	Misaan	1,106	21	991	2,118	278	2,396
	Total	26,891	1,499	36,896	65,286	10,715	76,001

Sources: Ministry of Social Affairs, annual statistics book 1425H-1426 H (2004/2005); Social Security Department records, 1425-1426H (2004-2005)

3.3 Welfare system and social policies for eradication of poverty in KSA

This section discusses the social welfare system in KSA, in particular, the governmental policies, representative of the Ministry of Social Affairs (MSA) and non-governmental policies, representative of the charity sector.

3.3.1 Welfare system in the KSA

Saudi Arabia does not possess a western-type welfare state. There are two National Insurance funds, covering public and private sector employees respectively. These are funded by employer and employee contributions, and pay retirement pensions and are possibly among the world's most generous pension schemes. Retiring employees receive a fortieth of a final salary for each year of service, so after 40 years in employment an employee can retire on full salary (see: Public Pension Agency, PPA, 2003 & General Organisation of Social Insurance, GOSI, 2000). The Saudi state provides free school education and free health care for all Saudi citizens. Thereafter the state system that addresses poverty is the Social Security system, and it is this system that is examined below.

There is no constitution and there are no laws that grant Saudi citizens the right to any minimum standard of living or income. Social security benefits are not based on independently assessed needs and there is no official poverty line. The system is Saudi specific, based on Saudi, Arabic or Islamic principles. The assumption is that citizens who cannot support themselves will normally be provided for by their families; otherwise they should be supported by charity. The state acts as a charitable agent. The social security budget is determined not by need but by what the state feels obliged and able to provide.

Figure 1 shows the structural organization of the Ministry of Social Affairs (MSA), the governmental body responsible for the issues of welfare and social support for the vulnerable categories of the population. The MSA is divided into two main branches: the Social Security Department which address poverty issues, and the Department of Social Welfare which addresses other categories of the dependent population.

Figure 3.1 The structural organisation of Ministry of Social Affairs

Ministry of Social Affairs

⇩

Department of Social Welfare and Development   Department of Social Security

⇩   ⇩

1-Social Welfare Department
- Public administration for care of orphans
- Public administration for care of the disabled
- Public administration for care of juvenile delinquents
- Public administration for care of the elderly
- Public administration for social protection
- Public administration for health care
- Administration of social benefits

❖ Public administration for pension and subsidies

❖ Public administration for the social investigation of cases

❖ Public administration services for beneficiaries

❖ Public administration for review and revision

2-Family Affairs Department

3-Social Development Department

➢ Public administration for social development centres.
➢ Public administration for charitable associations/organisations.
➢ Public administration for cooperative societies

Source: Ministry of Social Affairs publishing (2007).

3.3.2 Government Organizations and Non-Government Organizations in the KSA that work for the alleviation and eradication of poverty

As mentioned previously, the most important government body dealing with issues of poverty is the Social Security Department (SSD). The second type of organization dealing with issues of poverty and the poor in Saudi Arabia is the voluntary organization, which in this context means local charities and women's associations, and deals with both Saudi citizens and non-citizens.

Social Security Department (SSD)

The Social Security Department (SSD) was established in 1963 as the government body responsible for vulnerable and poor people in accordance with specific conditions and acceptance criteria. In 1975, the post of Deputy Minister of Social Security (DMSS) was created, which then became attached to the Ministry of Social Affairs as the main body (see Social Security Department, 2007).

According to the Social Security System Bill[22] there are two types of income support in Saudi Arabia. First, the Social Security Pension (SSP) is a regular sum of money assigned to the beneficiary in accordance with the stated articles of the Social Security System, for which the following types of persons and families are eligible: orphans, the disabled, senior citizens who do not have retirement pensions, women with no provider and families with no provider. Further categories can be added to the above-mentioned only through Cabinet resolutions based on a proposal made by the Minister of Social Affairs (Article 3).

There are conditions of eligibility required for the receipt of SSP which commence with an application that has to be submitted to the Office of Social Security and which should include all the information and documents needed. In addition, the application should show the extent to which the claimant is in need of the SSP, with proof of current situation through official documents, with field visits to some cases if necessary[23]. If the beneficiary retains another regular income, the amount of which is over one half of the pension received, then this amount will be deducted from the pension, on the condition

---

[22] - The Bill can be found in English at: http://www.mosa-d.gov.sa/daman/en/firstpage.html. Also, see "Social Security System: new updated Bill", Riyadh: SSD 2007.

[23] - In the Social Security Bill there are details for each category in terms of the conditions and required documents. In respect of widows, divorced, and abandoned women, and those whose husband is a prisoner, all should have an ID card, and official documents that prove their situations. Sometimes they have to get an official letter signed by the local mayor.

that the remaining amount of pension is not less than SR6000 ($1600) per year (Article 7). The following are not included under the types of income stated in Article 7:
1. Student awards
2. That which is given by an appropriate social or health institution to a beneficiary for the purpose of medication (money or material gifts)
3. Alms, charitable donations and gifts.

Second, the Social Security Subsidy (SSUB) is a decided sum of money to be assigned to the beneficiary in accordance with the rules of Article 13 of the Social Security System. These rules show that the Minister, or whichever deputy the Minister assigns, is authorized to assign a cash payment to any beneficiaries that he/she deems in dire need, on the condition that this money does not exceed the limit of SR30,000 ($8000) in each case. The SSUB can be provided to the following categories if they satisfy the conditions and requirements: the temporarily disabled, prisoners' families and families whose supporters are absent or have deserted them. The beneficiary should be not less than 50 years old (otherwise they are deemed capable of supporting themselves unless they qualify for a Social Security Pension) and should not be in receipt of SSP. In addition, he/she should satisfy the general conditions of Social Security. Assistance may be repeated after three years and subsidies are also provided during times of emergency or disaster (Article 18).

The last update to the policy occurred when King Abdullah Ben Abdul-aziz came to power (2005) whereupon he increased the SSP and SSUB by 73% (see the levels of compensation in Table 3.10).

Charities and women's associations

The charities in Saudi Arabia are voluntary organizations, but they are governed by the rules of the MSA. The Eighth Development Plan, according to the report of UNDP and MEP, emphasized the role that voluntary associations can play in the alleviation and eradication of poverty. These associations provide support and care to the needy throughout the country; in addition, they play an essential role that complements that of the relevant government organizations (UNDP & MEP 2005) without being under its restraint.

As shown in Table 3.7, the total number of charities and women's associations in the KSA in 2005 was 355. In the table, they are divided into charities where the administrative body is male, and women's associations that are administered by women. There is more interest focused on the issues of women and families among women's associations than there is in those organizations where the administrative body is male. However, the statistics show that there are far fewer women's associations, with 23 compared to 332 charities supervised by men. This may highlight a significant cultural dimension of Saudi society where the conservative traditional culture is still concerned with the separation between the woman's world and the man's world, which might increase the suffering of poor women due to the lack of institutions run by women. Table 3.7 also shows that there is a greater number of charities in those provinces with higher population rates.

Table 3.⁷ Numbers of charities and women's associations in the KSA (2004-2005).

	Province	Charities (supervised by men)	Women's charitable associations	Total
1	Al-Riyadh	62	4	66
2	Mecca	67	5	72
3	Al-Madinah	24	3	27
4	Al-Qasim	26	1	27
5	Eastern Province	34	5	39
6	Asir	41	1	42
7	Ha'il	22	1	23
8	Tabuk	10	1	11
9	Al-Baha	12	-	12
10	Northern Borders Province	5	-	5
11	Al-Jouf	5	1	6
12	Jizan	19	1	20
13	Najran	5	-	5
	Total	332	23	355

Source: Social Security Department records, 1425-1426H (2004-2005).

The work of the charities and women's organizations is based on the policy and legislation of the MSA. The Bill of Charitable Associations was passed in 1989 and deals with the policies, regulations and instructions related to the registration of charities and their framework. The charitable associations aim to provide social services and social support for the poor and needy. In addition, they provide programmes in education, childcare, health care, care for the elderly and disabled, charity housing and housing improvement (Social Security Department records, 1425-1426H (2004-2005).

3.4 Finances

This section presents financial issues relevant to SSD and charitable associations in KSA

3.4.1 Budget and financial allocations for SSD and charitable associations[24].

Referring to the SSD Bill (Article 18), the financial resources for the Social Security System are as follows:

- Money collected through alms
- Money collected by the public treasury
- Money collected through charitable works, donations, gifts, and endowments according to the established regulations in this respect
- Investment returns from the Social Security system's invested money.

Table 3.8 shows the 2005 figures for SSD spending, with $803,283,377.6 on financial support paid out to the poor as SSP and SSUB, with 85.5% spent on SSP and 14.2% on SSUB. The total amounted to less than 3% of all state spending, which accounted for 27% of GDP (see Saudi Arabian Monetary Agency, 2008).

Table 3.^ Budget and financial allocations of SSD paid to the beneficiaries as SSP and SSUB 1426-1425 (2004-2005)

Category	SR
Social Security Pension SSP	2,576,938,396 ($ 687,183,572.2)
Social Security Sub SSUB	427,107,472 ($ 113,895,325.8)
Collaborators expenses	8,266,798 ($ 2,204,479.466)
Total	3,012,312,666 ($ 803,283,377.6)

Source: Ministry of Social Affairs records, 2004-2005.

---

[24] - I relied on the available financial statistics of the MSA for 2005 and 2006.

The total income for charitable associations was $99,500,662.4; 44.5% from financial donations, whereas the MSA financial support was 9.4% of the total budget. As detailed in Table 3.9, the expenditure of charities in 2006 was $86,099,440 in contrast to $803,283,377.6 by the MSA. Financial support for the poor was $20,847,492.26, which comes to 24.2% of the total, whereas the majority of the expenditure was $53,834,793, being 62.5% of the budget for costs and administration.

Table 3. ٩ Budget and financial allocations of charitable associations paid to beneficiaries as social assistance 1427 (2006)

Total financial support	78,178,096 ($ 20,847,492.26)
Total in-kind support (non-financial)	39,002,050 ($ 10,400,546.66)
Housing/mosques cost	3,812,283 ($ 1,016,608.8)
Activities/demonstrator cost	201,880,474 ($ 53,834,793.6)
Total assistance	322,872,900 ($ 86,099,440)

Source: Ministry of Social Affairs records, 2006.

3.4.2 The Social Security System in the KSA: how income support has been determined and developed

It is important to examine the historical development of the social security system in the KSA. As mentioned above, the social security system (represented by SSD) was established by Decree 1382H (1963), which is regarded as a base year for the measurement of poverty. The Social Security Pension (SSP) was determined at that time as follows: for all SSD beneficiaries, the head of family received one Saud Riyal (SR 1) per day, making a total of RS 360 per year. Dependent family members received SR 1/3 (one third of a Saudi Riyal) per day for each person, making a total of SR 1450 per year for a family of seven members, which was the maximum number of family members that could be registered with the social security system (see Albaaz 2005: 50, 51).

The Social Security System has passed through several stages of development from 1963 to the present time. This development has taken the form of increasing income support allocations generally and for SSP in particular. The development process has been boosted by several royal decrees issued by successive Saudi Kings. The following table shows the SSP increases that took place between 1963 and 2005.

Table 3.11: Increases in SSP compensations for individuals and families from 1963 to 2005

Year	SSP annual compensation for head of family	SSP annual compensation for family (seven members)
1963	SR 360 ($ 96)	SR 1540 ($ 410.4)
1974	SR 1080 ($ 288)	SR 5400 ($1440)
1976	SR 1620 ($ 432)	SR 8100 ($2160)
1981	SR 2268 ($ 604.8)	SR 11349 ($ 3026.4)
1992	SR 5400 ($ 1440)	SR 16200 ($4320)
2005	SR 9400 ($ 2506.6)	SR 28000 ($ 7466.6)

Source: Albaaz (2005), and the Bill of Security System (2006).

Figure 3.2: Increases in SSP compensations for individuals and families from 1963 to 2005

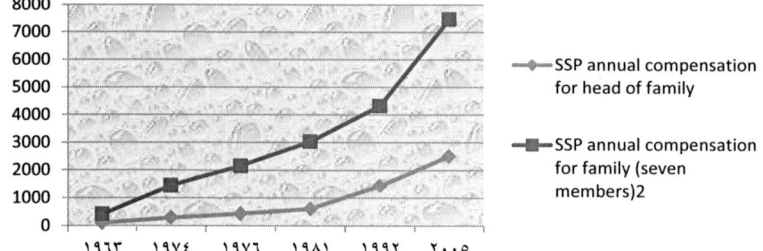

These figures need to be set in several contexts. Between 1974 and 2005, the compensation rate for a family of seven increased 5.18-fold. Over this same period, nominal GDP rose 7.4-fold, and real GDP 2.17-fold. Non-oil monetary inflation was 473%. This meant that the real level of benefits in 2005 was a little higher than in 1974, and had increased less rapidly than the GDP. Another set of benchmarks is that in 2006 the average annual salary in the private sector was $4428. The minimum for a clerk in the state sector was $5542 and the minimum for a teacher was $22,902. A single person on the Social Security Pension received just over $2500 (see Saudi Arabian Monetary Agency, 2008).

Under the recent boom of oil prices (which ended in 2008) and the increase in the state's income, the questions currently raised for the KSA are: how should the social security system be developed in response to the changing circumstances of the poor resulting from the current social and economic transitions? and how far should social security policy look beyond merely increasing fiscal allowances, enabling more substantial policies to be considered within a sustainable development plan?

3.5 Projects and programmes for the alleviation and eradication of poverty in the KSA

There are many governmental and non-governmental projects and programmes relevant to poverty elimination.

Governmental projects

3.5.1 The Eighth Development Plan

In 2005 the Eighth Development Plan (2005-2009) was issued, outlining an ambitious strategic vision for development, aiming to achieve the Millennium Development Goals (MDGs) by putting poverty reduction at the heart of public policy. The Eighth Development Plan defines poverty as follows: "Poverty is not limited to material deprivation, but has many other dimensions such as hunger, lack of shelter, inability to secure medical treatment, lack of access to education and schooling, illiteracy, and unemployment" (Eighth Development Plan, chapter 16).

Accordingly, Saudi Arabia puts raising living standards, improvements in the quality of life and the provision of job opportunities for its citizens, at the top of the twelve general objectives of the Eighth Development Plan. The plan also involves 22 strategic bases (see the Eighth Development Plan, Chapter 2) of which the first six bases are:

1. To increase the share of Saudi manpower in total employment in various sectors, by upgrading their efficiency and productivity through training and re-training, and to continue to substitute Saudi manpower for non-Saudis;

2. To place emphasis on women's issues, promote women's capabilities and remove the constraints that impede their participation in development activities;

3. To expand provision of health care and social welfare services to the entire population;

4. To take care of needy citizens and to pay attention to the management and reduction of poverty by concentrating on economic policies and programmes that will lead to higher economic growth, along with achieving balanced development for all regions in the Kingdom;

5. To develop all relevant aspects of education and training systems, adapting them to meet the changing needs of society, the labour market and the development process. In addition, to keep abreast of advances in knowledge and technology, paying special attention to the promotion and dissemination of culture.

6. To improve the quality of public services and increase their supply to meet the growing needs of the population, along with improving the performance of the responsible agencies.

In this way, improvements to the quality of life, poverty reduction and the welfare of women were established as central aims of the current economic and social development of Saudi Arabia.

3.5.2 National Poverty Reduction Strategy (NPRS)

A significant transformation occurred in state policy in terms of dealing with poverty as a serious problem when Prince Abdullah Bin Abdul-Aziz (the current king of the KSA) visited slums in the capital, Riyadh, in 2002. A royal decree was issued - 25/10/1423H (2002) – to establish the National Poverty Reduction Strategy (NPRS), which operates at the level of policy analysis and planning.

The report of the United Nations Development Programme (UNDP) & Ministry of Economy and Planning (MEP) (2005) introduces some features of the National Poverty Reduction Strategy as follows:

A. Fundaments of the Strategy:

• To provide the poor with opportunities to establish and enhance their material and human assets, through providing work opportunities, credit, education, training and health services.

• To enhance the ability of the poor to participate efficiently in economic activities.

• To improve the living standards of the poor through enhancing their ability to face health, natural and economic risks.

B. Themes of the Policies of the Strategy:

1. Macroeconomy: policies aimed at accelerating economic growth and distributing its benefits equitably among the regions and social groups.

2. Economic empowerment of the poor: policies aimed at providing the poor with their own means of production and raising their productive capabilities, as well as improving work opportunities.

3. Public services: policies aimed at improving health, education and municipal services.

4. Social protection: policies aimed at increasing the effectiveness of the social security network, and enhancing the role of benevolent and voluntary organizations in poverty alleviation.

5. Family property: policies and programmes aimed at solving housing problems and providing adequate housing for the needy

(see UNDP & MEP 2005: 21, 22)

As a result of the report of the NPRS, the Saudi Cabinet of Ministers issued a decree in 27/7/1427H (2006) to establish and develop a Supplementary Support Programme, the aim of which was to bridge the gap between the "actual income" of poor families/individuals living in extreme or absolute poverty, and the "poverty line". The state funded programmes with an annual budget of 264,000,000 RS (70,400,000 $) towards the following aims:

- To increase orphans' allowance, foster family allowance, disability allowance, marriage funds, and schooling funds.
- To support the foundation budget of the National Charity Fund (NCF) by providing 300,000,000 RS (80,000,000 $) annually.
- To develop an "emergency aid programme" which aims to support families who are under the absolute poverty line and who live in emergency

conditions that increase suffering such as the illness, death, or imprisonment of the family breadwinner.
- To increase the state funds for charities.

(See NPRS, 2008)

3.5.3 National Charity Fund (NCF)

The NCF was established in 25/10/ 1423H (2002) as an operational tool for the NPRS. Its aims are as follows:

- To offer interest-free loans for establishing small business projects.
- To develop individual skills by offering various training courses.
- To provide help with finding job opportunities.
- To raise awareness among the poor about how to improve their skills, including information about available training courses and help in securing jobs relevant to their skills
- To find "business incubators" for small business projects.
- To further develop the idea of the "productive families' project".
- To develop a sense of social participation towards poverty reduction issues.
- To help governmental bodies concerned with poverty issues to understand the educational, social, health, and housing needs of the poor.
- To enable voluntary organizations to participate in poverty reduction programmes.

Five main programmes have been established to achieve these goals, namely:
- Awareness programmes which aim to help the poor understand their problems and develop their skills.
- A "Small business project" programme.
- A "Productive families "programme.
- Educational scholarships and training courses
- "Job centre" programmes.

The current trend is towards work on the practical level, and therefore the NCF concerns itself with processes and programmes. Thus, many programmes for poverty reduction are launched by the cooperation of the NCF with several local partnerships such as private sector and voluntary institutions (see NCF, 2008).

3.5.4 Social Security Aid Programmes (Additional aid programmes provided by the Social Security Department)

Besides giving income support, the SSD developed aid programmes to help the poor to overcome difficulties of daily life. According to the SSD records, the programmes launched during 2007 – 2008 were:

- Programme of the Restoration of Houses
- Programme of the Discount Card, helping people with low income to obtain reductions or discounts on their food purchases
- Health Insurance programme: helping the poor to get free treatment and medications.
- Programme of Support for Electricity Bills: help in paying electricity bills.
- Complementary Aid Programme, providing the poor with a sum of money to bridge the gap between their actual income and the expenditure needs of daily life.
- Home Furnishing Programme, helping poor people to furnish and equip their homes
- Bag and school uniforms, which help poor people to meet the needs of school requirements for their children.

(See: Ministry of Social Affairs, 2008)

3.5.5 Saudi Credit Bank (SCB)[25]

The SCB was established in 1971 to extend interest free loans to Saudi citizens who have limited financial resources, in order to help them to overcome financial difficulties.

---

[25]- http://www.mof.gov.sa/en/docs/ests/sub_tsleef.htm

Its loans are extended in return for a sufficient mortgage or acceptable surety from a creditworthy individual or firm to insure the repayment of the loan. The SCB offers loans up to SR 20,000 (5,333.3 $), if the beneficiary satisfies the following conditions:

- A loan applicant must be in actual need of the loan.
- The applicant's annual income should not exceed SR 36,000 (9,600$).
- The applicant should not have any outstanding loans from the SCB, regardless of the type and amount.
- The guarantee should conform to the SCB's bylaws and its relevant instructions.

The SCB provides loans for marriage, home repairs, vocational pursuits, as well as other social endeavours, including family loans (See Ministry of Finance, 2009a; Ba-Gader 2008: 165).

3.5.6 Real Estate Development Fund (REDF)[26]

The Real Estate Development Fund (REDF) was established in 1974 and started its activities at the beginning of fiscal year 1975/1976 by providing loans to citizens to help them construct their own homes and for investment purposes. REDF began operation with a capital equivalent to SR.250 million. Since the start of its activities at the beginning of fiscal year 1975/1976 and up to the end of fiscal year 1998/1999, REDF has granted 443,842 private loans as well as 2,488 investment loans, with a total value of SR 120,144 million ($ 32,038.4 million), resulting in the construction of 555,866 residential units (See Ministry of Finance 2009b; Ba-Gader 2008: 166).

Non- governmental projects

3.5.7 Human Resources Development Fund (HRDF)[27]

The Human Resources Development Fund was established in 2000 as a legal entity that enjoys administrative and financial independence. The general objective of the fund is to prepare a national workforce and help them to gain employment in the private sector. In order to achieve the general objective, the HRDF offers the following:

---

[26] http://www.mof.gov.sa/en/docs/ests/sub_ests_dev_fund.htm

[27] http://www.hrdf.org.sa/hrdfnewsite/default.aspx

- Grants to those involved in the preparation, training and employment of a national workforce, especially in the private sector.
- A share of the expenses of preparing, training and employing the national workforce in the private sector.
- A percentage of the salary of any trainee who is hired by a private firm after he / she finishes training. The same applies for new recruits to the firm.
- Financial assistance to programmes in the field, projects, plans and studies aimed at employing Saudis and helping them to replace the expatriate workforce.
- Provide loans to private establishments that prepare and train the national workforce.
- Embark on studies and research related to activities in the field of preparing, training and employing the national workforce.

(see HRDF 2009)

3.5.8 Abdul Latif Jameel Community Service Programme (ALJCSP)[28]

The Abdul Latif Jameel Community Service Programme (ALJCSP) is one of the largest and most famous programmes in Saudi society and was established by the ALJ Company, the largest commission agent for TOYOTA. ALJ Company started its social programmes in the 1980s, but the Community Service Programmes were launched in 2003 with a view to developing many partnerships with local and international organizations. The most popular programmes are:

- ALJ funding for training courses for professional posts.
- ALJ funding for small business projects.
- ALJ funding for family productive projects.
- ALJ funding for social and health programmes.
- ALJ funding for international programmes.

---

[28] http://www.aljprog.org/ar/bernameg_abdulatif/ourprog.asp

3.6 Female poverty in Saudi Arabia

There is no clear picture of female poverty in Saudi Arabia. This could be explained by the lack of accurate statistics and data on poverty in general and poverty among women and FHHs in particular. Additional to this is the lack of studies on poverty, both quantitative and qualitative.

Regarding the studies of poverty among women, there are two studies of note as described below.

Alshibeki (n.d), in a study entitled 'The social problems of poor women in Saudi society', tried to investigate the extent of women's poverty and some related social problems. This study was based on an analysis of official documents. The findings showed that there has been a marked increase in the rate of poverty among women compared with men, and one piece of evidence showed that the number of women who receive social benefits and social support from both the SSD and from charitable associations, is greater than the number of men who receive support. The study highlighted some problems experienced by women, such as illness and the breakup of the family. Furthermore, poor women faced problems with the judiciary system due to the weak legal processes relating to women as well as the prejudice of some judicial rulings against them. In addition, poor women suffered from bureaucracy and the ineffectiveness of the regulations of the social welfare system.

In an unpublished study conducted among poor FHHs in Jeddah and the Kelease area[29] by King Abdul-Aziz University (2006), a survey was used to investigate a sample of 1500 poor FHHs that had been selected randomly from those who were receiving social support and social benefits from the SSD and women's charitable associations. The study aimed to describe the socio-cultural environment of these households, in addition to searching for the causes of poverty and poverty severity among FHHs. The results showed that 67% were illiterate whilst others had only a basic education, and 77% of FHHs were headed by divorced, widowed and separated women. The high rate of fertility was significant; a high percentage of households had children younger than 6 years old and a significant percentage of households had 7 members or more. In terms

---

[29] - Jeddah City is the second most important city in the Kingdom of Saudi Arabia. Kelease is a small town administratively attached to Jeddah City.

of reasons for becoming FHHs, they were sequentially: the death of the family's male breadwinner, his unemployment, his sickness, or abandonment of the family and all responsibilities. The study attempted to measure 'poverty severity' by using a measurement based on a 'derived variable' and tried to measure three levels of poverty among FHHs: poverty threshold (1.43% of FHHs in this level), relative poverty (92.11% of FHHs in this level) and absolute poverty (6.26% of FHHs in this level). The study identified some factors that affected 'poverty severity' in women-led households and identified a range of factors such as age, family status and the employment status of their husbands. Young women were more affected by poverty - they did not own their own house, they had small children or children of school age, or their husbands were unemployed, therefore the family's poverty was increased due to the fact that the women in this position were not eligible for 'lone mother benefit'[30]. The study suggested that it is important to have integrated social policies to deal with the demands of poor FHHs.

3.6.1 Women and unemployment

According to the Ministry of Economy and Planning (see Table 3.11), the rate of unemployment for Saudi females is higher than the rate of Saudi males. Female unemployment reached a peak of 26.27% in 2006. This figure raises a question on whether or not the increase in the unemployment rate among Saudi women, as compared to men, has a significant association with the limitation of job opportunities for women.

Table 3.11 also shows low unemployment rates for non-Saudis, compared with Saudis, which could be explained in a study by Alsreaha (2007) who researched the reason behind the unemployment rates of Saudis which were a result of their avoidance of certain jobs deemed to have a low social reputation. These types of job provide a good

---

[30] - The current SSD's regulations provide income support to lone mothers who are divorced or widowed; it seems difficult to support a poor woman with a spouse even if he is unemployed. In addition, there are no policies regarding support for unemployed people.

opportunity for non-Saudis who constitute the actual 'working class' in Saudi society and whose jobs are the most required by the labour market.

Table 3.11 shows the total rate of unemployment in 2007 among Saudis as 11.05%, although the media, the press, and some official reports increase the number to 30%. It is indeed possible that the problem of unemployment in Saudi society is greater than the governmental statistics reflect.

Table 3.11 unemployment rate by sex and nationality

Year	Saudis			Non-Saudis			Total		
	Males	Females	Total	Males	Females	Total	Males	Females	Total
2001	6.82	17.23	8.34	0.98	0.60	0.93	3.87	9.14	4.62
2002	7.57	21.70	9.66	0.82	0.62	0.79	4.21	11.51	5.27
2003*	8.00	23.18	10.35	0.80	0.79	0.79	4.36	12.51	5.56
2004*	8.39	24.40	10.97	0.77	0.93	0.80	4.49	13.36	5.82
2005*	8.74	25.41	11.52	0.75	1.06	0.80	4.60	14.07	6.05
2006	9.07	26.27	12.02	0.74	1.17	0.80	4.71	14.69	6.25
2007	8.30	24.70	11.05	0.40	0.5	0.43	4.24	13.21	5.63

*Estimates
Source: Central Department of Statistics and Information, Ministry of Economy and Planning (cited in Saudi Arabian Monetary Agency 2008).

Figure 3.3: Unemployment rate by males and females for Saudis citizens from 2001 to 2007

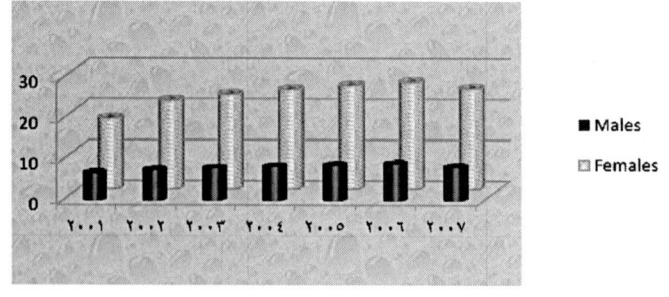

3.6.2 Government statistics on female poverty

According to the SSD's statistics for 2006/2007 (see Table 3.12); and after treating manually the numerical data in order to be able to display separately the number of poor women and FHHs from the total number of poor people, the results are described below. The number of poor women who are registered in the SSD for the SSP, in all the KSA (13 provinces) amounted to 273,137 women or cases (women could either be accounted for individually or as head of a family). The total number of the poor registered for SSP & SSUB in the entire Kingdom was 606,182, so the women in this case constitute 45% of the overall number. This ratio is relatively large and becomes problematic in the context of a society that is structured on the assumption that women will be supported by their male relatives.

Table 3.12 Numbers of beneficiaries on SSP & SSUB in all kingdoms 2006/2007

Kingdoms' Regions	SSP & SSUB	Women on SSP
	No. of all beneficiaries	No. of women beneficiaries
Riyadh	88,650	48,233
Mecca	121,449	58,030
Al-Madinah	46,041	18,636
Al-Qassim	26,693	11,715
East Region	65,911	30,966
Asir	84,806	34,283
Tabuk	19,979	8,730
Ha'il	28,776	12,350
Northern Borders	14,508	5,417
Jazan	54,556	21,434
Najran	18,221	8,066
Baha	21,746	9,033
Al-Jawuf	14,846	6,244
Total	606,182	273,137

Source: Social Security Department, Annual statistics book 2006/2007

The Statistics in Table 3.13 (below) also show that in terms of the Mecca province (Jeddah is located as one of the important cities in this province), the total number of poor who were registered in 2006/2007 on SSP only was 30,270; the number of women who received SSP was 17,352, thus women constitute 57% of poor people on SSP.

In terms of Jeddah City, statistics show that the number of poor who are on SSP is 9,107 of which 5,617 are women who thus constitute 61% of the total number of poor people in Jeddah who are on SSP.

Table 3.13: Numbers of beneficiaries on SSP in Mecca province 2006/2007

	Mecca region (the local towns and cities)	The beneficiaries of SSP	
		Number of All beneficiaries (including women/FHHs)	Number of Women/FHHs
1	Mecca	8197	4891
2	Jeddah	9107	5617
3	Tife	6181	3560
4	Misaan	343	213
5	Bani Malik	239	125
6	Al-Kunfutha	2044	926
7	Arada Ashamalyah	890	462
8	Al Layth	1405	447
9	Audum	37	6
10	Rabig	453	291
11	Ranya	533	281
12	Turba	841	533
	Total	30,270	17,352

Source: Social Security Department, Annual statistics book 2006/2007

The previous figures demonstrate that women comprise a high percentage of the receivers of official income support from the SSD in the entire Kingdom and that this is particularly high in the Mecca region and Jeddah City (the study site) compared with the number of men. There are significant indicators of the problems that women and FHHs face, therefore it would be important to study female poverty in Saudi society, in particular FHHs, in more in-depth.

Conclusion

The investigation of social policy in relation to FHHs must not be conducted in isolation from its social contexts. The subject of this research, social policies and FHHs in Saudi Arabia, exists within a specific Saudi social context, thus the subject is understood according that context. However, the Saudi context must then be paced within the wider social context of Arabic society, where there are shared historical contexts, cultural influences, social and economic factors, problems and obstacles, in particular those relating to issues of development, poverty and women. The Arabic context involves the Saudi social context in the Arabic cultural system; therefore this chapter has discussed both the Arabic and Saudi contexts in their respect of poverty, women, and other related issues.

This chapter has highlighted issues such as indicators of previous studies on poverty in the Arab region; the picture of the Arab region in the UNDP's reports; the Arab region and integrated social policies and female poverty in the Arab region. Studies reviewed here presented some indicators on poverty discourse in Arabic society where the problem of sustainable development is integral to this discourse. The UNDP's reports reflect the Arab world as having many problematic issues such as the fragility of the political, social, economic and environmental structures, characterized by a lack of people-centred development policy which in turn threatens human security, freedom and rights, leading to the marginalization of women and other vulnerable groups, high rates of illiteracy, unemployment and poverty. In terms of women's poverty in the Arab world, this has to be understood in terms of women's status in general, that is characterised, according to AHDR (2006) by low levels of education, health conditions and work opportunities for women and where the traditional culture impedes the progress of women's empowerment. Within this social context there is a prevalence of high rates of poverty and unemployment among Arab women and an infringement of their human rights and freedom.

The chapter has highlighted many sub issues relevant to the whole context of Saudi society such as the lack of poverty definitions, poverty measurements and official statistics on poverty and it has shown how the KSA is portrayed in United Nation Development Reports (UN-HDR 2007/2008). This chapter has also introduced the Saudi welfare system and some relevant financial issues. The chapter concluded by highlighting the reality of female poverty in Saudi society by providing numerical evidence on the rates of unemployment and poverty among Saudi women in comparison to Saudi men.

Overall, this chapter has looked at the available data and information on poverty in the Arab and Saudi contexts. The main objective was to highlight how women's poverty in Saudi society occurs as a result of several inter-linked socio-cultural factors.

This chapter has also demonstrated that there have been few previous studies on poverty and women in Saudi Arabia. Therefore this thesis is an in-depth exploratory study of the subject.

Chapter four

The Research Problem and Research Methodology

Introduction

As the previous chapter highlighted, the problem of poverty among women and FHHs is an important issue that overlaps with multiple social, cultural, and organizational determinants in Saudi society. This problem has not, to date, been examined sufficiently in Saudi society, where 'poverty' intersects with the factor of 'gender' and where this in turn needs more in-depth investigation. However, the increase in the incidence of poverty in Saudi society - and an increase amongst women in particular, as reflected in the statistics of SSD - is not just a social problem but also a challenge for policy makers. For policy makers, it is fundamental, if they wish to make efficient social policies for poverty eradication, to rely on strong evidence relevant to the social reality and the demands of different categories of the poor. It is important that decision and policy makers should not consider the poor of society within the same framework but treat them according to the different perspectives appropriate to their different categories. Therefore poor women and FHHs constitute a specific category of poor people who have their own specific demands and social conditions and will accordingly need specific policies.

This research focuses on poverty among women and FHHs in Saudi society where this category has specific social, cultural, and demographic characteristics. Also, these households and the female breadwinners have their social reality that reflects how these families interact on an everyday basis (inside and outside the household unit) and the barriers and difficulties faced. In addition, the research looks at their relationships with social policy and the welfare system, and whether this system provides adequate assistance and support compatible with the realities and needs of poor women and FHHs.

In this chapter I will address two elements: the 'research problem' and 'research methodology'. The research problem should accurately identify the research's key concepts, goals, and questions. Then, the methodology should identify how the research goals will be gained and how research questions will be answered. This includes the research design (approach), the data collection tools, the strategy for data analysis and the interpretation of results. This chapter benefits from the work of Frankfort-Nachmias, (1992); Outhwaite, (2007); De Vaus, (2001); Punch, (2005) and Patton, (2002).

4.1 The research problem

The importance of this research

Researching poor FHHs and social policy in Saudi society is of great importance because of the following:

1. There has been no previous research investigating social policy and female poverty in Saudi society. This research will be useful in highlighting the problem faced by FHHs in respect of their relationship with the social welfare system. This in turn will help to develop a guide for policies to enhance FHHs' lives.

2. In recent years, there has been increased interest from the government towards women's issues. Public opinion, particularly as represented in the media, has shifted towards giving women more social participation, probably as a result of an increase in recent years in divorce, family breakdown, loss of a family breadwinner, unemployment and poverty, as well as weakening formal and informal 'safety nets'. All of this gives great importance to the study of women's poverty in relation to social policy.

3. The combating of poverty in Saudi Arabia has in recent years become an important national goal, and there is strong interest in the media and the responsible governmental bodies towards the issues of the poor, development and the reformation of social policies, in particular the social security system. There are several categories of poverty which latterly have included women and FHHs. Due to the recent inclusion of this last category, the group has received little attention as a specific group of poor thus FHHs still suffer from social marginalization for two reasons: poverty and gender. Women experience poverty

differently because they are women and their burden is increased because they are heads of their households. This research will study the FHH category which so far has not received adequate attention from researchers.

4. Official statistics of the Social Security Department show that there are growing numbers of poor women and FHHs (divorced; widows; abandoned; prisoners' wives etc.) and that this category comprises a significant part of Saudi's poor. Although the social security policies deal with these women, those policies are still unable to keep pace with the needs of the poor and therefore need to be developed, taking into account the characteristics and needs of FHHs. Hence, this research will benefit policy-makers, helping them to improve and develop social security policies.

5. There are no previous in-depth studies which have examined social policies and the social welfare system in relation to poverty and women. There are also no previous studies on the relationships between the social security system, charitable organizations and FHHs in Saudi society. This research will provide a picture of the relationship between the social welfare system, poor women and FHHs in a transitional society such as Saudi Arabia.

6. This research provides description and interpretation of the reality of poor FHHs in Saudi society, as well as the relationship of these households with social reality and the welfare system. This will benefit those interested in the issues of poverty, women and social policy such as:
- Policy makers and decision makers who are interested in poverty in general and female poverty in particular.
- Decision makers and the head office of the 'Poverty Reduction Strategy' and 'National Fund' who aim to tackle poverty in Saudi Arabia.
- Officials and policy makers of the Ministry of Social Affairs (MSA) who deal with policies and regulations for supporting the poor and FHHs.
- Officials in the Ministry of Labour (ML) who are involved with labour legislation for women.

- Officials and administrators of charitable institutions and women's associations who work to support the poor and FHHs.
- Activists who are interested in women's issues in Saudi Arabia and wish to improve their social status.

7. There is a strong trend from the current government, led by the King, towards the need for social and economic reform of many social systems. The social welfare system has always provoked debate in terms of reformation and improvement of the legislation and policies of income support. This research is directly related to this interest.

Statement of the research problem

The research problem focused on the FHHs in Saudi society and aims to achieve the following goals:
- **Goal one**: (poverty profile) - studying the social, cultural and demographic characteristics of poor FHHs in Jeddah City.
- **Goal two**: (daily life) - studying how poor FHHs experience everyday life and how they interact with their social reality inside and outside the household unit.
- **Goal three**: (policy application in practice) - studying the relationship between FHHs, social policies and welfare systems: governmental (social security system) and non-governmental (charitable women's associations).
- **Goal four**: (recommendations for social policy) - giving or suggesting a guideline for making or formulating an effective social policy for combating poverty among women and poor FHHs in Saudi society.

Research operational objectives

The goals as outlined above were divided into the following operational objectives (sub-goals):
1. Identifying the social characteristics of poor FHHs.
2. Describing the social needs of FHHs.
3. Describing the barriers faced by FHHs.
4. Explaining how poor women deal with everyday life.

5. Analysing the social policies and programmes offered by the state and non-governmental organizations to support poor FHHs.
6. Appraising the social policies and programmes that are meant to alleviate poverty among poor FHHs.
7. Providing suggestions, recommendations or guidelines to help with the reform of, or formulating, effective social policies for the eradication of poverty among women and FHHs.

Research questions

Research questions derived from these objectives cover four levels as follows:

Poverty profile: social, cultural and demographic characteristics of poor FHHs

1- Who are these households and what are their social, cultural and demographic characteristics?
2- Who are these women who head the households and what are their social, cultural and demographic characteristics?
3- Why are these households deemed to be poor?

Daily life: poor FHHs and social reality of daily life

4- What are the social needs of poor FHHs?
5- What kinds of problems and barriers do poor FHHs face?
6- How do poor women deal with their social reality in everyday life?

Policy application in practice: poor FHHs and social policy application in practice

7- What is the relationship between poor FHHs and the official support system (social security system / SSD [Social Security Department])?
8- What kind of support, facilities and social benefits are provided by the official support system (social security system / SSD) for poor FHHs?
9- Are the support and facilities provided by the social security system for poor FHHs consistent with the FHHs' everyday requirements?
10- What is the relationship between charitable associations and FHHs?
11- What kind of social support is provided by charitable associations for poor FHHs?

12- Is the social support provided by charitable associations consistent with the everyday requirements of poor FHHs?
13- What are the strengths and weaknesses in these organizations regarding support for poor women and FHHs?
14- What are the features and characteristics of appropriate regulations and policies to support poor women and FHHs?

Recommendations for improving social policy: suggestions or guidelines for reforming, improving, or formulating effective policies for the eradication of poverty among FHHs

15- Critical reading of the regulations of the SSD and women's charitable associations in the light of the research findings.
16- To review any current or recent suggestions and guidelines for formulating an effective social policy for the eradication of poverty among FHHs in Saudi society (see Appendix G).

Research limitations

This research was undertaken within the following limitations:

- The three research visits took place between December 2007 and January 2009. The main fieldwork was undertaken for four months between October 2008 and January 2009 (see Appendix A).

- The research applies to the community of Jeddah City, which is representative of Saudi Arabia's cultural, racial, and ethnic diversity, as well as reflecting the problems of urbanization such as population congestion, slums, crime, unemployment and poverty. Jeddah, in addition to being the place of my residence, provides a model of Saudi transitional city in its modern phase. Its modernity hides the conflict between traditional values and values of modernity, which can clearly be seen in various aspects of social life.

- The research is limited to a particular category of poor, namely the FHHs. This refers to families headed by women who might be: widows, divorced, wives of prisoners, deserted or abandoned and married women whose husband is absent due to sickness, old age, addictions, disability etc. thus rendering the woman as head and breadwinner of the family.

- The research is limited to the category of poor women and FHHs in Jeddah City who are described as:
1. Receivers of income support and social benefit from social support institutions such as the Social Security Department (SSD) and charitable women's associations.
2. Non-receivers of income support or social benefit from the above institutions for various reasons.

- The research limited to the Saudi poor FHHs which means non-Saudi poor FHHs are not included.

- The Saudi households in this research are defined as :
1. Families where both parties, the man and woman, are Saudis, meaning that both have Saudi nationality.
2. Families where one party is Saudi and the other is non-Saudi. For example, the man is non-Saudi and the woman who is the head of family is Saudi, or the opposite where the woman is non-Saudi and the man is Saudi.
3. Saudi means in this context the holder of the Saudi ID / Saudi Nationality.

The position of men is determined according to their marital relationship with women where the women might be divorced, abandoned, widowed, a prisoner's wife or married.

How the 'Saudi family' is identified in this research

Family in Saudi society, like any Muslim, Arabic society is the greatest responsibility of the man who is responsible legally, socially and economically (financially) for his family, therefore the family carries his legal identity and nationality. This means that the Saudi family is defined traditionally and legally as the family that is headed by a Saudi male. In this respect, all family members are affiliated to the male head's legal identity, thus his children are Saudis, and his wife – if she is foreign - will be entitled to acquire Saudi citizenship providing she meets the requirements of the Saudi Home Office (the Ministry of Interior) and the husband's consent is given, which are the foremost conditions of the Saudi Naturalization Law (Act).

On the other hand, the family where the wife is Saudi and the husband is non-Saudi is traditionally and legally treated (or regarded) as non-Saudi. The Saudi wife in this case still retains her nationality and her legal right as a Saudi citizen. However, her husband and her children remain outside the framework of these rights because they are carrying the nationality of the male head of the family. In a case of the husband or children wishing to acquire Saudi nationality, the wife will not be able to give them access or permission as it is only the Saudi man who can grant this, in line with the procedure of the Saudi Naturalization Law (Act).

Generally, the naturalization of family members remains a problematic issue that faces Saudi women who marry non-Saudi men and this remains the subject of discussion and controversy for the media and activists in the field of women's rights. This problem has created many obstacles for women who are married to non-Saudis and if added to the fact that the women are poor, the problem will be more complicated, and when the families need social support from state institutions, they face many barriers and difficulties. For example, according to the regulations of the official support system, which means in this context the Social Security System (or SSD), the Saudi poor woman has the right to apply for income support and, if she satisfies the conditions, she can access the support system. However, her husband and / or children will be excluded from accessing support because they are non-Saudis, even though they are poor. In some cases, the poor Saudi woman will not be able to access the income support system due to her marital status and her dependency on a non-Saudi husband, so her family is classified as a non-Saudi family, therefore she would be excluded from formal social assistance in accordance with the regulations.

These factors constitute a dilemma for the broader category of Saudi women. Therefore in this research, these points could not be ignored, nor could the category of poor Saudi women who head their households and who married non-Saudis. This latter group constitutes an important category highlighting many gaps in the welfare system and social policies.

There is also another category of women heads of family who are married (or were married) to Saudi men, but they had not yet gained Saudi citizenship / nationalization. Such families and their female breadwinners were considered in this research to be Saudi families. Although the women were not Saudi, the family is officially classified as Saudi. This type of family also has its own special problems due to gaps in the social welfare system. I have considered the previous types of families as Saudi FHHs.

Operational definitions of the main research concepts

Poverty

Poverty is a loose concept and has multiple definitions, and it will be difficult to look at every dimension or even specify one to investigate. So this research will look at poverty as 'deprivation' where the research will investigate the deprivation within the Saudi poor FHHs. In this case, the research will look at what type of deprivation these women and households suffer and whether or not their necessities or subsistence needs are being met and what could not be met and why. Deprivation, like poverty, can be absolute or relative and it could also incorporate a feeling of being deprived. Also an individual can be multiply deprived (see Roberts 2009: 60).

Female poverty

Female poverty in this research means the 'poverty of a woman' where the concept of poverty is combined and associated with the implications of the factor of 'gender' within a specific cultural context as well as how this association has brought about the notion of 'feminine aspects of poverty'. Within this perspective 'woman poverty' will be investigated in Saudi society via deep investigation into the reality of FHHs.

In the Saudi context, women's poverty seems to be intersected and overlapped with the effects of many cultural and social factors linked to how Saudi society perceives or understands the differences in gender roles. Therefore, poor women in Saudi society may find themselves fighting the challenges of the socio-cultural context in addition to the fight against poverty. As a result, the reality of poor FHHs will be shaped differently from the reality of poor MHHs (male headed households) in terms of the quality of problems and challenges of daily life. Therefore, despite FHHs and MHHs appearing generally to have similar poverty conditions, in reality they face different challenges created by the social construction of society and how this society views and acts upon the differences in gender roles.

Therefore the key issues in this research relevant to female poverty are concerned with how women's experiences reflect feminine aspects of poverty and how these aspects are produced and mirrored in Saudi cultural contexts.

Poverty profile

This research attempts to introduce descriptive information about poor women and FHHs in Jeddah City. The information will provide an insight into who these women are and who their households comprise of. This includes their social, cultural and demographic characteristic (e.g. age, marital status, education level, job, income, number of children, living area, type of house, sources of income support) as well as reasons for their poverty.

Female-headed households (FHHs)

The definition adopted by the United Nations identifies female-heads of households as:
> 'Women (who) are financially responsible for their families' who are 'the key decision makers and household managers' who 'manage household economies on behalf of an absent male head' or who ' are the main economic contributors' (United Nations, cited in Sabra *et al.*, 2006: 459).

This research investigates the Saudi poor FHHs who have the following characteristics:
- The female is the head and manager of the family due to the absence of a male head for reasons such as divorce, widowhood, imprisonment or abandonment or due to illness, old age, addiction or disability etc.
- The female who heads a household could be divorced, widowed, a prisoner's wife, abandoned or married but the husband had no role due to being sick, elderly, addicted, disabled etc.

- The woman is the breadwinner or financially responsible for the family.
- The family is poor so the income is limited or absent.
- The family might rely on income support or social benefits provided by the SSD or women's charitable associations, or might be deprived of social support for various reasons.

Social policies for the eradication of poverty

This research refers to two types of policies for poverty eradication:
1. The policies and regulations of the SSD identified as the 'Social Security Systems bill'. This bill is representative of official governmental policies related to poverty and the poor.
2. The policies and regulations of charitable organizations and women's associations where social assistance is provided to the poor, especially women and FHHs.

Both sets of policies work together in Saudi society as part of the Social Welfare System, which also includes other policies related to health, education and social services.

Difficulties

Some of the difficulties that the researcher was faced with are outlined below:
- Researching sensitive issues (female poverty and social policy) in a specific social context such as Saudi society. As an example, some of the responses include: 'Do we have real poverty?' 'We are a rich society!' 'No women here need help'. 'All women are supposed to be sponsored by their families' 'Government helps but people are greedy!!!'. 'Why are you investigating such an issue?' 'It concerns men...it is better for a woman to stay at home and look at something easy.'
- Being a female researcher, e.g. many social and cultural expectations governed my role as a female researcher in terms of my appearance, behaviour and speech. On the other hand, being a female researcher allowed the women to speak more freely to me. My gender as a woman investigating social policy

issues was an issue but my position as a postgraduate PhD student undertaking a study of social policy at a major European university gave me a certain status, especially when meeting elite people.

- Being an insider researcher sometimes meant that I was suspected of being a government agent!
- General difficulties were experienced such as a lack of poverty statistics, other data and information, and the bureaucracy of the governmental bodies.
- In Saudi society there is no public transportation (e.g. buses, trains or underground systems) so the cost of a private driver with a car was a large proportion of my money. Transport around a Saudi city is very difficult for people without a car or private driver. The culture and lifestyle in Saudi is different from that of the UK, so without public transport, it is difficult, but especially so for women without their own private driver or car. The only alternative to a private car with driver was to catch a taxi but this was mainly a waste of valuable time and, in addition, this behaviour is culturally unacceptable for women.
- There were some difficulties in conducting some case studies or gaining access to some places without help from a gatekeeper, or without prior personal relationships.
- There were some difficulties in maintaining a balance between the objectivity and subjectivity of a researcher, especially since this was a unique experience that revealed the dark side of a patriarchal society in which poor women are fighting to maintain livelihoods for their families, despite the difficult circumstances facing them.
- There were difficulties in managing my time and budget in order to collect all information and data during one year in which the researcher conducted three visits for this purpose. The research involved travel between the four cities of Jeddah, Mecca, Madinah and Riyadh (see Appendix A). To travel, most of the time alone, between these cities to collect data and meet some research participants was not an easy task for a female researcher, especially from many cultural considerations. In order to conduct a meeting with research participants in Riyadh, the researcher had to take an early flight from Jeddah to Riyadh,

which took approximately one and a half hours, then attend a meeting with them in their official offices and then to return to Jeddah on a flight that same day.
- There were difficulties in transcribing the interviews, especially with women, where the researcher gathered 112 cases including 50 in-depth interviews. The researcher was unable to ask for help with transcribing due to the ethical considerations of the interviews including private issues. The researcher destroyed all audio files once they were transcribed.

4.2 Research methodology

To achieve the research goals and to answer the research question (see p. 109) it was important to identify from the beginning the research design (approach) that would be the logical framework or structure for data collection, data analysis and interpretation. A qualitative approach was selected and accordingly three parallel strategic methods (keys) were applied to address the research goals and questions. The strategic methods were:
1. Comprehensive reading of all available materials (literature and relevant data and information)
2. Meeting with research participants: Saudi experts, officials, academics and decision makers who worked with, or were interested in, poverty, social policy and FHHs. (see Appendix F)
3. In-depth qualitative study (in-depth investigation) of FHHs.

Research design and approach (the logical structure for inquiry)

This thesis is a descriptive, exploratory, qualitative study. The research aim was to explore and describe the reality of poor FHHs in Saudi society, as represented in Jeddah City. In doing so, the research also sought to understand and interpret the social reality of poor FHHs, especially in their relationship with the social welfare system. This highlights gaps in the social policies for the eradication of poverty among women and FHHs.

The research is 'theory building', so it does not aim to test theory, but instead seeks to build upon it by using 'induction', a theoretical framework for obtaining data, observations, and relevant evidence collected in the field. This research is based upon the notions of 'inductive inquiry', collecting data and related evidence on poor FHHs in Jeddah City in order to explore, understand and interpret their social reality and their relationship with the social welfare system. The thesis aims to conclude with the introduction of a 'theoretical framework' or explanation that synthesises the details into a coherent text and highlights gaps in the practice of social policy. This framework has to be compatible with the Islamic, Arabic and Saudi contexts (as explained in the previous theoretical chapter).

All aspects of selected methods, strategy and data collection tools depended on the research questions and the sort of data and information that were required. Given the research questions, the best method for this research was the qualitative method.

Qualitative methods are methods of social research that employ no quantitative standards and techniques; they are based on the theoretical and methodological principles of symbolic interactionsism, hermeneutics and ethnomethodology (David & Sutton, 2004: 35). Qualitative data can also be defined as data that expresses, usually in words, information about feelings, values, and attitudes (Ibid. 35). Because this research focuses on describing the everyday life of poor FHHs, as well as highlighting women's experiences with poverty and the social welfare system while also analysing the gap between the theory and the practice of social policies, the qualitative method has been used and qualitative data was collected in this research.

The reasons for selecting a qualitative approach to this research

Overall, the qualitative method was selected for the reasons outlined below:

1- The study posed 'what/how/why' questions (e.g. open-ended) to investigate how poor FHHs deal with everyday life and how this experience may shape or be shaped by their social characteristics as well as investigating how a woman understands the meaning of her poverty and her position as a breadwinner for the family. The study also explores how poor FHHs deal with society and the social welfare system within a specific cultural context.

2- The study uses many complex indicators, variables and concepts in respect of poverty and how it is understood within the Saudi context.

3- Women and poverty, especially in a context such as Saudi society, is a sensitive and complex issue, so an in-depth investigation would be appropriate.

Within the qualitative approach, three parallel strategic methods were applied as main keys to achieve the research goals, and are as follows:

1. Comprehensive reading

Because of the difficulty of a lack of data and information on this research subject, the researcher collected and examined available literature on poverty, social policy and FHHs. The researcher undertook comprehensive and extensive reading of the literature on poverty and FHHs on three levels: globally (international), territorially (Arabic region) and locally (Saudi society). The researcher examined many articles and previous studies and available data, information and statistics on poverty in Saudi society and Jeddah City in particular. The researcher used the database of the University of Liverpool, King Abdul-aziz University (Jeddah), and Umm-alquar University (Mecca) to investigate the updated articles and studies on the subject. The researcher also collected published and unpublished items on the subject in both hard and soft copy (electronic data) and also looked through the official documents and databases of governmental and non-governmental bodies, in the particular the SSD and women's charitable associations from where the main sample was drawn. The researcher's aims in this extensive reading were: to highlight the background of the research subject and to get ideas on the most important relevant variables, themes, and issues on poverty and FHHs as well as to establish a good framework for data analysis and interpretation. This reading continued during all stages of the research and during the three main visits.

2. Meetings with research participants: experts, officials, academics, and decision makers (referred to as elite informants)

The aim was to meet a group of informants (elite) who are working in the poverty area or interested in policies and programmes for poverty eradication in Saudi society, such as experts, officials, academics and decision makers. The main purpose of the meetings was to highlight, explain and interpret the problematic issues that were raised by the interviews with FHHs. It was important to balance the views of the FHHs with those of the specialists in this area, specifically those people who worked in proximity with FHHs.

The priority was to select officials and specialists from the institutions that were most suitable to collect samples from. The academics, experts and decision makers were selected according to their careers and interest in poverty issues. The researcher listed the most important people as the interviews progressed, along with the important issues that would come under discussion (the interviews and questions will be discussed in more detail later in this chapter).

The elite informants occupied different positions according to their careers (see Appendix F). In terms of the social support institutions, they were divided into two categories:

1. Those who were working in top positions in the administrative hierarchies of the institutions, e.g. at the level of policy and decision making.
2. Those who were working in middle positions such as executive managers or administrators, who had closer connections and communication with the beneficiaries.

Although the researcher met with decision makers from the first category, she found the second category more important for the study as those individuals were closer to the reality of the poor and accordingly they were able to give a realistic picture of the environment of working with the poor and FHHs.

The researcher was able to connect with the elite informants in two ways:

- Through official connections where a formal request for an appointment had to be made (normally requiring a verification fax of CV, SCB letter and research goals as confirmation of the researcher's identity and position as a postgraduate student).
- Via personal relationships, where word-of-mouth helped introductions as a field researcher, particularly in the academic field and social work area where many good relationships helped in all stages of the research. It helped that some gatekeepers were amenable and helped to make the task easier by assisting with the bureaucracy.

The number of elite informants was 18 (see table 4.7) and they were chosen from the following governmental and non-governmental bodies:
- Main head office of the Ministry of Social Affairs (Riyadh City).
- Branch of the Minister of Social Affairs (Jeddah City).
- Main office of the National Poverty Reduction Strategy (NPRS) (Riyadh City).
- Main office of the National Charity Fund (NCF) (Riyadh City).
- Main head office of the Social Security Department (Riyadh City).
- Main office of the Social Security Department in Mecca Province (Jeddah City)
- Jeddah Urban Observatory (JUC).
- Jeddah municipality.
- Head offices of the main three charitable associations in Jeddah (FWWS, KWS, and BWS).
- Head office of Dar Al-Rahmah House (private charitable residence).
- King Abdu-aziz University (Jeddah City).
- Taibah University (Madinah City)

3- In-depth qualitative study (in-depth investigation) of FHHs

This research faced several difficulties in relation to the nature of the research problem and the methodology of the study. The problem of the research, the main concern of which was the social policies and FHHs in Saudi society, had not been investigated previously in any depth, so there was no preliminary data or raw data that could be relied upon.

In terms of the methodology, the approach selected was the 'in-depth qualitative approach'. This approach depends on the method of in-depth interviews that explore the phenomenon associated with the subject. In order for this approach to be successful, there must be some data on the phenomenon that would enable the researcher to build and design the data collection tools as well as to formulate appropriate questions. In this case, there was no suitable basis of raw data; therefore such data had to be collected in the field.

To deal with this problem and to obtain background knowledge and basic information and data as well as build research tools, the researcher designed and undertook three visits to the research field in just over one year - from December 2007 to January 2009 -

where these visits were linked and dependent on each other systematically. These visits, as table 4.1 shows, respectively were: visit 1 (the initial exploratory study), visit 2 (the pilot study), and visit 3 (the main fieldwork).

Table 4.1: the procedures and methods of the in-depth qualitative study via the three research visits

No	Main goal	Date	Methods of investigation/ and data collection tools					
			Survey documents	Interviews with FHHs	Meeting with elite informants	Focus groups	Comprehensive reading	Observations & collection of field notes
1	Exploratory study	Dec.07 -Jan.08	100 files	7	11	No	Yes	Yes
2	Pilot study	Mar-Apr. 2008	No	12	7	3	Yes	Yes
3	Main fieldwork	Oct.08-Jan.09	No	112	18	No	Yes	Yes

3.1. Prior preparations (procedures)

There were prior preparations that had to be undertaken before starting the visits. One of the basic things was to agree the main goals and plan of the study with the supervisor for this thesis. Communication with governmental and non-governmental bodies in Saudi Arabia (Jeddah City) had to be established due to the researcher wishing to collect data from the Social Security Department, the Ministry of Social Affairs and charitable associations in order to get approval for the research.

The initial contact with these bodies located in Jeddah City was by phone, e-mail and fax from Liverpool in order to find out the basic requirements for the research visits. In a society like Saudi Arabia, the researcher was required to understand prior procedures and to get approval from the concerned sectors to conduct the research. It transpired that the following was necessary:

1. A formal letter from the university department, and a formal sponsor letter from the Saudi Cultural Bureau (SCB) in the UK. The official letters were to include the following data: researcher's name and ID number, name of the university

and department, course title, the title of the research, the type of work to be undertaken and the type of information required along with the name of the institution or targeted body. All letters needed to be signed and stamped and original copies.
2. A brief of the research proposal including the objectives, timing, nature of the data required, the method and a copy of the questions and other tools for collecting data.
3. A formal request from the researcher, tailored to each official body, explaining briefly the nature of the research and the type of assistance required.
4. A CV.

These requirements were sent in advance to the Social Security Department and the three charitable associations in Jeddah: al Bir Welfare Society (BWS), First Welfare Society (KWS), and al Faisalya Women's Welfare Society (FWWS). It took two months of their procedures to provide official approval to conduct the research; each subsequent visit meant repeating the same procedures to renew the approval.

3.2. Administration of the qualitative study: the three research visits

The three research visits for conducting the qualitative investigation of FHHs in Jeddah City are detailed below.

Visit 1: the initial exploratory study (December 2007- January 2008)

The main goal was to explore the field of study and all related data and information.

The objectives of the exploratory study

1. To collect data, statistics, policies and legislation from several governmental and non-governmental institutions.
2. To collect and list the poor families who were in receipt of social support and benefits from the Social Security Department and charitable associations in Jeddah.
3. To choose only the FHHs from the previous list and classify them into categories according to the marital status of the female head of the family.
4. To conduct an exploratory study of poor FHHs in Jeddah City through meetings.

5. To survey a sample of FHHs to gain an understanding of some of their socio-cultural and demographic characteristics.
6. To determine the position and names of the officials, decision makers, experts, and academics who were required to be interviewed and to set up meetings.
7. To conduct comprehensive reading and collect up-to-date published and unpublished data and publications.

Types of information and data required at this stage
- Data and information on structural organization, policies, regulations and frameworks of the GOs and NGOs that worked on the alleviation and eradication of poverty in the K.S.A.
- Statistical and numerical data relevant to poverty in K.S.A in general and poverty in Jeddah in particular.
- Collection of available data to make a primary analysis of the social, cultural and demographic characteristic for a sample of FHHs who were receiving Social Security Pension (SSP) or social support from the SSD and / or charitable associations.

The places from where the data and information were drawn:
The data and information on FHHs were collected from the SSD and the three women's charitable associations: BWS, KWS, and FWWS.
In terms of the elite group, the interviewees were from governmental and non-governmental organizations:
- Ministry of Social Affairs (MSA) (branch of the Mecca region).
- Social Security Department (SSD) (main office of Mecca region).
- Office of Women's Supervision in Mecca Region (OWSMR)
- The following charities and women's associations: Al Bir Welfare Society (BWS), Al Faisalya Women's Welfare Society (FWWS), and First Welfare Society (KWS).
- Ektefaa association (EK)
- Jeddah Urban Observatory (JUC)
- Care Committee for Prisoners' Families (CCPF)

The result of the exploratory study

The overall number of poor in Jeddah City who were officially registered in the records of the social support organizations (SSD & charitable associations) for 2007-2008 was 37,753 families. The poor families could be divided according to the institutions from where they drew support as follows: SSD (28,764), FWWS (3,615), FWS (1,748), BWS (3,626).

The overall number of poor FHHs in Jeddah City was derived from the overall number of poor. The data was collected and classified manually, with no electronic databases in the institutions with the exception of the SSD. Accordingly, the overall number of FHHs from 2007-2008 in Jeddah City was as depicted in table 4.2:

Table 4.2: Number of poor FHHS in Jeddah 1429-1428 (2007-2008)

SSD	BWS	FWWS	KWS	Total
5,688	170	740	2,823	9421

Sources: SSD, BWS, KWS, FWWS records

A questionnaire was designed in order to survey the socio-cultural and demographic characteristics of a sample of FHHs. It was difficult to obtain a sample of poor women who were heads of their families directly from the institutions (SSD and charitable associations) where no systematic databases existed. There was also the matter of data confidentiality, thus it was difficult to contact the FHHs directly. However, during a visit to the SSD and other charities / women's associations, there seemed to be similar indicators in all records, which would mean that if data were collected systematically, it would reflect a consistent picture of the socio-cultural and demographic characteristics of FHHs. So a design with the same indicators of social, economic, educational, and demographic status was made and then applied to 100 cases (files) which were chosen randomly: 40 from the SSD and 20 cases from each charity / association (FWWS, KWS, and BWS). Each person was given a table with number and codes. The overall indicators were: age, marital status, education status, occupation, monthly income, source of income, monthly expenditure, living area, family members (their gender/age/education), type of house, ownership of house, number of rooms, code of

family and entitlement for SSP. After conducting an SPSS analysis, the results illustrated those FHHs in Jeddah city seemed have the following characteristics:
- Mostly the head of family was a lone mother because of widowhood, divorce, abandonment, or the wife of a prisoner.
- Illiteracy and low education were prevalent.
- Mostly, they were housewives who did not work.
- There was insufficient income and therefore a low rate of spending.
- The main source of income for 70% of FHHs was social security assistance. This could raise questions about the rest on their non-entitlement for assistance: for instance, why they were not included into the aid system although they were citizens and needy.
- They were mostly large families, concentrated in the south and eastern parts of the city where the poor districts, slums and immigrants were found. The majority lived in traditional houses and mostly they were renters rather than owners.

Eleven elite informants were met, in addition to six women heads of households.

Visit 2 (the pilot study: March - April 2008)

The exploratory study (visit 1) highlighted some important findings that needed to be taken into account in the next stages and are outlined below:

1) The exploratory study highlighted sufficient indicators of the social, cultural and demographic characteristics of FHHs in Jeddah City. These characteristics were to be taken into account in the selection of the main sample for the study; therefore a matrix was designed (table 4.3) which indicates the characteristic and estimated numbers of the main purposive sample of FHHs to be selected.

Table 4.3: The matrix shows the distribution of a purposive sample for 60 FHHs according to the area of the city, age and marital status.

	All housewives						
	South Jeddah			Rest of Jeddah			total
	Y < 40	M 41-60	O 61>	Y <40	M 41-60	O 61>	
Widows	2	2	2	2	2	2	12
Divorced	2	2	2	2	2	2	12
Prisoner's wife	2	2	2	2	2	2	12
Abandoned	2	2	2	2	2	2	12
With husband	2	2	2	2	2	2	12
Total	10	10	10	10	10	10	60

2) The matrix (table 4.3) indicated that the main sample would be selected purposively to represent the following characteristics: all female heads of households should be housewives; they should be selected from the beneficiaries of SSD and / or women's charitable associations; they should be selected from all Jeddah City's districts; all age categories should be involved (young - middle-aged - old); they should include all marital statuses for women (widows – divorced - prisoner's wife – abandoned - married). In each cell of the matrix was an estimated number (2) to be selected, therefore the overall estimated number of the purposive sample was 60 cases.

3) Visit 1 showed clearly that poverty issues should be taken into account when designing the research tools and research questions. Therefore, research questions which were designed for the focus groups and interviews were to be tested in the pilot study.

The goal of the pilot study

The pilot study was between March and April 2008 where the main goals were to test and develop the research tools. These goals were divided into the followings objectives:

1. To design and conduct focus group sessions to examine the current reality for poor FHHs in Saudi Arabia.
2. To analyse the findings of these focus groups and to develop questions for a qualitative study.

3. To conduct in-depth interviews with (at least) five female heads of households.
4. To analyse the finding from these women's interviews.
5. To develop interview questions for the main fieldwork.
6. To continue comprehensive reading.
7. To continue the meeting with elite informants.

How the work was organized

One of the women's charitable associations, Al Fasylaya Women's Welfare Society (FWWS) was contacted in advance to make arrangements regarding the pilot study. All conditions to obtain approval were met with in order to apply the pilot study. They were provided with a plan and requests and expectations regarding the work environment with poor women and FHHs.

The focus groups and interviews were conducted in the FWWS. All cases were selected from FHHs who were beneficiaries of FWWS and also some beneficiaries who were registered with the SSD for social income support.

At the beginning of the work, the researcher met the general director of FWWS and discussed the plan; after this, the researcher was referred to the head of the Social Work Department who dealt with the poor. Information was given regarding work in the department with some essential regulations (written and unwritten) that organized working with poor FHHs.

The work within FWWS lasted for three weeks and the researcher was in attendance every day during working hours (8.00 am to 2.00 pm) to work alongside the charity's employees in their normal working environment. They provided a desk within the social work section, in addition to another area for interviews and focus groups.

Inside the charity, women who were representatives of poor families were allocated numbers according to a structured timetable, stipulating the time for them to receive their assistance. On arrival, they waited in a large waiting room until their numbers were announced, and they then received their assistance and signed a receipt.

The work started with an inspection of the documents and case files, then choosing appropriate cases and listing names and codes. By referring to the file codes, the FWWS social worker was able to collect the names of women from the timetable for that week; and after receiving their allocations, those women were sent to the researcher's office.

The interviews started with introductions to the researcher and the research aims, and checking that the women were willing participants in an informal conversation. Most women had no objection to this, although they were sometimes quite reserved. The ethical issues of the research were emphasized, stating confidentiality and the sole use of the information for scientific purposes without the revelation of any personal information. Through this process, twelve representatives of FHHs were interviewed, where five cases were in-depth interviews and others were with three 'focus groups' as follows: the first with six cases, the second with two cases and the third with two cases. There were also some less structured conversations with other women who were sitting in the waiting room.

During the pilot study, the researcher met with six officials, experts and decision makers in Jeddah (from the MSA), and Riyadh (from the head office of the National Poverty Reduction Strategy – NPRS and the office of the National Charity Fund - NCF).

<u>The findings of the pilot study</u>

The focus group method was unsuccessful with poor women in the Saudi context. This maybe explained by several reasons:

- Some were afraid of being known to others and so some women did not uncover their face veils.
- Some women seemed unhappy for other women to learn details of their story which made them more taciturn.
- Some women were afraid that criticizing the authorities might cause problems for them.

The interviews with individual women were more successful; this method highlighted many overlapping factors in respect of the reality facing those women, and their relationships with their private realm (family, personal histories and experiences) and the public realm (state, society, culture and the welfare system). The findings showed that the women had similar experiences in some aspects of the public realm but they experienced quite different private realms. The findings of the interviews raised a question about the existence of 'hidden poverty or silent poverty' among FHHs who were suffering from poverty but had no access - for various reasons - to the official support system (SSD) or charitable association services.

Visit 3: the main fieldwork (October 2008-January 2009)

This final research visit lasted approximately four months from October 2008 to January 2009 (this stage will be explained later in more detail).

Based on the results of the pilot study, it was important to adopt the following amendments in the final plan for the main fieldwork:

1- Cancelling the focus group method and just focusing on the following methods: interview (semi-structured in-depth interview and open interview), official document analysis, researcher's field notes and field observations.
2- Improve the research questions and develop the interview technique and interview schedule.
3- Pay more attention to the possibility of 'hidden or invisible poverty' among FHHs. Thus it was necessary to consider another sample of poor FHHs who are not involved in the official support system (SSD) or women's association services. The 'snowball' strategy was to be used in this context.

The main goal was to collect the primary qualitative data via the interview. The objectives of this visit can be shown as following:

- To conduct in-depth interviews with a sample of FHHs according to the previous matrix (see table 4.3).
- To continue the comprehensive reading.
- To continue meeting with the (elite) informants.

The GOs and NGOs where the main sample (FHHs) was obtained

The poor women who were heads of their households were drawn from the beneficiaries of government and non-government social support institutions in Jeddah City.

Alongside these women were the poor FHHs who were non-beneficiaries and accordingly had not received any social support.

The following outlines information about these institutions in Jeddah City:

Social Security Department (SSD)

The main SSD of Mecca Province is located in Jeddah City. The SSD provides its services through 11 offices that cover Jeddah and other cities and local areas of the province. The main building is located in South Jeddah and is where many beneficiaries apply for benefits or update their information. Monday and Tuesday of each week are specifically for female visitors.

Charities and women's associations

In Jeddah City, there are many charities and women's associations but the two most important for providing support to poor and needy families are:

First Welfare Society (KWS)

This was the first women's association and was established in Jeddah City in 1962. The purpose was to offer social support and social services for the poor. The association provides several types of service, such as health care, childcare, care for the elderly and the disabled, support for poor families and poor FHHs, building charitable residences, training and rehabilitation. The association covers the districts of South Jeddah from the head office and a branch office (K3).

Al Faisalya Women's Welfare Society (FWWS)

This society was established in 1975 to provide social, health, religious, cultural and rehabilitation services for needy and poor families. In addition, it is interested in the development of human resources in the community. It also aims to foster social solidarity through care programmes that include sponsoring orphans and the disabled. The association covers the northern and eastern districts of Jeddah City.

Charitable housings (Repat/Arbeta p. l)

There is much charitable housing in Jeddah called 'Arbeta'. This type of housing is considered a kind of waqif (endowment) which is specifically for the benefit of the poor and needy and in particular, poor women and FHHs. There are many charitable housing associations in Jeddah, some of which are supervised by the local authority via the Ministry of Endowment, or the Ministry of Social Affairs (MSA). Therefore it is known as 'public charitable housing', but some units are supervised by the donor and are called 'private charitable housing'.

3.3 Sampling

Research population: all poor FHHs in Saudi society.

The sample frame: where the FHHs were drawn from included all Saudi poor FHHs in Jeddah City who were receiving social support and social benefits from the SSD and charitable associations alongside those who were not involved in the social support system for various reasons.

In other words, the sampling frame involved the following:

- FHHs who were beneficiaries of the Social Security Department (SSD) in Jeddah City.
- FHHs who were beneficiaries of two women's charitable associations: al Fasylaya Women's Welfare Society (FWWS) which serves the northern districts of Jeddah City; and the First Welfare Society (KWS) which serves the rest of the Jeddah districts.
- FHHs who were living in charitable housing (or charitable residences) but who were not involved with the services of the SSD, FWWS or KWS (the snowball technique was used in order to draw a sample).

Sample type and sample strategy

This research used the 'purposeful sample'. This sample was adequate for the research purposes and aims, therefore two main strategies or techniques were used to select this sample: the 'quota' and 'snowball' techniques.

The quota sampling technique was used to draw up a purposeful sample of FHHs from the SSD and charitable associations, so this sample was selected according to the characteristics of the matrix in table 4.3. This ensured the selection of representatives from each category of age, marital status and neighbourhood. This research needed another sample from poor FHHs who were not involved in the social support system, so in this case the snowball technique was used to find this sample with the same level of matrix characteristics and this sample was located within charitable housing. So both techniques, 'quota' and 'snowball', considered the same level of matrix characteristics, the only difference was regarding the variable of 'receiving' or 'not receiving' social support.

Size of sample

Although there are no rules regarding sample size in qualitative enquires, a matrix of 60 cases was designed. During the fieldwork, this number expanded, so that 112 women were interviewed (see table 4.4). In starting the fieldwork, the initial plan in collecting cases was to look, firstly, through all records of the SSD, FWWS, and KWS, and then to choose appropriate cases that would match the matrix characteristics. This plan failed because of the following reasons:

- Apart from the SSD, the institutions lacked a database and systematic information tools.
- Even within the SSD, the database was confidential and it was not permissible for a researcher to look through the beneficiaries' information or to try to contact those cases.
- There were several categories of FHHs and each one had its own problems, so in this sense the subject had an effect of increasing the number of cases for some categories.
- The number was increased due to the involvement of the snowball sample.

The solution seemed to be for the researcher to become involved in a daily work environment within the three institutions. This meant attending during working hours in order to select and meet the women, and 112 interviews were conducted with women who headed their own households; 50 of these were in-depth interviews. As Table 4.4 shows, there is one field that remained incomplete (marked with 0).

Table 4.4: The number of FHHs who were interviewed during fieldwork

	All housewives						total
	South Jeddah			Rest of Jeddah			
	Y < 40	M 41-60	O 61>	Y <40	M 41-60	O 61>	
Widows	٠	٤	٠	٢	٦	٠	27
Divorced	٩	٧	٤	٠	٧	٢	34
Prisoner's wife	٠	٠	0	٢	٢	١	15
Abandoned/ Absent husband/ Separated	٣	٣	٢	٢	٢	٢	14
With husband	٢	٣	٢	٦	٧	٢	22
Total	24	22	13	17	24	12	112

The sampling unit (unit of analysis)

The key issue in selecting and making a decision about the appropriate unit of analysis is to decide what you want to be able to say at the end of the study (Patton 2002: 229). Therefore, the sampling unit in this research was the "woman" who was a breadwinner for a poor household; these women were to be representative of themselves and their families in the study.

Table 4.5: the distribution of FHHs / women who were interviewed according to the institution from which they were drawn

Institutions	No of FHHs/women
Social Security Department (SSD)	50
Women's charitable associations (FWWS & KWS)	32
Charitable residences & private residences	30
Total	112

How work was organized and how the researcher engaged in the field

The work was not easy in such an environment, where a female researcher faces greater difficulties than would a male researcher, because of various cultural considerations relating to gender issues. In addition, the researcher had to contact the administration bodies of all government and non-governmental institutions in order to secure official approval for the work. This took a long time due to the bureaucratic procedures involved. Some departments such as the SSD remain exclusively restricted to male employees, which raised the problem of how to become involved in such male-only work environments (which could both break the rules and also might embarrass the administering body). Another difficulty was caused by the lack of public transport, which resulted in having to spend a large portion of the budget on renting a car with a driver.

The work was organized as follows:
- After gaining approval from the Saudi Ministry of Social Affairs, the researcher worked from the hours of 8.00 am to 3.00 pm in the offices of the SSD, FWWS, and KWS.
- SSD is an official department that deals specifically with all income support applications. This department receives male and female beneficiaries, but at different times. Saturdays and Sundays are for male beneficiaries, whereas Mondays and Tuesdays are for female beneficiaries and Wednesdays are for disabled people. Inside the SSD building, the main offices consisted of transparent and glass walls which meant a lack of privacy. There is no women's section in the SSD, so the women have to deal directly with male staff; therefore, ethical considerations relating to gender relationships have to be taken into account in such a work environment.

- The first day at work at the SSD began with a staff meeting called by the Head of the Department with introductions to each employee and an overview for them of the research aims. He also explained the roles of the various team members, with particular emphasis on the team that served women and FHHs. This team later referred female beneficiaries to the researcher. Each interview commenced with questions that helped to ascertain whether or not the case would be continued with for an in-depth interview (if the beneficiary matched the matrix characteristics, she was considered as a sample unit). Although more than 50 cases were seen each day, only two or three cases would match the matrix characteristics. A total of 50 women were interviewed at the SSD.

- Within FWWS and KWS, the work was easier than at the SSD although there was difficulty relating to the beneficiary records, which were organized by both associations only according to area of residence and number of family members. This made it difficult to identify cases appropriate to the sample, thus it was once again essential to become involved full-time in the work environment. However, the beneficiaries attended the women's associations on weekdays according to a schedule that involved their file number and they were required to come at the allotted time in order to receive their assistance or to update their data. The researcher was allocated an appropriate room with an office desk. The work commenced with the collection of ID cards from beneficiaries, showing their data and file numbers; appropriate cases were chosen according to beneficiaries who matched the matrix characteristics and an interview was conducted with each. A total of 32 interviews were conducted with women from FWWS and KWS.

- As the prior pilot study had shown, there remained hidden (or "invisible") poverty in Saudi Society. Many Saudi FHHs are poor; nevertheless, they are not involved in the established support systems of the SSD or the charitable women's associations, because they do not satisfy the eligibility conditions of those institutions. The researcher aimed to seek out some of those families who were outside the SSD and women association's beneficiaries – and fortunately, through personal contacts, was able to access some charitable housing areas where many poor FHHs live. Some of this charitable housing is owned by the local authority of Jeddah City, while other sections are privately owned, but all this charitable housing is designated for poor families and FHHs.

- With support from a gatekeeper, a colleague and PhD researcher in charitable housing, the researcher was able to identify a snowball sample from five charitable housing areas located in the northern and southern areas of Jeddah City. The gatekeeper explained the aims and mission of the research and asked whether they would mind becoming a subject for in-depth interviews. Women agreed because they trusted the gatekeeper (although the researcher was not known to them) – thus this colleague became an access point to learn more about the daily environment of these poor women[31]. All interviews were conducted in her office, and each interview lasted from two to three hours. The women would sometimes bring a friend or family member, which in turn led to further cases. These interviews proved very significant, highlighting very important points relevant to the women's environment, and their difficulties in coping with cultural, social, and judicial systems. A total of 30 women were interviewed from the five charitable housing agencies.

Data collection tools

1- Interview (semi-structured in-depth interviews, and open interview)
2- Documentary research.
3- Observation and field notes.
4- Digital records were made in most interviews with women, but not with the elite informants.

1. Interview

Semi-structured in depth interviews with FHHs

- Semi-structured in-depth interviews were used with women who headed their households. The aim was to collect two types of information: personal data on the characteristics of these women and their families and in-depth information on their experiences of everyday life and their relationships with the social policy and welfare systems.

---

[31] - With support of this gatekeeper I was able to meet many significant cases. In addition, she acted as a conduit for meetings with various decision-makers. She was 45 years old, researching a PhD in "charitable housing" in Jeddah City at the Department of Sociology, King Abdul-Aziz University. Also she worked as an administrator at a private charitable house, Dar Al-Rahmah (DAR: literally "Mercy House"), which is a modern well-appointed building established by one of the city's most wealthy and powerful businessmen. The building contains 36 flats, all furnished. In her office on the first floor, she received applications from families who wanted to live in DAR. If the applicants satisfied all eligibility conditions, then they would be accepted.

- The interview schedule (guide) addressed the topics and themes that are listed in Table 4.6.

Table 4.6: topics and themes of the in-depth interview schedule (guide).

Topics	Theme(s)
Personal data Age, education, marital status, work, monthly income, source of income, area of living, family members (their gender/age/education), type of house, ownership of house, entitlement for SSP, entitlement for charitable association social support.	Poverty profile
In- depth information **Women's experience of poverty:** Understanding the implications of being poor- before, during, and after the crisis - and dealing with everyday life. **Women's experience with the family:** Understanding the implications of being head of the family – the barriers and difficulties – and understanding their needs.	Daily life
In- depth information **Social policy and poor FHHs in Saudi Society:** FHHs and the relationship with the SSD. FHHs and the relationship with charitable associations. How do FHHs judge the social welfare system?	FHHs and social policy applications in practice

The above schedule shows the main topics of the interview. Personal data was collected according to the semi-structured questions involved in the first part of the interview schedule. These questions were in tabular design so each case had one table with all personal information in addition to code, date and place of meeting. The in-depth interviews dealt with the rest of the topics according to each case where each interview lasted between 1.5 and 2 hours. These interviews were conducted more than once with some cases. The topics involved detailed questions in accordance with each case and the unique circumstances of that individual.

All in-depth interviews were conducted with the women in the institutions from which they drew their benefits but they were held in a comfortable place that ensured a degree of privacy. Some women preferred to be met in their houses and many were met in the office in Dar al-Rahm.

The interviews began with a general conversation with the women and progressed to personal information. The next phase was about the women's experiences with poverty and heading a family. This structure was flexible and in-depth according to the topic and the details of the women's stories. Significant details could lead to a reconsideration of some of the issues or to an additional question about some of the issues related to the women's lives.

In all of the interviews, there was much ethical consideration given to the privacy and confidentiality of the information.

The number of in-depth interviews totalled 50 cases; the rest were interviewed just once in open and flexible meetings. In the in-depth interviews, there were more details and the timescale was longer, some of them having been met twice.

The open interviews mostly concentrated on issues that filled the gaps in some of the cases of the in-depth ones. In the open interview, the individuals were met just once for between 1 – 2 hours.

Most of the interviews were recorded after seeking prior permission (approval) from the women. Some women did not want to be recorded and some women asked for the recording to be stopped when they discussed sensitive details of their stories. Afterwards, these interviews were transferred to a computer and were transcribed into a word document, once the digital files had been deleted. It took a long time to transcribe the stories but due to the ethical considerations, where these stories involved many sensitive and private issues, help with transcribing could not be sought.

Informant (elite) / face-to face interviews

A total of 18 elite informants were met with (see table 4.7). The purpose of the meetings with the elite participants was to explain and interpret some problematic issues that had been raised by women during the interviews. To achieve this goal, open interviews were conducted with the elite informants; therefore the interview schedule was designed with open and flexible questions. The meetings were as flexible as conversations. The subjects of these conversations were problematic issues that were raised during the fieldwork.

The interviews with elite informants were conducted in their offices but two participants visited the office in Dar al-Rahma. Each interview lasted between 1.5 and 2 hours.

Before each meeting, the following preparations were made:

- A detailed topic guide was prepared that included: 1- **general issues** that were raised by the women such as the policies and regulations of income support and how they could be applied in some cases; the reform of the welfare system and whether this could solve some problems for FHHs; poverty reduction strategies and programmes regarding the elimination of poverty among FHHs; FHHs and SSD regulations; FHHs and the regulation of women's associations etc. 2- **specific issues** focused on the role and perspective of the interviewee towards poverty and FHHs.
- Information on each interviewee, biography, career history etc. was collected.
- The participants were sent the required documents - CV, research proposal etc - in advance.
- Travel plans were managed in advance, in particular with those interviewees who were in different cities.

During the interviews, there were no digital recordings of any sensitive matters and due to the public positions of the elite informants; they were not able to talk with any freedom if the meetings were recorded. Therefore during the interview, notes were taken and were written up in more detail afterwards. The open questions enabled flexible conversations. Many of the interviewees took the opportunity to ask questions about the research subject and to what extent it could contribute to the development of the welfare system and social policies. Offers were received from two decision makers of consultancy work with teams who worked in the area of policy development. The participants expressed their institutional needs for specialists in poverty and social policy. They declared that the results of the research would benefit the development of social policies in Saudi society, especially in terms of SSD and women's associations' policies. They asked to be provided with a full copy of the research.

There was a need to be aware of the 'power dynamic' between the interviewer and the interviewees. Because these elite participants were important, the interviews had to be carefully managed in a way that enabled the achievement of the goals and the balance of power in the meetings. Therefore all questions were answered clearly by the researcher who also exchanged dialogue at the same level of understanding to give the participants a good impression on the research mission.

There were no serious difficulties when meeting the elite informants, which was both unusual and unexpected. These well-placed contacts were, for the most part, highly educated and open-minded, and offered a great deal of support. Surprisingly, the researcher's gender as a woman helped and it seemed that people were surprised that a Saudi woman was investigating poverty – an area that male researchers have found difficult to explore. Moreover, the researcher's position as a postgraduate PhD student undertaking a study of social policy at a major European university gave a certain status, particularly since no prior researcher had investigated social policy and female poverty in KSA. Therefore, as many of these decision-makers observed, Saudi Arabia is now a society in which women will be able to prepare the setup of a new age and a new direction for social change and social movement, in particular where this is relevant to women's issues.

Generally, the interviews with the elite informants gave some indications about what was happening in reality, rather than merely what was supposed to be happening. Meetings with the elite group continued throughout all stages of this research.

Table 4.7: Elite informants who were interviewed during the fieldwork

	Jeddah	Riyadh	Mecca	Madinah	Total
Officers. GOs departments	6	3	1	1	11
Officers. NGOs departments	6		1		7
Total	12	3	2	1	18

2. Documentary research

The following types of documents were investigated and researched:

- Official records and files of the poor women and FHHs in the SSD and charitable associations.
- Policies and regulations of the SSD.
- The regulations of the charitable women's associations.
- The statistics and numerical data on the poor in the SSD, MSA, and charitable associations.
- The official hard copies and soft copies (electronic), both published and unpublished, of the government documents of some official bodies such as: the Ministry of Social Affairs (MSA), the National Poverty Reduction Strategy (NPRS), the National Charity Fund (NCF), Jeddah Urban Observatory (JUO), the Ministry of Economy and Planning (MEP), the Central Department of Statistics & Information (SDSI), Saudi Arabia Monetary Agency (SAMA), General Organisation for Social Insurance (GOSI), Public Pension Agency (PPA).
- The publications and statistics of the 'United Nations Economic and Social Commission for Western Asia ESCWA' on poverty, social policy and FHHs in the Arabic region.
- The publications and statistics of the 'United Nations' (UN) and the 'United Nations Development Programme' (UNDP) on poverty in Saudi Arabia.
- Theoretical information on poverty in Islam and Islamic jurisprudence.
- Empirical data and information from previous studies on poverty and FHHs (at international, Arabic, and Saudi levels).
- Studies of poverty in Arabic and Islamic contexts.

3. The field observation

Unstructured observation was used to collect data during all research visits. This observation was in the following areas:

- Observed the social reality of Saudi society during the time of study.
- Observed what was published or raised in the press and media especially on poverty, women, and the welfare system.
- Observations on the women and FHHs who were interviewed.
- Observation on the social support institution from where data was collected.

- Observation of the elite informants and their work environments.
- Memoirs and field notes that were regularly written during all visits.

Data treatment and data analysis

Managing data

1. Digital records of the interviews were downloaded to a PC; these digital records were transcribed (in Arabic language) into documents suitable for analysis.

2. All documents and records were then organized into main folders and given codes according to the names of the institutions.

3. Each main folder was divided into subfolders that involved cases organized according to the marital status of the women.

4. Every main folder contained each case that was organized horizontally according to the following: date of interview, institution code, case code, name of subject, marital status, age, education level, number of children, SSD assistance, charitable assistance, area of residence, contact details.

5. Another table was designed for all data from all others tables, in order to produce the final table (see table 4.4) that maps the final numbers of FHHs into the basic sample matrix. This made it easier to work with each case because the number, code, and location of each one, were managed.

6. In terms of the official documents that included policies, regulations and governmental publication, all were organized in accordance with the subject and area of investigation.

Data analysis

1- Comprehensive reading

All the material was collected, managed and organized according to the type of information and data and its relevance to the research structures. This information was used to formulate the theoretical chapters that developed according to the logical structure from the broader context to the narrowest context: poverty concepts in the western framework, poverty in Islam and poverty in the Arabic and Saudi contexts. Statistics, regulations, and policies were analysed thematically and the findings are in the analysis chapters.

2- Meetings with the elite informants

The data collected from this group was treated as qualitative data, so it was organized into Word documents and given codes and numbers. The thematic approach was then used to analyse the data in the same way as the women's interviews, and the similarities, differences, themes and patterns were considered. The findings were used to highlight, explain and interpret the ambiguous issues relevant to FHHs and the welfare system. Women's stories reflected the 'practice' of how social policy works in reality whereas the elites' narratives might mirror the 'theory' or the theoretical level of how these policies were formulated. Both the theory and practice are important to introduce the research findings within a holistic framework for analysis and interpretation. The findings of the elite group meetings will be discussed in the analysis chapters.

3- The qualitative investigation for FHHs (the in-depth and the open interviews)

- SPSS was used to display the socio-cultural and demographic characteristics of the FHHs in a quantitative picture. This was used to analyse the first part of the interview schedule that focused on the personal data. The findings are presented in the analytical chapters.
- The rest of the qualitative data was analysed using the thematic approach. In this context, the models of Miles and Huberman (1994) were followed where they identified three concurrent flows of activities for qualitative analysis: data reduction (summaries; codes; divided themes; clusters; categories), data display (diagrams; pictures; visual forms; text), conclusion and verification (interpret displayed data; look for comparison and contrast; note and explore themes, patterns). The findings are presented in the analytical chapters.
- Nvivo8 was used in some stages of data analysis to help organize and code some data.

- Poverty among women and FHHs in this research was investigated, treated, and analysed within three inter-related cultural contexts: Arabic, Islamic and Saudi contexts.

How the researcher dealt with the issue of language and translation from Arabic to English language: with consideration for what has been translated and when and what difficulties arose in translation.

During this research, all the interviews with women and informants were conducted in the Arabic language. The interviews were recorded then transcribed into Microsoft Arabic documents. As researcher, I looked at these documents as 'social texts', which means that I viewed the texts as reflecting a specific 'frame of meaning' where language carries social and cultural symbolic implications (or indications). At this stage of the research, the choices were to either a) translate the texts into English or b) work with them in their original Arabic state.

I realized that by translating the documents into the English language would mean the loss of a lot of the rich and symbolic meanings; the Arabic language is very rich and complicated and the women's language is associated with many social circumstances that generate a specific discourse. Thus it was preferable for the women's language to be understood and analyzed within this context and within its temporal and spatial framework. The first stage of the analysis was therefore in the Arabic language and was afterwards translated to the English language.

The analysis work was developed in the following way:

1. I started the analysis by using the Arabic language and 'Arabic framework of meaning' to look through the texts and documents. I then identified many indicators, themes, and issues relevant to the research questions. I categorized and classified the significant themes under titles and subtitles appropriate to the research goals.
2. The Arabic documents included rich women's stories; therefore many quotations from these stories were identified for inclusion under the appropriate sections and titles.

3. The first draft of the analytical outline was completed, then this primary outline was translated into the English language.
4. This primary analytical outline – at this stage fully translated into English - was then enhanced according to the growth and development of themes, codes and research discussions.

During the translation from the Arabic to the English language, there were some difficulties that had to be addressed. Women talked according to their local vernacular, so the words and phrases carried a lot of meaning and connotation which varied according to local dialects, class and family background (e.g. Bedouin, rural, urban). In this context, there were many words and phrases which have no precise equivalent in English, words linked and associated with the cultural context of Saudi society, for example:

(Hareem): the translated word is 'women', but this word in the Saudi context takes a cultural meaning for how society classified women positively or negatively, depending on the context. *(Mahram)*: this word translated into 'guardian male' but the word in the Saudi context is more complicated in its meaning, reflecting a process of formulating the gender role of men and of women. *Mahram* could be understood in a positive or negative way as well as in accordance with how a man understands and plays his role and how a woman accepts, or not, this role as well as how society introduces the 'ideal type' of this role.

(Khula): translated into 'divorce at insistence of wife who pays compensation'. This is not the typical divorce or separation but might be classified as another aspect of divorce. There are many other problematic words, sentences, and phrases found in the analytical chapters and translated into the nearest English that could explain the meaning. Although the precise meaning could only be understood within the social, cultural, ethical and religious context of the language, I tried to portray as closely as possible the Arabic meanings through the medium of the English words and phrases. I believe that although a researcher with the aim of being neutral and non-invasive or influential, what helped with the matters of accurate or honest translation was the fact that I belong to the same society as these women and I have a good background in Arabic language and

local dialect, which enabled me to understand the circumstances and complexity of women's speech.

Ethical considerations

The Statement of Ethical Practice of the British Sociological Association, 2002 and 2006, provided more knowledge about ethical considerations such as research approval, relationships and responsibility towards research participants, anonymity, privacy and confidentiality as well as relationships with the sponsors.

Research approval and responsibilities towards research participants

- The researcher, with the help of her supervisor, managed the plan of the fieldwork, informed the sponsor (SCB) of the plan of the fieldwork, sent a formal letter to clarify the research's title, site of study, the plan and timing. This was supported by a letter from the supervisor. Accordingly, SCB provided official approval to stay in Jeddah for 3 to 4 months to conduct the fieldwork and also provided official letters when approval was needed from government and non-government organizations relevant to the research work.
- Organizations were contacted in advance to gain approval for conducting the research. The organizations were visited to ascertain how to manage the task in suitable conditions. They were provided with all original documents such as the SCB letter, the study plan with emphasis on the ethical issues of the research such as anonymity, privacy and confidentiality as well as the security of information regarding the participating institutions,
- The administrators of the institutions were met to discuss how the work would be conducted and how the meeting place should be comfortable with a guarantee of a degree of privacy.
- Also discussed (with the administrators) were details regarding the right of individuals (FHHs) to understand all information about this research and their right to agree to or reject being interviewed. Accordingly, the interviewees' approval (consent) was crucial, therefore a pro-forma was prepared to be signed by the women that stated that those women understood the explanation and gave consent for the interview(s).

- The pro-forma was discussed with the administrators of the SSD and the women's charitable associations because the individuals were transferred to the researcher's office by the administrators. It was therefore important to discuss this with them and to make sure that they understood this point. In application, the pro-forma did not work, so the administrators replaced it and instead the women were given spoken explanations without signing the pro-forma due to two reasons :
    1. Most women were illiterate
    2. Many women were afraid to sign an official letter where they thought it might be used against them
- The researcher discussed with the institutions and individuals their right to know the findings of the research. All institutions asked for completed copies of the research as well as Arabic translations of the conclusions and findings.

Relationships with participants

Before each interview was conducted, the interviewees were given explanations of the purpose of the study, placing special emphasis on confidentiality as a basic ethical rule. It was explained that their data, stories, narratives and voice recordings would not be disclosed under any conditions; that instead they would be used only for scientific purposes and would be destroyed after completion of the study.

The women agreed to become subjects for interviews; they often hoped to find someone who could help them out of their miserable conditions and thought that the researcher might be able to help in this regard. This expectation made the mission harder, giving an extra challenge of how to help the women who placed trust in the researcher and who revealed intimate information about their private lives. The mission was clearly stated with emphasis on the fact that the findings of the research would be sent to the social welfare institutions and decision makers and that it might help to improve regulation and services.

Another difficult situation was when the women burst into tears, which happened quite frequently during the interviews, when they recounted the painful experiences that were still shaping their current reality. According to their stories, they suffered a great deal from discrimination, oppression and injustice caused by the actions of their men, their families, society and the judicial system.

Obviously, the situations described above present particular challenges in terms of ethical research. It was also clear that the gender of the researcher played a significant role in this process: for example, the women would not have spoken as freely with a male researcher as they were able to talk to a female one. On the other hand, there were more restrictions as a female researcher, particularly by cultural boundaries. The research had to safeguard against tempting involvement in other issues, where the researcher felt a strong sense of compassion for the situation of the women, but could not play an active role in resolving their complicated issues, as this would have undermined the research plan.

Chapter five
The socio-cultural and demographic characteristics of poor female headed households in Jeddah City (poverty profile)

Introduction

The aim of this chapter is to give a brief description of the research sample; in other words to highlight the profile of poor FHHs who were interviewed for this research. This profile relies on socio-cultural and demographic indicators that indicate characteristics of these households and their female heads. The FHH profile should be set within its own socio-cultural context, thus there will be a brief introduction to Jeddah City as a multicultural city, outlining the number of poor people in Jeddah City within the study time scale according to the records of the institutions from where the research sample was selected.

5.1 The study site: Jeddah City, the place, the culture and the people

Jeddah is a port on the Red Sea, located mid-way along the Western coast of the Kingdom of Saudi Arabia. Jeddah's location on the ancient trade routes and its status as the seaport and airport for hajjis visiting the Holy City of Mecca have ensured that Jeddah is the most cosmopolitan of all Saudi Arabia's cities. By the end of the 1970s, the population of Jeddah was estimated to be close to one million. By 1986, the estimated population was 1.4 million. With an estimated annual growth rate in excess of 10%, the population by 1993 had passed the 2 million mark[32.] The most recent population of Jeddah, according to the 2004 census, was 2,821,371 with 1,442,788 Saudis and 1,378,583 non-Saudis. Among the Saudi population, there were 697,895 females and 744,893 males; thus females comprised 48% of the Saudi population in Jeddah City according to the 2004 census.

---

[٣٢]- http://www.saudinf.com/main/b6.htm.

Figure 5.1: Map of Saudi Arabia and the geographical location of Jeddah City

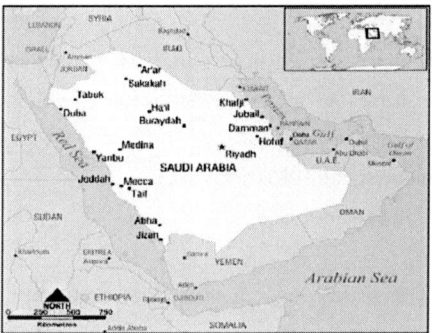

Source: *world-geographics.com*

It is important to understand what constitutes the physical environment as well as the social and cultural context of Jeddah City in which the Saudi poor FHHs live and interact in their daily lives. There are many reference books about Jeddah City and its social history as one of the most important cities on the Red Sea. For this brief introduction, the researcher relied heavily on two sources: Alanssari (1982) who wrote about the history of Jeddah, and Bagader and Alturki (2006) who conducted a recent anthropological study and analysed the social history of Jeddah City by studying changes in family relationships over several decades.

According to Alanssari (1982), Jeddah City was characterized throughout its history by two significant features: being an attractive port for trade and for migration. Because of its location on the Red Sea's coast, Jeddah became an important port for traders and an important gateway for the two Holy Mosques in Mecca and Madinah. Accordingly, the city gained significant commercial and religious importance that made Jeddah an attractive point for immigrants from outside the country who were traders and/or pilgrims from different countries who then settled in Jeddah (Alanssari, *ibid.*). The oil boom period experienced by the country during the 1970s increased the importance of Jeddah City; like other Saudis cities, it expanded and became an attractive place in terms of opportunities for employment, the buoyancy of trade, and the presence of governmental and educational institutions. With an increase in the internal migration of people from the surrounding villages and towns, Jeddah became a cosmopolitan city (Bagader and Alturki, 2006).

Migrations to Jeddah have formed a part of its modern history. There were two significant phases or waves of migration during the few last decades which have affected the city:

1. The migration during the 1960s and '70s, and
2. The migration during the 1980s.

During the '60s and '70s there was the first phase of migration by traders and pilgrims who came from both inside and outside the country and settled and integrated within the indigenous population and local communities of Jeddah. The second phase was during the '80s which saw the peak of the oil boom, characterized by the import of a large number of workers, especially from Arab, Asian and Hindi countries. The immigrant workers, who formed the working class, often worked in particular types of employment that did not attract the indigenous people such as domestic work, petty trade and crafts, so these new arrivals changed the demographic and socio-economic profile of the city. The immigrant workers increased the problems of the city where pressures on services resulted in the inability of the city to absorb the larger population. The immigrant workers also formed sub-cultures that could not merge or integrate with the local communities of the city. This led to a clear difference of social class, and therefore social and cultural differences among the population. This was mirrored by the separation of the districts of the city which were divided into a high class area, a middle class area, and traditional poor areas. After 1985, a belt of residential areas grew up around Jeddah City; these areas were regarded as a belt of poverty which included the immigrants from the countryside to the city who did not find suitable living areas in the city, so they lived on the outskirts in poor traditional districts that lacked many services and facilities (Bagader and Alturki, 2006: 72).

Thus the modern city of Jeddah was formed from a mixture of different races and ethnicities that have shaped the multi-cultural identity of the city and features of its class divisions that are reflected across the marginal areas: the poverty belt and the slums in Jeddah. Using this framework, a sample of poor FHHs was selected and interviewed, and in this chapter some features of their socio-cultural and demographic characteristics will be presented.

5.2 Number of poor in Jeddah City at the time of the field study (2009)

Table 5.1: Total number of poor in Jeddah City 2008- 2009 according to the organizations from where the sample was selected

Categories of poor by household unit head	GOs and NGOs			
	SSD	FWS	KWS	total
Divorced	556	250	204	1010
Widows	4,502	427	402	5331
Prisoners' families	713	30	18	761
Abandoned	150	25	26	201
MHHs	24,085	1089	448	25622
Others	-	-	91	91
Total	30006	1821	1189	33016

Source: the fieldwork study, figures and data collected from SDD, FWS, and KWS records 2008- 2009.

Table 5.1 shows the total number of poor in Jeddah City at the time of the fieldwork, between October 2008 and January 2009, as 33,016. The distribution of poor in the table is according to two factors. The first factor is the names of the organizations from which data was collected which were the SSD, FWS, and KWS. The second factor is the category of households which were: FHHs (those families headed by females such as divorced women, widows, abandoned women and prisoners' wives) and MHHs (those families that were headed by males) and others (disabled people, for example).

With reference to the above table, the official number of FHHs in the organizations from where data was collected was 7,303 who comprise 22% of the entire official number of poor people. The poor MHHs and others numbered 25,713, so FHHs constitute a significant percentage of the poor of Jeddah. The table indicates that the largest number of FHHs was affiliated to the SSD and that the largest number of poor, according to the category of family, was widows' families, then divorced women's families.

From the total number of poor FHHs, the researcher selected 112 to be interviewed for this study, as explained previously in the methodology chapter (see chapter 4). (FHH in the tables below refer to the study sample and not the total official number.)

5.3 Description of social, cultural and demographic characteristics of the sample

A total of 112 women were interviewed for this research, so in this section some of their characteristics will be displayed. These characteristics are based on the first part of the interview schedule that involved semi-structured questions investigating some socio-cultural and demographic indicators such as age categories, marital status, educational level, employment status, income sources, area of residence, number of family members, type of house, ownership of house, the place from where the sample was selected, receipt of support from the SSD and/or women's charitable associations, the nationality of the female head, the tribal background of the female head, the woman's ethnicity, the family's geographic background, the husband's (if any) nationality, and finally the origin of the woman's family.

The raw data was processed using SPSS and the results are as follows.

Educational levels

Table 5.2: Distribution of FHHs according to the educational level of the female heads

Education level	Frequency	%	Cumulative Percent
Illiterate	44	39.3	39.3
Read & write	8	7.1	46.4
Primary	33	29.5	75.9
High school	12	10.7	86.6
Secondary School	10	8.9	95.5
University degree	5	4.5	100.0
Total	112	100.0	

Source: the researcher's field work (2009)

According to table 5.2, the majority of family heads were illiterate or had basic educational levels such as read and write only, or a primary school certificate, and they comprised 76% of the total sample. Twenty-four percent of the sample had a medium level of education and a small percentage had an academic degree. This statistic raises the questions about why this 24% of women were not in employment, and where were the training programmes targeting this category?

Job/work

Table 5.3: Distribution of FHHs according to the job of the female head

Job	Frequency	%	Cumulative Percent
Housewife	104	92.9	92.9
Employed (in low paid work)	4	3.6	96.4
Retired	2	1.8	98.2
Beggar	1	.9	99.1
Cleaner	1	.9	100.0
Total	112	100.0	

Source: the researcher's field work (2009)

From the above table it is very clear that almost 93% of the FHH sample were housewives. The table shows that a very low percentage (3.6%) was employed, in all cases in low paid work.

The main source of income

Table 5.4: Distribution of FHHs according to the main source of income

Main income resource	Frequency	%	Cumulative Percent
SSD	48	42.9	42.9
Charity	13	11.6	54.5
SSD & Charity	18	16.1	70.5
Relatives	13	11.6	82.1
Job	6	5.4	87.5
Pension	4	3.6	91.1
Donation	4	3.6	94.6
SSD & Pension	6	5.4	100.0
Total	112	100.0	

Source: the researcher's field work (2009)

Table 5.4 shows that the social security department (SSD) was the main income source for 43% of the FHHs. When taking into consideration the category in receipt of benefit from both the SSD and charities, the percentage rises to 59% of FHHs that relied on the SSD as a main income source. Charities supported almost 12% of the sample, but when considering the category that benefitted from both SSD and charities; this increases the percentage to 28% of the sample who benefitted from charities. Relatives supported almost 12% of the sample whilst FHHs who relied on a job and/or state pension constituted just 9%.

Where FHHs live

Table 5.5: Distribution of FHHs according to their living area

Area of living	Frequency	%	Cumulative Percent
South & East Jeddah	68	60.7	60.7
North	44	39.3	100.0
Total	112	100.0	

Source: the researcher's field work (2009)

The above table shows that almost 61% of the sample was living in districts located in southern and eastern Jeddah, and 39% were living in districts located in northern Jeddah. Those districts are mostly poor and lack services needed by the population such as water, electricity and sanitation in addition to lacking educational, health and social services.

Family members

Table 5.6: Distribution of FHHs according to the number of family members

No. of family members	Frequency	%	Cumulative Percent
1-3	24	21.4	21.4
4-6	48	42.9	64.3
7-9	34	30.4	94.6
10-12	5	4.5	99.1
12<	1	.9	100.0
Total	112	100.0	

Source: the researcher's field work (2009)

Table 5.6 shows that 42.9% of the sample had 4-6 family members and 30.4% had 7-9 members, thus a combined total of 73.3% of FHHs had between 4-9 family members with 5% having 10-12 family members. It can be deduced that 78% of the sample headed very large or fairly large families.

Type of house

Table 5.7: Distribution of FHHs according to the type of their houses

Type of house	Frequency	%	Cumulative Percent
Traditional / old house	32	28.6	28.6
Flat	71	63.4	92.0
House	9	8.0	100.0
Total	112	100.0	

Source: the researcher's field work (2009)

Table 5.7 indicates that the majority of FHHs (63%) were living in a flat (most with 2 or 3 bedrooms). Nearly 29% of the FHHs lived in old traditional houses which tended to need a lot of maintenance and renovation in order to become and remain habitable. Only 8% of the sample lived in good, detached houses.

Ownership of the house

Table 5.8: Distribution of FHHs according to ownership of their houses

Ownership of the house	Frequency	%	Cumulative Percent
Owner	8	7.1	7.1
Tenant	76	67.9	75.0
Free charitable house resident	11	9.8	84.8
Non- free charitable house resident	17	15.2	100.0
Total	112	100.0	

Source: the researcher's field work (2009)

Table 5.8 shows that only 17% of the sample did not have to pay house rent because they were already either owners of their houses or lived in free charitable houses. The majority of the sample (83%) had to pay rent for their houses because they were tenants or lived in non-free charitable homes and were therefore liable to pay partial rent for their residences.

Where the FHHs were selected from

Table 5.9: Distribution the FHHs according to the places from where they were selected

Code of place	Frequency	%	Cumulative Percent
FWS	17	15.2	15.2
KWS	15	13.4	28.6
CH	30	26.8	55.4
SSD	50	44.6	100.0
Total	112	100.0	

Source: the researcher's field work (2009)

Table 5.9 shows that nearly 28% of the sample were recruited from two women's charitable associations: the FWS and KWS. Approximately 45% of the FHHs were selected from among the Social Security Department's beneficiaries (SSD). The remaining 27% were selected by a snowball technique from the residents of charitable housing who did not benefit from SSD or women's charitable associations.

Obtaining official support from the SSD

Table 5.10: Distribution of FHHs according to receipt of SSD

Official support from SSD	Frequency	%	Cumulative Percent
Yes	75	67.0	67.0
No	37	33.0	100.0
Total	112	100.0	

Source: the researcher's field work (2009)

Table 5.10 shows that 67 % of the sample received official support from the SSD whereas 33% of the sample did not receive any support from the SSD despite being poor.

Obtaining support from the charitable associations

Table 5.11: Distribution of FHHs according to being supported by charitable associations

In receipt of support from charitable associations?	Frequency	%	Cumulative Percent
Yes	54	48.2	48.2
No	58	51.8	100.0
Total	112	100.0	

Source: the researcher's field work (2009)

The above table indicates that approximately 48% of the sample were in receipt of benefits and support from charitable associations, whereas almost 52% did not receive any benefits or support from charities, despite their status as poor and needy.

The nationality of the female head

Table 5.12: Distribution the FHHs according to the female head's nationality

The nationality of the female head	Frequency	%	Cumulative Percent
Saudi	86	76.8	76.8
Naturalized	21	18.8	95.5
Non-Saudi	5	4.5	100.0
Total	112	100.0	

Source: the researcher's field work (2009)

Table 5.12 shows that almost 77% of the families' heads were Saudis. The table also shows that 4.5% of the heads were non-Saudi, while the 'naturalized' category (non-

Saudis who were in the process of becoming Saudi nationals) stands much higher at 18.8%.

The tribal background of the family

Table 5.13: Distribution of the FHHs according to their tribal backgrounds

Tribal background	Frequency	%	Cumulative Percent
Bedouin / tribal	35	31.2	31.2
Urbanites / non-tribal	77	68.8	100.0
Total	112	100.0	

Source: the researcher's field work (2009)

The table above shows that nearly 69% of the sample were urbanites, meaning they were non-tribal. However, 31% were Bedouin, so in other words, 31% of the sample were tribal.

The female head's ethnicity

Table 5.14: Distribution of the FHHs according to the female head's ethnicity

The women's ethnicity	Frequency	%	Cumulative Percent
Saudi Arabian	72	64.3	64.3
Saudi Asian	3	2.7	67.0
Saudi African	12	10.7	77.7
Arabic (non-Saudi)	23	20.5	98.2
Asian	2	1.8	100.0
Total	112	100.0	

Source: the researcher's field work (2009)

From the table above it is clear that 64% of the female heads were Saudi, which means that their root was Saudi. On the other hand, 36% of the female heads had different ethnic backgrounds such as Black (African), Asian, and Arabic.

The residential areas of the respondents' families

Table 5.15: Distribution the FHHs according to the places of residence of their families

The place of residence	Frequency	%	Cumulative Percent
Jeddah	68	60.7	60.7
Western region (Mecca & Madinah area)	14	12.5	73.2
Southern (Jazaan & Najraan)	29	25.9	99.1
Middle region	1	.9	100.0
Total	112	100.0	

Source: the researcher's field work (2009)

Table 5.15 indicates that almost 61% of the sample's families resided in Jeddah City. The remaining 39% lived in different provinces and regions of Saudi, from where it is likely that they had migrated and settled in Jeddah City to search for work or to be near the holy places of Mecca and Madinah. The figures in the table show that the highest percentage among immigrant families was 26% and represents those whose families resided in the southern provinces of Saudi, where Jazzan and Najraan are the poorest provinces[33]. The table shows that 12% of the sample's families resided on the outskirts of Jeddah, where the western villages, towns, and countryside are located near Jeddah City. Only 1% were from the middle part of Saudi, which is the location of the central government and all official governmental bodies.

---

[33] - See for example the series reports on poverty in Jazaan conducted by 'Riyadh Daily Newspaper', Friday 03 January 2003 No. 12614 Year 38 :
http://www.alriyadh.com/Contents/03-01-2003/Mainpage/COV_439.php

The husband's or ex-husband's nationality

Table 5.16: Distribution of FHHs according to their husband's or ex-husband's nationality

The husband/or ex-husband nationality	Frequency	%	Cumulative Percent
Saudi	101	90.2	90.2
Non-Saudi	11	9.8	100.0
Total	112	100.0	

Source: the researcher's field work (2009)

Table 5.16 shows that 90% of the FHHs had (or used to have) Saudi husbands. This means that the FHHs were either Saudi women or non-Saudi women who had obtained Saudi nationality through marrying Saudi men (as indicated in table 5.12). The table also indicates that 10% of the female heads were Saudi women but they had married non-Saudi men, which means that these families would be treated as non-Saudis by legal and bureaucratic systems.

It should be noted that the 10% in table 5.16 who were Saudi women who had or formerly had a non-Saudi spouse, plus the 23% in table 5.12 who were non-Saudi women who were or had been married to Saudi men, total 33% of the sample. They can be regarded as a group with specific conditions or problems relevant to their identities as Saudi or non-Saudi, and could thus be considered a type of minority group. These types of families are treated by the researcher as Saudi families (as explained in the methodology chapter), but it is understood that these families could face, alongside their poverty, deprivation of official support because one part of the family was non-Saudi or could not attain Saudi nationality.

The origins of the women's families: where these women came from

Table 5.17: Distribution the FHHs according to origin of the female heads

The origin of the female heads	Frequency	%	Cumulative Percent
Saudi Arabia	86	76.8	76.8
Yemen	10	8.9	85.7
Egypt	7	6.2	92.0
Syria	2	1.8	93.8
Somalia	1	.9	94.6
Pakistan	1	.9	95.5
Palestine	2	1.8	97.3
Morocco	1	.9	98.2
Boukharstan	1	.9	99.1
Indonesia	1	.9	100.0
Total	112	100.0	

Source: the researcher's field work (2009)

The table above shows that 77% of the female heads were women whose family origins were Saudi. However, the other 23% had family origins that were non-Saudi. This means that their backgrounds were in various Arabic and non-Arabic minority groups, as represented in the table. The largest percentages were women who had come from Yemeni and Egyptian communities.

Conclusion: typical poor FHHs

Most of the FHHs had specific characteristics that can be summarised as follows. The FHHs were mostly heading large families – approximately 73% of the sample lived in families with between 4-9 members. The male head tended to be missing from family life so the family was headed by the female. The women had suffered divorce, widowhood, imprisonment of their husbands, abandonment, the husband suffering sickness, old age or unemployment. These female heads were mostly uneducated or had a low or basic level of education. This was mirrored in the children as the fieldwork revealed high levels of school dropout. These families mostly had no regular earned incomes because the heads had no jobs. The majority of the FHHs were tenants and lived in small flats. A significant number of FHHs were deprived of both official supports from the SSD and from women's associations. Some of these women were regarded legally and socially as minority groups because of their ethnicity, family backgrounds and/or nationality.

The quantitative indicators (statistics in the tables) raise questions about some minority groups who have specific circumstances that might increase their poverty due to:

a. Regional dimension: for example, the FHHs and/or their families who came to the city as immigrants, especially from the Southern region, seemed simply to transfer the same culture of poverty and poverty conditions from their original poor region.
b. Race and ethnicity dimension: non-Saudi citizens could find themselves marginalized because of their position as minorities.
c. Gender dimension: the various sub-groups of the FHHs, depending on their particular marital statuses, could face, besides their poverty, many difficulties relevant to their gender as female heads of their families.

The following chapter will examine the everyday lives of these FHHs.

Chapter six
The social reality of the everyday lives of poor female-headed households

Introduction

The previous chapter described the socio-cultural and demographic characteristics of poor female-headed households (FHHs) in Jeddah City. This chapter will focus on another research goal: the description and explanation of how poor FHHs experience poverty and deal with their daily lives. As explained previously, FHHs can be classified into five sub-categories according to the marital status of the female head, which are: widows' families divorced women's families, abandoned women's families, prisoners' wives families and married women's families. The aim of this chapter is to describe how these categories of FHHs deal with poverty in their everyday lives, which in turn will show the social suffering, problems, and social needs of these families, as well as the similarities and differences among the categories.

The chapter is divided into the following sections:

1 – Definition of concepts and terms such as 'categories of FHHs' and 'daily life'.

2 - Discussions of the interviews with the study sample and a description of each category in terms of poverty as an experience in daily life, focusing on several dimensions, such as how the families became poor, how the women became breadwinners or female heads for their own families, how the families and female heads dealt with social problems and the most important social needs and requirements in their daily lives.

In the discussion of the above issues, some stories and quotations from the women's interviews are presented as examples and as representative of other similar stories.

6.1 The definition of some terms

6.1.1 Female-headed households – sub-categories of the research sample

The research sample was divided according to the marital status of the female heads and formed five sub-categories or sub-groups which were: the families of widows (23 cases), the families of divorced women (34 cases), the families of abandoned women (16 cases), the families of prisoners' wives (12 cases) and the families of married women (27 cases). The five categories had two common features: poverty and being headed by females. However, within each group there were varying conditions relevant to their everyday lives such as how they experienced poverty, the barriers and difficulties they faced, their social needs and their relationships with social support systems. It seems to be the case that the sub-groups of FHHs and their female heads share the common features of poverty, gender and the cultural context which frames their social worlds as women. On the other hand, they are distinct (or different) in their own life details, characteristics and the factors affecting their experiences.

6.1.2 The daily lives of female-headed households

The daily life of FHHS refers to the social reality of FHHs and their female heads, the requirements of daily life and interactions with others, both within and outside the household unit. The term daily life in this research includes the experience of poverty as faced by FHHs and their female heads and how this experience was understood and dealt with within the social conditions surrounding them. An understanding of daily life requires an understanding of the cultural and social contexts and how these frame the details of the daily life of FHHs and their relations with others. It also requires an understanding of how the poverty experience is structured within a particular social context (Saudi - Arabic - Islamic). Thus, the analysis of the women's interviews and their experiences within the framework of everyday life reflects the phenomenon of poverty in Saudi FHHs in its special features (those relevant to each category separately) and its general features that reflect the similarities between sub-categories.

6.2 Interviews with the study sample
6.2.1. The case of widow's families' category: home without pillars.
6.2.1.1 The stories of the heads of widows' families

Widow 1: Um-jabrah, 75 years old, illiterate with three daughters
".....My husband died of disease more than 30 years ago ... he was from Jazaan and I am Yamani. He married me when I was 17 years old. We lived in Jeddah for a long time.

My husband was working as a taxi driver in his private car. I haven't got Saudi nationality because my husband did not make this happen and I did not ask him to. In that time, I did not need anything because my husband provided us with what we needed as a family. We were poor but we had shelter and the basic requirements of life and this was enough for me. After his death, I was shocked and scared and the important thing was how I would be able to look after my three daughters, how to feed them and how to pay the rent on my house. We were four *hareem* [women] alone, I experienced a difficult time. I used to stay at home so I had no knowledge of the outside world and whether the government could help me or not, but *Alhamdulillah* [thanks for god] the God did not forget us; my neighbours helped and collected money for me. They continued sending food, clothes and money as a donation for my orphan daughters. In that time I thought about work so I cooked fried potatoes near my house and sold to people who passed in the street. They liked it, especially the children who were playing in the street near their houses. After a while two of my daughters got married and one remained with me. She is 40 years old now and she applied for SSD support several years ago. SSD accepted her for a monthly allowance but rejected my application because I am not Saudi. Frying potatoes for many years has badly affected my lungs. I am old now and very ill, I need health care, treatment and medications. The public health sector rejected me because it is for Saudis so I have to pay for private health care. My daughter and I are now dependent on her SSD monthly allowance but it is not enough for us to eat, to pay rent and to buy my medications..."

Widow 2: Fatimah S, 62, illiterate, has 6 sons and daughters

"My husband died of a stroke three years ago; he was an employee of Saudi Arabian Airlines. I was the second wife and I have 6 children (3 sons and 3 daughters). My children are now married except the youngest girl who is 23 years old and lives with me. My husband had another wife with 7 children so the family was very big compared with his modest salary. When my husband was alive he was able to handle everything so he provided us with a good life with the basic things like good food, clothes and house equipment. He could also build a small traditional house and he divided it between me and his other wife. After his death, I received with my daughters our share from his retirement pension which was 1725 Real per month [about £287]. His first wife got more than me because she has more family members. Our share is not enough for my and my daughter's needs so I went to the SSD to apply for social support but unfortunately they told me that we were not eligible for support because we already have a 'retirement pension'. I tried to explain that this pension was not enough but they did not understand. I am very sad, do you know that! Everything is becoming more expensive; the bills for the telephone, electricity and water as well as my daughter's university tuition fee because she could not get a free place. She also needs expenses for her studies, clothes, transport, and other things girls need. When I think about all these matters, I cannot sleep at night. I do not know why the SSD bothered to take account of our little bit of retirement pension which is not enough to feed us dry bread. Everything is getting worse than before. For example, the university used to give students monthly awards, but nowadays there are no more places for students so if students can't get a place their families have to pay tuition fees. Not all families have enough money. I try with difficulty to collect and calculate *kirsh* with *kirsh* [a penny with a penny] just to pay my daughter's tuition fees..."

Widow 3: Faten B, 46, educated, has one son and three daughters
"My husband died four years ago of a heart attack. He was not Saudi and he was working as a shop manger with a good salary. We were not rich but we were not poor. We lived well and did not feel that we were missing anything. I have three daughters and a son who at that time was a student at the university. Thanks for God who made things easy for my son to get Saudi nationality. Generally it is not easy for a Saudi woman to give her children her nationality. In my case I applied officially many times to the Home Office requesting Saudi nationality for my children. After a long time, my son was accepted but my three daughters were rejected. To be honest, the most important was the son because at the end he will be the breadwinner of the family; the girls will get married sooner or later. The death of my husband changed everything. I faced difficult times where I had to think about many things like house rent, the cost of living, school requirements, the bills, food and a lot more. My husband did not leave any savings. Also I did not have a good degree that enabled me to find paid work. My son suspended his studies and sought a job. He found one as a seller in an electronics shop; it was very low paid work with long hours. I tried to cook traditional food and sell

it to my neighbours and friends but it did not work out. A friend advised me to apply for SSD and after a while they gave me a monthly allowance of 850 SR (£141.60) but they rejected the applications of my daughters because they are non-Saudis This affected my daughters - they were not able to get a fair opportunity in education, employment, public health care and other social support and facilities. This makes me very sad and I cry when I think of what will happen to my daughters when I am dead! My close relatives support me as much as they can and I appreciate that a lot but I realize they have their own lives so they will not be expected to support me forever..."

Widows 4: Salmah S, 40, Alyaa S, 67, and Hameidah S, 58 are three Bedouin widows. They are friends and neighbours and they were interviewed when they were renewing their registration data at the SSD. They belong to a famous Bedouin tribe that is located outside Jeddah in a village called Alkhamel. Most Bedouin people were farmers and they left their home villages a long time ago and settled near Jeddah after the drought hit their lands.

Salmah S: "I came with my neighbours today to SSD to renew our data. My husband was an old farmer who was dependent on SSD income support. He died of a heart attack 10 years ago. At that time I was a young woman with 7 children of different ages. This was a great responsibility and the income allowance of SSD was not enough for us so my relatives supported me. My oldest son is now 24 years old. He tried to work but he has not found a job yet. He is uneducated, so he prefers to work as a taxi driver. He needs a car and there is no money for that..."

Alyaa S: "My husband died 15 years ago. He received SSD income support since he left the village after the land was hit by drought. We and other farmers lost everything. Here in Jeddah, most ex-farmers get support from the SSD. They live in the same community. After the death of my husband, his income support was divided between his three wives and their children. I was the third wife and I have got three boys and three girls. Our share of the income support was not enough so I couldn't manage the daily requirements for my family. Relatives and neighbours supported me a lot. My sons did not like their school so they abandoned education after the elementary stage. Two of my sons are now married and work as militaries (soldiers). The youngest son, who is 25 years old, still lives with me; he has no education and no job. Two of my daughters are married and one remains with me; she graduated two years ago from the university but unfortunately she has still not found a job..."

Hameidah S: "My husband died 13 years ago. He was a taxi driver and was also on SSD income support because he had a large family: two wives and 13 children. I was the second wife and have 3 sons and 3 daughters. I had no problem when my husband was alive but after his death, life became bleak. I had to face life alone with my children. The SSD income support divided between the two wives was not enough for both of us. My brothers supported me a lot. Unfortunately my sons dropped out of school and now they are unemployed and live with me. The daughters are better as they graduated from the university then applied for public sector jobs as teachers but are waiting to hear. I suffer the lack of income and though I think about it a lot, I haven't found a solution. I have a large plot of land in my village but it is abandoned and not suitable for agriculture or for sale. All my children have no work. I cannot work outside my home or even go to the women's charitable association. That would be embarrassing in my case because my father was an ex-tribal sheikh. He is dead now but I have to protect his reputation..."

Widow 5: Muteiba Z, 63, illiterate with 6 daughters and sons

"My first husband died 30 years ago in a car accident. At that time I was a young and beautiful woman with four daughters aged 14, 12, 10 and 6. My husband worked as a broker. His large family was in the southern region of Saudi and he came a long time ago to stay and work in Jeddah, then we got married. After his death, I was very sad, terrified and shocked. During the funeral, I was just thinking about life for me and my daughters and what I could do! After the funeral, my husband's brother called me to say that he and his other brothers would take responsibility for my daughters' cost of living. They paid the rent for my house and sent me a monthly income. I felt safe and comforted but I was not surprised because this ethic is widespread between good families. After six months, my brother informed me that the brothers of my dead husband (they were three) would come to see the girls. A few days later, they visited us and my brother made a big *Azeemah* [a big dinner with some close family and friends in honour of the guests]. After they left, my brother told me that my daughters' family wanted my four girls to live with their granddad. The three brothers informed my brother to discuss this with me. They wanted me to agree to it saying that I could see the girls any time I wanted to. They also said that if I wanted to go with my daughters, one of them would accept me as a wife. My brother asked me to think carefully about this and he recommended the second option. I thought a lot about it and asked advice from some close friends. I know how the tradition is strict towards honour and that the family needs to be raised and looked after and protected. The tradition gives the men the right and I could not break this rule. If I disagreed or complained to the court the judge would have given the grandad the right to take them because he was their guardian. I finally agreed to marry the youngest brother (who was 40). He had a wife and 5 children but my condition was to live in Jeddah near my family and he agreed. He was and still is a good father for my daughters and a good husband for me. I now have 2 more sons. My daughters and sons are now married to their cousins..."

6.2.1.2 Analysis of the widow's families' category: homes without pillars.

Widows' families are an important category of poor Saudi FHHs. The research sample consists of 21% who were widows who lost their spouses for various reasons including car accidents[34], heart attack, stroke, chronic disease and old age etc. The stories of the widows' families are divided according to the matrix of the sample into three age categories: the young age category – widows who were less than 40; the middle age category – widows who were between 41-60, and the older

---

[34] - Some official statistics and press reports mention that Saudi Arabia has the highest rate of car accidents in the world. Women are not allowed to drive in Saudi which makes men more likely to die in car accidents than women and also makes women more likely to be widowed by losing their husband to a car accident.

age category – widows who were 61 and older. This diversification of age groups aims to ensure that the sample includes members from all age ranges. This section addresses several issues on how this category became poor and how widows became the breadwinners or heads of the family. The families' problems and their most important social needs are also addressed.

The social reality of widows' families: how the family became poor and how widow became the breadwinner and head of the family

The widows' stories reflect how the traditional and popular culture portrays the man as a 'house column' and his position in society as a social and cultural symbol in family life. Therefore when the man dies, family life becomes unbalanced. The man is the 'social and economic symbol' and is considered the basis of social protection for the family, even if he is poor and/or unemployed. The loss of the man has a negative impact on the life of his wife and family.

According to Shari'a law, a woman whose husband dies has to spend a period of time - four months and ten days - in mourning for her departed husband. This period is called in Islam '*iddah*'. The widow has to respect the memory of her departed husband during *iddah*, so she has to stay in her house and show the manifestations of mourning in her behaviour and appearance. During this time, it will be clear if the woman is pregnant from her husband. If she is not pregnant, she can marry again after *iddah*, but if she is pregnant, she has to wait until the baby is born before she is free to marry.

The widows' stories indicate that their lives with their husbands were relatively stable and secure and the main reason for this was the existence of a man in their daily lives. The man was the breadwinner of the family and the one responsible socially, culturally and legally for all family matters. The man also has a great responsibility to secure all life requirements for his family such as shelter, food and cost of living. The man is also the legal representative of his family in things relevant to the law, legislation, social and governmental institutions. Thus the man is the guardian of the women and his family and is called in the local vernacular *'wally alamar'* or *'mahram'* which means 'the official male guardian' (see also chapter 4).

Most widows' stories highlighted that the death of the husband brought about a great gap in family life where the widow was then forced to take responsibility to occupy that gap, but most evidence shows that the women (widows) are still not able to occupy the man's role, especially in Saudi society, where many aspects of social life are controlled by the traditional culture and differences in gender roles. According to their gender role, the widows used to deal with the internal sphere of family issues within the household unit, so the women have little interaction with the public sphere which is generally limited for women in Saudi society. Therefore after the death of her husband, a widow, in trying to occupy the position of the family's head, will face many barriers that hinder her efforts. According to the widows' stories and interviews, these barriers could be related to two main factors:

1- The traditional culture that controls and directs the whole social context.
2- The women themselves lacking education, skills and capabilities, which impedes their interactions with the outside world.

In the interviews, the widows presented much evidence to illustrate the above factors in the struggles of widows in their social reality and daily life such as:

A. The lives of these women before their widowhood showed that, according to the culture, they were fully dependent on their husbands. Socialization within their original families was based on being sponsored by the family (father, brother or other close male relatives) until she married and then became the responsibility of her husband. Accordingly, the most important roles for women are as a good wife and a good mother, whereas the significant role for men is to sponsor his family (wife/wives and children). The culture here plays a significant role in dividing and shaping gender roles and gender differences. The culture also identifies an 'ideal type' for these roles. For example, to be a good wife means more than playing the gender role; the woman is required to be patient, more supportive of her husband if he is poor or ill and not complain or cry about the misery of her life. Salwa D. (aged 40) said:

"My husband had a crisis in his career; he lost his job as a bank accountant. He lost all his savings in the stock market crisis of 2006. We had nothing and then everything got tragically worse - my husband got ill and lost his leg because of his diabetes; his health condition was serious and he went to hospital. I have three children so I returned to live with my family. I was desperate and crying all the time, especially when I thought about our previous life. My dad was always reminding me that all these sad events were just a test of my faith and that it was an ethical test for me as a good wife and therefore I had to have more patience and be more supportive of my husband. I was told that I should not complain or cry because it was the will of God. My husband died. I hope I was really a good wife..."

B. As a result of the prevailing cultural trend, the women seem uninterested in developing their skills for gaining paid work, despite their disadvantage in having low educational levels.

C. The husbands, according to the widows' narratives, seemed unprepared for (or had no interest in preparing) their wives for facing the external social reality in the case of any emergency. Therefore these women were mostly unaware of the regulations, laws and social and governmental institutions or even the systems that could support them. The Saudi man, according to the dominant traditional cultural trend, tries to keep his wife away from direct contact with the public domain. Some men – usually those who are well educated and open-minded - let their women know about and learn how to deal with the public sphere. The traditional culture and socialization of Saudi society endorses the man's reservation with his wife, especially in issues of money and business, so the Saudi man does not encourage his wife to ask or learn about his income or work issues. It is not culturally and socially acceptable for a woman to assert herself on such matters.

Therefore, it appears from the widows' stories that the trauma for a woman after the death of her husband is related to how she will face the outside world. For example, the early stage is the transitional period after the death of her husband when there are many issues to be resolved such as the funeral preparation, the inheritance issues - especially if the man has more than one wife who has borne him children - and the procedure for getting the pension if he was in paid work. All these issues are problematic for the Saudi widow for the following reasons.

1- The illiteracy and low educational level of these women which prevents them from communicating effectively in the public sphere.
2- The masculine nature of Saudi society, where most social and governmental institutions deal basically with males, so the women have to be represented by their male relatives if they need any service from these institutions. Some issues such as rent contracts and paying utility bills add to the problematic issues for these women in their transitional period.

The widows get help mainly from their close relatives and neighbours who sometimes work as guides for these women in the governmental and non-governmental organizations that provide social services and support.

6.2.1.3 Barriers and problems faced by the widows' families

The interviews with the widows who were heads of their families demonstrate that they faced many barriers and problems in their daily lives: problems such as life requirements, children's needs, male-led culture, societal institutions, regulation and legal identity.

Life requirements

Many widows expressed their inability to cope with the life requirements of their families (e.g. food, rent, clothes, utility bills, school requirements etc.) where the high cost of living and the rise in prices were serious problems. Some widows on SSD benefit explained that their benefits were not significantly increased in line with inflation and the increase in prices for everything, and this had contributed to making their situation worse.

A widow with 4 children said:

> "My kids used to drink Nido milk, but after the prices went up, I could not buy Nido any more. The price is now 120R (£20) for the big Nido whereas it was 50R (£8.30) last year. I replaced it with a cheaper milk, but the kids did not like it and did not drink it..."

A widow on SSD benefit said:

> "I do not want any increase in my income support if that would increase the price of our food. What benefit can I get from that? In the past I bought my shopping from PANDA [a big supermarket store similar to ASDA]. Now I shop in low price shops. I have replaced our Basmati rice with a cheaper version but my children don't like it. The King increased our benefit by 15% last year but the prices go up threefold..."[35]

Another widow said:

> "I wish I could buy a car for my son to be able to save the cost of transport, but I don't think I could...how can I get the money? Even coming here to the SSD and returning to my house will cost me 60R (£10)..."

---

[35] - According to many official reports in Saudi newspapers the dramatic increases in the price of rice that started in Saudi in late 2007 was associated with a global problem relevant to the countries that export rice crops such as India and Thailand where they increased their own prices for world consumption. The price of 'Basmati rice' at the time of my fieldwork (2009-2010) was: Indian Basmati rice No1 (45k) was priced at 300R (£50) but in the middle of 2007 it had been 120R (£20).

Children's requirements

1. A widow has a great responsibility to her children, to support them and to provide their life requirements which vary according to their age groups, from childhood to adolescence to young adulthood.

> **Salwa** said: "The expenses of my children and their school and life requirements are the biggest problems for me. I cannot sleep when I think about that. I now have insomnia."

> **Awatif,** who is on SSD income support said: "I have three daughters and they need many things...you know how girls' requirements are. They need to be like their friends in school and university, with good clothes, shoes, bags and makeup. Also there are tuition fees for my oldest daughter who could not get a free place, so I have to pay for her. I cannot let her feel she is less than her friends at university. Although I feel my daughters do not ask me for too much, the problem is where I can get enough money."

> **Um-ahmad** is 43, a widow with four children: "Last year, when my son was 25 years old, I decided to get him married. He is the eldest of my sons, with no work and not a good education and I noticed that he started spending time away from the home. He is a young man and I was afraid that he would fall into the ways of *haraam* [to have wrong sexual relationships] so he needed to be married. If his father was still alive, he would do the same as I did. I borrowed money from some relatives and friends and discussed marriage with him. I chose his cousin to be his bride because her father would not ask a big dowry. I provided an acceptable wedding party and gave him a room in my house. He is now trying to find a job and he must pay off our debt..."

> **Fatimah,**40, said: "I wish I could take my kids on a trip to the beach with some relatives who take their kids but I have to think about how much it would cost me! For example, I have pay for a taxi, drinks, ice-cream, burgers, sweets and games etc. With four kids and our SSD income support

being barely enough to feed us, how can we go on a trip? I told my kids we will go in Eid [the Muslin festival day]..."

2. Widows face the problem of the 'legal status of her children as orphans'. According to some widows' interviews, many social and governmental institutions that have relationships with these families require the widows to send the *wakeil* (the 'male guardian' who represents the widow and her children) before the local and legal authorities. Usually this person will be a close relative of the woman or her children such as the grandfather or the uncle, or the father or brother of the widow. The widows cannot always find such people for various reasons: there may simply be no existing relatives; if relatives do exist she may not be in a good relationship with them. Some of the stories showed how the widows suffered from a fear of losing their children to close relatives, especially if they were female children (for example, see widow story 5). The Saudi traditions and cultural heritages support this behaviour and make it easy for male relatives to take the children even though Shari'a law might support women's and children's rights. Thus the strength of the traditional culture and the lack of legislation and personal/family laws deriving from Shari'a law make it easy for women to find themselves wronged and oppressed in such circumstances.

Zahra, 33, said: "After the death of my husband three years ago, my mother-in-law asked me to sign an official document for her son [Zahra's brother-in-law] who is the uncle of my children, to make him the legal *wakeil* [official male guardian] for me and my kids who were at that time 10, 8 and 6. That document enabled this man to take all our financial benefits and the financial rights of my husband from his work company. It was about 150,000R (£25,000). I did not see the money - they took it and built a two room extension in the roof of their house for me and my children. My mother-in-law and her son and daughter treated me badly. They swore at and beat my children. When they learnt that I was going to marry another man they were very angry and threatened to throw me in the street and take my kids. I'm very scared. I do not know what to do. My family is in Yemen and they will not be able to do anything..."

Naiemah, 27, said: "When my first husband died six years ago, my kids were small (2 and 4). I lived near my parents-in-law and after two years I got married. My parents-in-law refused to let my kids go with me and took them. After a while when they visited me, I noticed marks on their bodies and they were weak. They cried and told me that their grandfather beat them and put them in a locked room with no food or drink. I was shocked; I cried and told my husband. Then we decided not to let them return to their grandfather. The next day, he came with the police and took them. I was screaming and crying. After that and with support of my husband, I sued my father-in-law. After two years, the judge ruled in favour of me so I won and got back my kids again."

3. Some widows found themselves in trouble with governmental bodies because of mistakes made by their husbands. For example, many widows narrated how they were informed by the SSD that their identity card or family card had not been declared in the governmental data system. This is problematic in terms of their national ID numbers or family card. The widows were recommended to resolve the problem in another governmental department called 'The Home Office: The Agency of Civil Affairs', responsible for all citizen ID matters.[36] In Saudi Arabia, such issues take time and have complicated procedures; the fact that it is a male's task means the widow has to rely on the male head of the family or the *wakiel* (male guardian). In addition to this disadvantage, most widows have a low level of education so they find it difficult to understand procedures. Being poor makes them more vulnerable and unable to cover the cost of the procedure. There is evidence that some widows stopped attempting to receive SSD income support because of these barriers.

---

[36] - In Saudi Arabia there are two types of National or Citizenship ID card: 1- the "Family Card" which basically belongs to the man who is head of the family; this card is an official document and includes the name of the head of the family with his personal photo, and also the names of all his family members (wife/wives and children) in addition to their dates of birth and national identity number for each person. 2- An individual ID card which is held by adults, both male and female, and which includes a photo, name, date of birth, and the national identity number of the holder.

4. Widows suffered financially due to having to cover the costs of education for their children. The children needed items such as uniforms, bags, shoes, stationery, lunch, transport to school and money. The children at university or college also had specific needs. With higher educational institutions aiming to reduce the number of full-time students due to the inability of the current Saudi universities to cope with the growing number of students, the students were directed towards other types of learning such as distance and online. The problem with the alternative systems was that students had to pay tuition fees, thus poor students were disadvantaged (see for example widow 2).

> Another widow said: "The University nowadays is just for whoever is able to pay. The rich can pay but we are poor so we cannot pay. I would have to pay 6000R (£1000) or more for an academic year for my son, but I would rather use that money to feed my children or pay my house rent..."

Culture and society

The women's stories reveal that widows and other women who have no male figureheads are treated differently from others and appear to be like 'a house without a fence or door' as the women expressed it. During contact with some men in public, social, and governmental institutions, the women could be subject to harassment. For example, some men could indicate to the women using a shameless word or sign directly or indirectly. Such behaviour is strongly insulting and although illegal and totally unacceptable socially and culturally in conservative Saudi society, most women are unable to complain publicly because the sensitivity of such issues has a bearing on the family's honour, so some women suffer in silence.

> A widow, 35 said: "Look, it is not just me but other women face this. For example, a man is supposed to serve women in such institutions but he harasses them instead by behaving in a certain way. It is as though he is sick and not afraid of God because he uses his position to use vulnerable women. I wish I could complain to his manager, but he will say that I am lying and he could hinder my application..."

Another widow, 40, said: "I went every six months to the office of [a famous rich man who has an office in his company for distributing *sadaqah* – charity - to benefit widows and orphans] to pick up my allowance. He is a good man, but his officer on the desk who distributes the money allowance for the women is not a good man. I noticed how he was looking at the women and he was interested only in the women who were uncovering their faces and talking and laughing with him. Because some women are not like that, he would not deal with them and ignored them until the end of the day, even though they arrived early."

Another widow, 28, said: "After my husband died, the landlord frequently called. I would talk with him from behind the door. Sometimes he asked for the rent, sometimes he needed to see if there was anything wrong in the flat. Another time he asked if I and my children needed any help. I did not like this man and I worried about the way he behaved so I asked my brother to search for another flat..."

Because of much social and cultural pressure on the single woman, some widows married again just to escape this pressure and to find a man who could help them with the responsibilities of daily life. Not all remarriages were successful and some women experienced painful divorces and other problems. This is discussed in detail in the divorced women's section.

Widow, 29, said: "If I find a good man I will get married. I need one to help me in my life. I cannot sign a contract to rent a flat; the landlord said this is not allowed without a *maharam* (male guardian). When I applied to get a charitable flat, the demonstrator asked me to bring a *maharam*. How can I take a *maharam* if my husband is dead and my family are far away and my son is just 10 years old? Traditions here force women to look for a man to support them.."

Women, family and civil identity

There are complications around nationality issues for a Saudi woman whose dead husband was non-Saudi: the government deals with the widow as a Saudi citizen whereas her children are treated as non-Saudi. The widow has to try to resolve the problem of the civil identity of the children who, as non-Saudis, will not be eligible for free education, public health care, and social services. Evidence from the widows' stories shows that non-Saudi children are excluded from SSD income support and are not able to stay legally in the country unless they satisfy the conditions of the Saudi Home Office. The widows were faced with the same type of problem faced by the non-Saudi widow whose dead husband was Saudi. Non-Saudi widows are not eligible for public health care, social services and income support until their civil identities are resolved.

Family and the needs of vulnerable people

Widows' families have multiple layers of suffering if there is also the need to deal with vulnerable people with specific requirements such as the elderly and disabled people, or people with chronic diseases of the heart and kidney, those with diabetes or terminal illnesses such as cancer, as well as the mentally ill. Those categories need specific health care in terms of treatment, medication, and supervision. Thus widows' families find it very difficult to deal with specific care for such vulnerable people in the light of their own disadvantages as well as the following factors:

- Shortages and inefficiencies in the public health services.
- The high cost of private health services, usually only available for people who can afford it or who already have health insurance. The health insurance services are available for the categories of the population who are in paid work or who can afford this service.
- The lack of public and civil society organizations that support the various categories of vulnerable people.

Elderly widows and specific needs

Elderly widows who head their households have many problems relevant to their age such as:

- The increase in health problems and the high cost of medical care. Widows discussed the futility of going to the local health centres because they only provided basic health care and no free medication or health benefits. If the women had an urgent health situation, they only had these alternatives: 1) - going to an emergency section at the public hospital with long queues or being given a long-time clinic appointment; 2) - going to the private hospital where good health care is provided at a high cost.

- Some stories reflected how elderly widows needed physical help to manage their household matters or to do their shopping. In addition, these elderly women needed a specific carer to look after them, especially if there were no relatives living with or near them. In many cases, the elderly widow would hire a maid to look after her and the house. The minimum monthly salary for the maid, usually female and non-Saudi, was 1000R (£167) not including the cost of living, therefore if the monthly SSD allowance for a widow was 850R (£142) this solution was out of the question.

- Some elderly widows reflected on how families became less responsible towards the elderly. They complained in particular about their ungrateful sons who showed no financial or moral responsibility towards their mothers. Some elderly women sought excuses for their children such as how busy they were or that their own poverty prevented them from supporting their mothers. Some studies have in fact shown that Saudi society, as a transitional society, has been influenced by many economic, social, and cultural factors that have affected family relationships and responsibilities among Saudis (see for example Fadaak 2003, Bakader 2003).

> A widow, 65, said: "I live in my small house alone with my maid. I rely on SSD. Although my son is employed he has not visited me and does not know whether I am still alive or if I've died. I think the reason is that his wife does not like me..."

> A widow, 70, said: "My son works as a security man in a shopping centre. His monthly salary is only 1500R (£250) and he has five kids. He does not visit me like before. I am very sad, but I have not blamed him because I feel he may be embarrassed because he is not able to

pay my flat rent or my bills. I have my own SSD income support, so I do not want anything from him, I want just to see him and his kids..."

- In Saudi society, there are no official civil society organizations concerned with elderly issues and there are no public or governmental bodies that provide qualified social and health care services for the elderly. The only ones are 10 centres called 'Residential Home Care for the Elderly' which cover the entire Kingdom, and these provisions belong to and are supervised by the Saudi Ministry of Social Affairs. According to many press reports, these centres have limited resources and services, so are undesirable and elderly people prefer to live with their families if possible.
- The elderly usually occupy a respected position within the typical Saudi family. The social changes during the last few decades have affected the structure of the typical Saudi family so that it has changed from an extended family - where all members of the family live together - to a nuclear family shape, where just the parents and children live together. These changes have affected the position of elderly women who usually live with their sons, or prefer to live in their own houses with a maid. The elderly who have no families live in the governmental home care system. Most elderly widows who were interviewed reflected on their situations as being poor and elderly along with a sense of loneliness and isolation. They criticized the lack of social concern for their issues.
- The elderly widows discussed the level of help they needed in their house matters.

In Saudi society, a care system does not exist so any widows who are elderly, ill, disabled or, for example, have Alzheimer's, often lack a specific system of care. In Saudi society, this role, according to the traditions and culture, should be carried out by close relatives; in particular the daughter or another relative who can provide a maid to look after her but in reality this is not available for all.

Summary of the special features and needs of widows' families

The widows' families suffer as a result of losing the male head of the household. Their needs depend on the types of problems they face in many aspects of their daily lives. The following table is a summary of the barriers to accessing regular support and to enjoying a worry-free daily existence.

Table 6.1 Summary of the special features and needs of widows' families

	Sector/field	Problems and barriers	Social need as expressed by the widows
1	Housing.	High cost of rent. High cost of bills for water, electricity.	Free accommodation or support with the rent. Free electricity and water services or supporting the cost of bills.
2	Daily life requirements.	High cost of living, especially the prices of basic food commodities.	Increase the SSD income support (the monthly allowance). Support the price of basic food commodities to make them more affordable for poor people, or present free baskets of food to the poor and needy.
3	Children's requirements.	Lack of basic life requirements (shelter, food, clothes etc). Lack of health care, education, social care and entertainment.	1- Support the cost of the children's requirements especially milk, diapers and school items such as uniforms, stationery and school meals. Alternatively, provide

			these requirements free to the poor and needy.

2- Provide free health care and dental services for children.

3- Provide a welfare allowance for poor children.

4- Facilitate the acceptance of attendance at university for children from poor families.

5- Provide training and work opportunities for the children of the poor. |
| 4 | Elderly widow. | Lack of health and social care. | 1- Improve the national health services for the elderly. Also provide health benefits (for prescriptions, dental care, sight tests and glasses).

2- Provide nursing and local health care services for the elderly (local health centres).

3- Establish, provide, and facilitate a carer's system for the elderly or provide them with a carer's allowance. |

6.2.2. The case of divorced women's families

6.2.2.1 The stories of the heads of divorced women's families

Divorced woman 1: Aysha, 48, 5 children - was granted a divorce by the court 6 years ago.

"...we are a black Saudi family. My tragedy started with the death of my Dad who left five orphans with me the eldest at 13. My Mum was young and she liked to enjoy her life so she married another man. She divided the house and gave us two rooms because she didn't want us to bother her new husband. My sisters and brothers and I suffered a lot with that man - he was very cruel and did not like us. After a while, he forced me to marry one of his relatives. That man was always drunk and I lived a miserable and unhappy life. He was unemployed and took all my wedding gold. I argued with him many times and returned crying to my Mum asking to be divorced. Although I had just an elementary education, I realized from the beginning that the marriage was a failure and that I would get into trouble if I got pregnant to such a man. My Mum argued with me and her husband slapped me and returned me back to my husband. I lived many years in horrible and poor conditions, I had four children which were a burden. I was poor and tried to collect our food from the charity. I made Arabic perfume to sell to my neighbours. I was fed up with everything and asked my husband again for a divorce and when he refused I went to the court, pregnant with my fifth baby. There, I told the judge my story and asked him to help me to get divorced or I would kill myself. Although I had a strong faith, I truly meant that. I was very desperate and hopeless. My dream was just to get my divorce and that would enable me to get the SSD income support, so I would save my face's water (meaning keep her dignity and self esteem from asking help from others). The case took around six months in the court and in the end the judge ruled in my favour and I got my divorce. Then I applied for SSD income support and for charitable housing. I got one with two rooms including the utilities. When my ex-husband knew my address, he came and made trouble and took my daughters (20, 18). I informed the police but they could not do anything."

Divorced woman 2: Lolo S, 35, educated, 2 children.

"I divorced a long time age because my husband had no responsibility towards our family. If a man was like that from the beginning of the marriage, it is not worthy for a woman to live with him and make a family. When I married, I was just 16; he looked a good and religious young man, he worked as muezzin (the man who works in a Mosque to call for prayer). A few months later, he left his job and was absent from home for long periods of time without leaving money for food or life requirements. I was pregnant at that time and there was not enough food; I was also afraid because the landlord was ringing the bell many times asking for the rent. My husband was always busy with his new friends who I think spoiled him so he became uncaring of me and our new baby. I talked then argued with him so many times when I needed money and his reply was to borrow from my family. Finally I became fed up, as you know my family affiliate to *al-ashraaf* [37] (a descriptive title of a noble family, their root to the prophet Muhammad family's tree) so I have to protect my family's dignity. My husband did not respect this, so he unfortunately put me in a miserable and pathetic status that made people think I deserved charity or a donation. This strongly hurts the dignity of my family because we are people not allowed religiously to eat charity, even if we were poor.[38] All these events forced me to return to my family home, telling them what I faced and insisting on a divorce, but divorce is not an easy decision, especially in my family, so they gave my husband a chance to revise his life and correct this situation. After one year, he came with some of his family, telling my family that he was a new person and he would like to start again, so my family agreed. I then returned to my

---

[37] - In Saudi society, as in other Arabic societies, the family and tribal affiliation is an important determinant of the identity of the individual and group. Family background and family origin has a significant influence on the social life of people, especially in issues of marriage relationships. Therefore some terms and concepts like: tribal or non tribal, Bedouin or urban, *shareef* (noble) or non *shareef* are used as descriptive words or indicators for the family affiliation. According to Arabic and Saudi culture, the use of these terms is socially acceptable and mostly would not take any negative or racist meaning, the reason behind this acceptance is because Arabic society in general is based on tribal affiliation, so the Arabs have their specific concerns with genealogy and family trees.

[38] - In the *Hadith,* the Prophet mentioned that it is not allowed for his family (grandson's root) to take charity but they could take gifts. In Saudi society, those families are known very well and according to my investigation, their poor do not mind applying for SSD support. Some also received support as gifts from some rich people who appreciated these families.

house and unfortunately the same thing happened – I became pregnant again and I faced the same miserable conditions so I went back to my family and got a divorce. My failed marriage resulted in two children and I was very sad when I thought about their future. My family supported me a lot. I also applied for SSD income support; I think it is my right as a citizen and the state sends it directly to my bank account, so this is not charity but accordingly I do not mind taking it. My brother supported me with my rent and utility bills and I also worked temporarily as a teacher for Qur'an in the nearby Mosque. My children are 18 and 16 years old now. I try my best to offer a good life for them but frankly I feel they need many things; they missed the role of a good responsible father in their life."

Divorced woman 3: Fatemah S, 34, divorced twice, 5 daughters.
"My father married again after the death of my mother. His new wife was a cruel woman and she treated me and my brothers badly. After a while, she made my Dada agree to give me as a wife for someone...I was just 14 and studying in school. They forced me to get married. My husband expected a mature woman, but I was just a kid and I would often run away to my dad's house. One year later, I got a baby girl and also got divorced. I was happy to return to my family home but my dad's wife was very upset and angry. She refused my baby so I left her with my ex-husband. I lived in horrible conditions where I was treated like a maid. I was not allowed to visit my friends or use the phone, so when another man proposed to me I accepted directly because I wanted to escape from that hell. The man was a Saudi and I was Yemeni so I was very happy by this marriage. With time, I experienced many horrible things: my husband shouted at me, he argued with me and swore a lot at me. He travelled often and left me alone. He had affairs with other women. I found out from his family that I was not his first wife - he was married and divorced twice before me. I lived many years in another hell; the only two positive things were my four daughters and I got Saudi nationality. I made a great effort to be patient because of my children, but everything got worse: my husband became very stingy so we did not have enough money or food, he started to beat me and when I collapsed many times, he took me to the hospital saying I was crazy and mentally ill. At home, he was giving me pills to make me sleep all day. In the end, God inspired me to stop taking the pills, then I felt better and started

to see how evil things were so I took my daughters and escaped to my family home, asking for a divorced from that devil man. Several months later, I got my divorce but without official documents. He did not give me any ID for my girls. After a while, my father asked to look for another place for me and my daughters...I experienced a difficult time, but with the support of some friends I applied for SSD income support which required me to present the following documents: 1- official divorce document, 2- the ID of my daughters, 3- an official document from the court to prove that my daughters are living with me and that I am their sponsor. My ex-husband refused to give me any ID for the girls and refused to go with me to the court to testify that he is not financially responsible for the girls. After many months, I received my divorce documents and applied for SSD income support but without my daughters, who were excluded until they could satisfy conditions 2 and 3. The Women's Charitable Association provided me with a free basket of food every six months and helped me to get a free flat in charitable housing (Rebat) so I moved to live there with my daughters. The flat was not so bad but the area was horrible, with drug dealers and addicts. The neighbours are not friendly and their children fight with knifes and have broken windows. The police are always around [she cried]. I just wanted to live in a safe area and need income support for my daughters to live like other normal people."

Divorced woman 4: Safaa, 35, educated, 4 children

"...I am from Egypt. My family is a poor farmers' family, so when a Saudi young man came and proposed to their daughter, they were very happy. At that time I was 16 and he was 25. He came with his two brothers to Egypt. After the marriage, I came to Saudi (Jeddah City) and lived in a room at his parents' house. After a while I noticed that my husband's reaction and behaviour was abnormal. He would sometimes smile and talk to himself and suddenly become irritable, angry and could destroy everything around. I could not understand what was wrong with him, so I asked his mother who said this was his personality. We were dependent on his family because he had no work, and when I asked him to work he became angry and tried to beat me. I did not like to ask for everything from his mother, so I decided to work, especially as I have a secondary school certificate. I found a job as a 'receptionist' in a local health centre near our house. My job was to deal with female patients, therefore my husband and his family agreed for me to work. After that we moved to our rented house but were still receiving support from his family because my salary was not enough. During that time I had three daughters and a son. Over time, things started to become clearer about my husband's health situation – that he was, unfortunately, mentally ill (a kind of schizophrenia). His family knew but they hid this fact when they came to my family and proposed me for their son who had been rejected by many relatives' girls. According to his doctor, his situation could improve or get worse, but the important thing was to keep taking the medication. I experienced a difficult time. There was no way to return to my home country and take my children (legally or illegally). I have Saudi nationality now and a job, so my position here would be better than with my poor family in my home country. So my rational choice was to stay with my children and wait for the possibility of my husband's situation improving. I found it difficult looking after my children and working, as well as keep my eyes on the changeable situation of my husband. Although all this [she laughed with tears] predestination worked against me - my husband's situation became worse; he became very aggressive and I could not control the situation. He beat me and the children many times. One day he put a knife on my neck and said he would kill me like a chicken; I was terrified. My children were screaming, the neighbours started knocking on the door, then he left me and escaped. I informed the police and told his family, but nothing positive happened. I asked his family to help me to get a divorce. When he learnt of this, he came angrily to the house and took our passports and ID and tore them. He said if I asked for a divorce again he would kill me. I lived in fear with my children and we slept in a locked room. One day, with the support of my friends, I planned an escape from the home. First, I made a request for a leave of absence from my work for a month; second, I prepared a temporary safe place to stay which was one room at the top of my friend's house. I waited for a suitable time then I took my children and some clothes and important documents, got a taxi and disappeared. I stayed three days in the room and then went to the Ministry of Social Affairs with my children to complain of domestic violence. I knew from TV and newspapers that the Ministry has a section called 'The committee for family protection'. I met the manager of the social protection section, then he put me through long procedures that started with taking my information to the committee of the human rights; also the police informed me that my husband called the police to put me on the black list because I kidnapped his children. After that, my case was transferred to the court. During this long process the Ministry of Social Affairs provided me with a furnished flat in a special building surrounded with high security and full of women and female headed households in similar circumstances. The families have to stay inside the building until their problems are solved legally via the governmental process. I was provided with all requirement and buses took the children to their schools. I officially informed my work of my situation and I transferred my children to another nearby school. My case took nine months then the court ruled in my favour so I got my divorce with the right of the custody of my children. The charitable women's association offered me a charitable flat with reduced rent. Also my children registered for SSD income support. I am still working but at another health centre near my new flat. My ex-husband went into hospital, then he got out and I have now heard that he tried to reach me and my children. His family tried to contact me via the Ministry of Social Affairs, but I refused in order to protect my children. I struggled to offer my children a good and safe life; there are still many things missing and I'm also fearful of everything around."

Divorced woman 5: Um-Majed. 40, divorced twice, 6 children
"I got divorced from my first husband after 25 years of married life. He was Yemini and he was a good man, but unfortunately he couldn't find a job therefore he was always broke. I could not endure all that and I asked for a divorce. I returned to my family with my children. Afterwards, I married a Saudi man who was 65 years old. I thought he was generous and would offer me and my children a comfortable life but unfortunately he was very stingy. We fought a lot and after two months he drove me away from the house and took all my stuff. I complained to the court and asked for a divorce. My case took long time, then the Sheik told me that if I wanted a quick divorce I would have to request it as divorced by *Khula*, which means that I have to return the dowry to my husband in exchange for a divorce. I agreed, so I paid the money, which at that time was R10,000 (£1,666) but still left R15,000 (£2,500). He had paid me as a dowry R30,000 (£4,166). Two months after my divorce, I received a formal notice from the court informing me that I had to pay the rest of the money to my-ex-husband or I would be subject to legal action that could lead to prison. I was terrified, so I investigated and asked a lawyer and found out it was compulsory to pay. I had no money so the

alternative was to ask for benefit from the Royal fund issued recently by the King to help divorced women who cannot pay for divorces. I felt happy and went to the judge explaining my position of not being able to pay and asked him to put me in touch with the King's Fund. The Judge refused and told me that my case did not satisfy the conditions of the Fund because it dated to before the Fund was released. I argued with him, saying the Fund is from the King not from the court, so the court was supposed to help all relevant cases and facilitate difficulties that divorced women face! The judge became angry and asked me to leave the courtroom. I now live in bad circumstances, reliant on SSD income support. My children are excluded from income support because they are non-Saudis and I have to pay for their costs of living, their education, their health care and their staying permission (*Iqamah*) to be able to stay in the country otherwise they will be deported to Yemen. I also have to pay the rest of the money to the court or I would face prison. The court put me through that horrible process of *Khula* and then did not help me to benefit from the King's Fund. What should I do now?!"

6.2.2.2 Analysis of the divorced women's families' category: Birds without wings

Divorce is a serious social problem that threatens the institution of the family in Saudi society, where divorce rates rose, according to a recent study to 18 per one thousand (see Alaqeil, 2007). Alaqeil (2007) said that divorce in Saudi society could be caused by many factors such as demographic, social, economic and cultural. He identified the most important reasons for divorce in the contemporary Saudi family such as the pressure of economic problems, the age gap between spouses, the differences in the social, educational and cultural backgrounds, domestic violence and the weakness in religious and moral commitments.

In this research, the largest number of the sub-categories was poor families headed by divorced women, numbering 34 cases which comprised 30% of the total sample. As mentioned previously, the categories of widows and divorced women were top of the other sub-categories entitled for SSD income support. Despite the fact that the divorced families' category received various types of social support, they faced many problems associated with their marital status.

This section highlights the interview findings with the divorced women's category which includes the experience of poverty in their daily lives as well as barriers, difficulties and their social needs and requirements.

The social reality of divorced women's families: how the family became poor and how the widow became the breadwinner and head of the family

Interviews with divorced women who head their household show that the divorce occurred as a result of a breakdown of the family for several reasons: addiction of the husband to drugs and alcohol; domestic violence against women and children; marriage with another woman; an affair with another woman; unemployment of the husband and lack of income; the incompatibility between the couple because of a forced marriage. The interviews with divorced women heads of household showed how these women can be classified into two categories, as outlined below.

First category

Women who found themselves divorced against their will because of the man, for example the husband no longer wants to be married to his wife or he might have married another woman and the first wife became less desirable. In this case the man could divorce his wife, so in such a situation and under unclear legislations, these women often find themselves in a situation where they lose their home, their safety and their right to live secure and decent life and thus fall into poverty and need. Three examples of women caught in this situation are below:

> Basmah, 55, divorced, 3 adult children: "I supported him when he started his business from scratch until he made his current fortune. I gave him three sons. I was patient about a lot of his irresponsible actions and after all that, he divorced me after 30 years of marriage. From living in a villa and having many servants, I lived alone in a small flat that my children paid the rent for. Where are my rights from all the previous years ...is that fair?!"

> Nahla K, 45, divorced, 5 children: "My ex-husband had a good job at Saudi Arabian Airlines. We lived a wonderful life for 17 years until I discovered that he was cheating on me with other women. I faced him with the evidence

and our married life was broken. Our life changed and the problems developed until we got divorced. He did not allow me to live in our house. I found myself with nothing and lived in poor conditions, relying just on the SSD income support, whereas he lives in our luxurious house with his new wife."

Nahla S. 38, divorced, 2 children: ".I agreed to be his third wife and had two children (2, 4). He did not comply with the conditions of our marriage contract that emphasised offering me respectful life conditions. He always left me for long periods of time without paying the flat rent or leaving any money for food. He had bad moods but I was always patient because of my kids. Once he disappeared for nine months and during that time he divorced me by default [without informing her] and left me with my daughters without any things."

Second category

This category consists of women who suffered injustice, oppression and difficult life conditions that prevented them from continuing with their spouses. Those women then reached a critical stage (a point of no return) where they were forced by hard and painful circumstances to ask for a divorce as the result of for example: alcoholism or drug abuse, domestic violence, mental illness and unemployment.

Kadeja F, 52, divorced, 2 children: : "When my first husband died and left me with two children, 14 and 12 years, I felt how life is very hard for a lone mother. I had to do a lot of things every day and I felt how much I needed a good man to help me with these matters and to be an alternative father for my children, therefore I married again. After a while, I discovered that my new husband had deceived me – that he did not have a job, a car, a house and income - he only wanted to live with me to get the benefit of my income support and my free charitable house. I expelled him from my house and sought a divorce, telling him that I would complain in court to get my late dowry, so I got my divorce."

Bashaier, 22, divorced, 2 children: "He was a drug addict and always brought his friends to the house. I was afraid and many times I argued and disagreed about it but he hit me and drove me out of the house. I was crying and would then go to the people next door to call my mother and she took me to her house. My mother and I complained to the court and I got a divorce several months later. My mother said that divorce is safer than staying with an irresponsible man."

Redah, 37, divorced, 4 children: "For me, I can accept from my husband any disadvantage but not affairs with other women; this is *haram* and not acceptable religiously, so when I found him cheating on me I asked for a divorce and got it and I have no regrets."

The stories of Aysha, Safaa and Lolo presented earlier in the divorced women's stories fit into this category and show how these women had to seek divorce because their marriages were unacceptable.

From the interviews and divorced women's narratives, it became clear that for many cases the divorce was not the beginning of the suffering, but was the middle linkage between two stages in those women's lives. The first stage was the period prior to the divorce where the women experienced painful daily lives with their husbands and had to bear plenty of burdens to keep their children and their lives safe. The divorce happened usually when the situation reached a crisis point but not all cases obtained an easy divorce and many women had to endure complicated procedures to get their divorce. The second stage is the transitional period that comes after the divorce, where women often experience hard times and many found themselves in a similar situation to homeless people, without a home, money or social protection as well as the issue of providing sanctity for their children.

The stories of the divorced women showed that some women before the divorce accepted their fate in living with their husbands, despite these men's disadvantages. The divorced women thought it important to keep the 'social front' of their family which naturally includes the existence of the husband. Traditional culture portrays the man as the wings for the woman's bird. Thus, some women prefer to live with damaged or broken wings, just to keep the social image of their families protected. When the divorce occurred, some women felt unhappiness because they had lost their wings. On the other hand, there were many women who could not afford to cope with the difficulties of their lives so they refused that sort of 'stereotype' or image of the man's role set by the traditional culture and these women chose to 'cut' their wings rather than stay unhappy and divorce was a better option than staying with abusive husbands.

>Fatemah B, 65, divorced, 3 children: "I got divorced when I was 40 at a time when divorce was more difficult than today but to be honest, I have a strong personality so I did not like to be humiliated by a man, even my husband. He was a violent, powerful, and oppressive man and I lived in tension, moodiness and misery and my life was hell. I remember when my grandmother told me once "listen daughter, the woman without a man is like a pigeon with no wings so keep your wings even though they do not work, it is better that being without them". I understood the meaning later, but I preferred to get divorced and I did not regret it, it is not important to have such wings if they hurt me and anyway, my children are my real wings."

>Kadeja F, 55, divorced, 2 children: "When I remarried again after the death of my husband I thought I had found a gentleman who could support me in my life but unfortunately I discovered that he wanted me to support him so I asked for a divorce. People say "shadow of man better than shadow of wall" but according to my experience, I could say the wall is more beneficial than a useless man, so my divorce document was the key to SSD income support."

How divorced women who head families face the requirements of daily life

Evidence from the interviews indicates how the divorce, even if requested by the woman, is still a difficult matter, especially when faced with the traditionalist view that women without men have lost their supportive wings. Divorced woman have to deal with many new things such as organize the family's internal issues and deal with external issues such as local authority, legal issues associated with governmental and social institutions as well as providing for everyday living.

As the interviews reflect, divorced women who head their household referred to some sources for support. The first source was close relatives or kinship relationships of the woman or her children, but sometimes those divorced women had no relatives or had relatives who were poor or could not support them. The second source of support was the neighbours who often played a significant role in supporting the woman and her family. The local Mosque was another source of support where in some cases, the divorced women referred to the Mosque's *Imam* (the person responsible for prayer and religious issues in the Mosque) for advice or help in their situations. The imam mostly transferred them to some social institutions or put their name on the list of poor families entitled to *zakah* and *sadaqha*. The SSD and charitable women's association were other sources of help and many women did not know about these institutions unless informed by their friends or neighbours. The interviews also showed how some women tried to increase their income by doing some simple work from their home such as cooking, dress making, hairdressing, henna tattooing and other similar things.

> Ajebah, 45, divorced, 6 children: "I do not have a certificate but I know how to make henna tattoos. I encouraged my daughters to learn hairdressing so I presented hairdressing and henna services for women from my home. This increased my income but I'm scared because I do not have official permission from the municipality and this is a very difficult process and needs a lot of money, so if they find out I will be in trouble. At the moment I have no choice; I have to continue to feed my children."

> Fatemha, 44, divorced, 4 children: "What can a divorced uneducated woman do to earn money especially if she has 4 young kids? I cooked samosas, Arabic pastries and cookies particularly in Ramadan and Eid. This cost me a lot of money and effort and at the end the profit was very small, many times I made the food for sale but my kids ate it."

Lolo, 49, divorced, 5 children: "I learnt sewing/dressmaking a long time ago. After my divorce, I wanted to increase my income so I thought I would open a tailor shop for women's clothes, but I do not have enough money for this business. Unfortunately I could not find a financial supporter. All the governmental and non-governmental institutions that advertise themselves as supporters for small projects or microfinance refused to give me a loan; they have complicated procedures and also asked me to bring a financial guarantor, so I stopped thinking about it."

Evidence also showed that some divorced women remarried just to escape the social pressures that surrounded them and some would divorce several more times. They thought marriage would be the solution to their problems, but on the contrary, they found themselves with the same problems in different circumstances, as will be explained later in his chapter.

6.2.2.3. Barriers and difficulties faced by the divorced women's families

The interviews with divorced women who head their households indicated many problems and barriers faced by these families on a daily basis. Besides everyday living requirements and the needs of their children, that are similar to other lone families such as widows' families for example, the divorced women's families have their own set of problems associated with the marital status of their heads as divorced women. Divorced women's families face social, economic, cultural and psychological barriers as outlined below.

Society, culture, and civil law

The evidence from the interview and women's stories showed that the relationship between divorced women, society, culture and civil law is reflected through two themes (or pointers):

Divorced women and social stigma

Divorce in Saudi society, as in other Arabic societies, carries a social stigma, especially for women, where the label of 'divorced woman' in the cultural and social sense is considered to have negative connotations. The divorced woman is blamed socially and culturally for the family break up, so this woman, according to the social perception of society, might be labelled as not able to satisfy her husband, or as failing to deal with her marital problems. After getting a divorce, a woman is often faced with a social assessment of her status as divorced, so her large family (parents, brothers and sisters) put her under a kind of supervision, trying to limit her social activities in order to protect the family's reputation against gossip.

Divorced women's rights between shari'a and civil law

The divorced women's stories revealed that there was a kind of injustice in dealing with these women's legal issues, despite the fact that Islamic law (shari'a law) is based on justice and the protection of human rights in general and women's rights in particular. This raises the question as to why there is a gap between theory and practice. In light of this law, it is useful to understand aspects of the reality of divorced women's lives.

Most divorced women, despite having serious problems in their marriage, did not seek to be divorced. After the divorce, most of these women were stripped of their rights to live in dignity, for example finding themselves without a home or social protection.

If the law is supposed to preserve and protect divorced women's rights, it was clear from their stories that there is no civil law in Saudi society protecting women's rights in such cases. What is found and applied is the shari'a law which is a set of flexible legislations derived from the Islamic texts. Although shari'a law deals with women's issues fairly, as explained in chapter two on women's rights in Islam, the application of shari'a law vary and could at times take an unfair position, especially in divorced women's issues as illustrated in their stories. Divorced women who head their households believed that they lost everything due to the divorce and that they were also denied the right to demand anything from their ex- husbands.

> Basmah, 52, divorced, children: "He divorced me and asked me to leave the house so I complained to the court and asked the sheikh [judge] to leave me in my house with my children. The sheikh said the house belonged to him and I am now a divorced woman with nothing except my nafaqah [the cost

of living for three months of the waiting period/ Iddah] or the late dowry. I think this was unfair."

Bashaier, 22, divorced, 2 children: "The court gave me my divorce with rights of custody of my two children. Also the court ruled that my ex-husband has to pay monthly the cost of living for the children but he did not pay anything, so I returned to the judge complaining, but he said this is another case and I have to raise another suit! I was shocked because this will cost me a lot of money and effort while I think the first ruling of the court was supposed to be obliged!"

Nahlah S., 38, divorced, 4 children: "I got divorced by default [without her knowledge] and nine months later, I knew I had been divorced. I asked my ex-husband to send me the official divorce document but he ignored me, then I went to the court requesting official documentation of my divorce. It took me about 15 months to get the official document then I was able to apply for SSD income support. During that time I experienced very poor living conditions because I missed my right to income support for more than two years."

It seems to be the case that divorced women were victims for several overlapping factors such as the man's oppressive behaviour, the traditional culture's discrimination against women, a lack of women's awareness of their legal rights according to shari'a law and the injustice of the judicial system where it adopted conservative and strict interpretations of shari'a law in terms of women's cases. All these factors have impacted on the social reality of Saudi women in general and divorced women in particular. This finding could support other studies' findings on how the position and rights of Muslim women in many Muslim societies have been changed since the early Islamic period. This is probably a result of re-reading and reinterpreting the religious texts against the interests of women and also that traditional cultures tend to be patriarchal, strict and very conservative regarding women's issues (see Ahmed, 1992, Sonbol, 1996, Abu-Sikah, 1990).

Due to the existence of the following conditions: 1- a lack of civil law or personal status law as derived from shari'a law and 2- a lack of family law or family policy that protects the rights of vulnerable family members such as the elderly, children and women, it is easy to understand how women quickly find themselves in poverty and miserable living conditions after being divorced.

According to the evidence from the divorced women's interviews and the details of their cases, it appears that the judicial system did not disadvantage any of the men in the divorce proceedings with the exception of that mentioned by 'fikh's books'[39] such things as: the expense of the iddah period (the cost of living for the waiting period after a divorce which is three months), the rest of the woman's dowry, the cost of living for the children and any rights that have been written into the marriage contract. Divorced women in this research criticized the judicial system because they expected more support, for example the first category of women as mentioned above who found themselves being divorced against their will and suddenly losing everything. This category expected to be treated more fairly in these circumstances and that the law would protect women from falling into poverty after their divorce as well as seek appropriate compensation for them from the ex-husband to ensure a suitable standard of life after divorce.

> Basmah: "When a woman like me found herself divorced after 30 years of marriage and being asked to leave the house...is that fair? Do I have a right to his money that I helped him to make during 30 years of marriage? I do not want money; I just wanted to stay at my home! I said that to the she Sheikh in the court when I complained against my husband but the Sheikh said he could not force him to give me the house or anything with the exception of iddah expenses. It is just the cost of living for only three months so what should I do after that? I do not think the shari'a law said I have to go on the street. Imagine if I served all that time as a maid? At least I would have a right to benefits at the end of service."

---

[39] - Those books refers to the whole Islamic school or Islamic jurisprudence, you can find more explanation on this point in chapter 2.

Samar: "He divorced me after 17 years and gave me the rest of my dowry - R30,000 (£5,000). Returning to my family house, I felt very sad because I lost everything and became a burdensome guest there. I gave my brother my money to pay the late rent on their house and I had nothing."

In the case of the second category of divorced women who sought the divorce, the interviews showed that those women face many barriers that prevent them from getting an easy divorce procedure which would then impede their applications for SSD income support. Although some women seemed to have a certain right to get a divorce, with strong reasons support their claim that do not contradict the rules of shari'a law, those women found difficulties and barriers associated with the following: getting the divorce; documentation for their divorce and getting an official document; getting the right of custody of their children; getting cost of living expenses for their children. All these barriers increase the problem of divorced women who head their households.

The judicial system, women, and the complexity of divorce issues

Divorce in Saudi society is a systematic process generally claimed by the man who pronounces divorce and then follows that with documentation of the divorce in an official document certified by the court. This is the systematic process for divorce and is often not problematic but according to the interviews with divorced women, problems arose if there was any defence or fault in the process of the systematic divorce. This defence could arise from two factors:

1- If a man refuses to divorce his wife, the wife has to raise a divorce case in court. In this case and according to the evidence from divorced women's stories, such cases could continue for many years. Although some cases provide strong and clear reasons for divorce, for unclear reasons, the process became complicated. There are several explanations for why theses complications faced women during their divorce claim in the court, including: i) the bias of the judiciary and the traditional culture responsible for women's issues; ii) to protect the family institution against disintegration - the prevailing trend of the court was not to facilitate divorce by women. The result of these complications are: a) women spend many years in court proceedings, which has a negative impact on the life of the woman and her children and increases their poverty because the mother is unable to apply for official income support until she is divorced;

b)- many cases showed how the divorce turned into what is known as *'Khula' divorce'* which means 'self-redemption' where the wife should return to her husband all the dowry or give up her rights to a divorce. Many women mentioned that the Sheiks (the court judges) recommended the women to take this choice for a quick divorce. Women accepted this option but only with the later realization of how this method forfeited a lot of their rights.

> Divorced woman 1: "I raised a divorce case against my husband who was unemployed, alcohol addicted and a violent man. My case lasted four years then the *sheikh* of the court told me that I had to think about *Khula* if I need to finish my case quickly. I rejected that because I thought this would lose my rights and would allow my husband to take my money. I believed that the court would guarantee my right but the case continued for two more years, so my divorce lasted 6 years."

> Another story was from Um-Majed, as featured in the divorced stories section, who found herself in trouble because she accepted *Khula*: "I accepted what the judge recommended, so he put me through the *Khula* process, but I could not pay the money and I could not get help from the court, therefore I had to pay or I would go to prison."

2- When men divorce women orally without an official document. In cases like this, many women needed their divorce documents, but they were not available, sometimes because the man did not want to provide them. If divorced women need to satisfy the conditions of social support institutions like SSD and/or women's charitable associations, they have to get an official divorce document. The only way available for these women is to raise a case in the court asking for their official document which is another process and includes routine procedures such as bringing the ex-husband to court. If he does not show, the case would take another direction and it could be a long time until the woman gets her divorce document. The interviews reflected how women criticized these long routine procedures and how their lives were affected negatively as they missed their opportunity to apply early for the official income support, dramatically increasing their poverty.

Divorced woman 3: "When I raised my divorce case, my husband did not attend the court sessions, which delayed the case for many months. I asked the judge why he did not bring my husband in mandatory, but he replied that it wasn't the court's business to. I was in that position for two years and the court could not solve that problem. During the two years I suffered severe financial needs as I had no income resource. If I had been able to divorce earlier it would have prevented a lot of sad things."

Divorced woman 4: "The most horrible thing is when a woman goes to court asking for a divorce or for her document of divorce. I spent five years obtaining my divorce document. My husband wanted to hurt me, so he did not attend the court sessions. The judge kept suspending the case every time. I was very upset and I was feeling a lot of frustration, so after five years, I spoke to the judge explaining that my claim was acceptable and that my husband wanted to hurt me. I explained that I needed my divorce in order to support myself and keep me away from the harm of *Haraam* [the wrong way for a woman to gain money i.e. through means of a sexual nature]. I lay this on the judge's conscience and two months later I received my divorce and had a divorce party to celebrate the occasion."

Divorced women and legal issues relating to children: custody, and the cost of living

According to Islamic legislation, after the divorce, a woman has the right of custody of her children and it is obligatory on the father to pay for their cost of living and take all responsibility for their nafaqah (obligation maintenance). Despite this, many women faced difficulties in getting their ex-husbands to meet their responsibilities and some interviews with the divorced women showed how some were denied the right of custody of their children and how their children were deprived of their right in nafaqah by their fathers. Many stories showed how the man tried to harm his ex-wife by threatening to take the children, where the prevailing social customs and traditions give the man this right if the children were aged over 7 years, regardless of the flexibility of the Islamic

Madahbs (the four Sunni Madhabs)[40] which generally give the priority to the mother in the custody of her children after divorce.

In some cases, according to the interviews, the men did not want to uphold financial responsibility towards his children so the divorced women tried to get SSD income support for their children. This was not possible: divorced women have to satisfy the SSD conditions that stress the necessity for official documentation from the court as proof that the children have no sponsor or provider. In many cases, the women took legal action through the court to get the document which in turn required the children's father to attend court. As the interviews illustrated, those men in general did not attend court, leading to the disruption of court proceedings in providing documents and therefore divorced women failed to get SSD income support for their children.

> Divorced woman 5: "I got my divorce because he was an alcoholic. I asked him to pay the cost of living for the children but he refused and said if I think to complain to the court he will take the children for ever. I know he can do that, so I did not ask him any more. Now my 4 children and I live only on my income support which is not enough for us."

> Divorced woman 6: "When the court gave me the divorce, the judge said my ex-husband had to pay the cost of living for our two children. Later, he failed to do so and I returned to the court but the judge said the only way is to make another complaint case. I did not have the money, energy or time to spend years in the court. I feel that the court should enforce his financial responsibility towards the children."

Divorced women and the impact of the surrounding pressures and challenges of daily life on their psychological well being

The divorced women's interviews reflected how the social environment and difficulties in their daily lives impacted the psychological well being of the divorced women who head their households. Before getting divorced, the woman has to undergo the family break up; during the divorce, she faces a lot of pressure socially, psychologically,

---

[40] - See some more details on Fiqh books, and Sunni Madhabs in chapter 2.

culturally and economically, associated with the collapse of her marriage. After divorce, she is faced with problems related to how to settle her life again, the children's custody and their cost of living. Not all divorced women find support from their extended family, which could be due to having no relatives at all, or having relatives who could not support or might not want to support the divorced woman. These pressures and difficulties have a terrible impact on many of the women. I met with some divorced women who suffered mental disorders as a result of such overlapping problems causing psychological and behavioural disturbance, asceticism and isolation from life and from others, for instance the case of Safaa S., Bassemah, Fatemah S., Najah, Naeemah S., Intssar and Lolo S.

Divorced women and the search for a safer life: experiences of failed marriages
The interviews illustrated that one of the methods that divorced women adopted to look for safe harbour was to get married again because they believed that men symbolize the safe life. The evidence reflected that some divorced women remarried more than once, but unfortunately those marriages also failed. The act of re-marrying several times is considered, in such conservative Saudi society, as undesirable and it is unacceptable culturally and socially for women to have diverse marriage experiences. From the interviews with divorced women, the reasons that push these women to engage in further failed marriages and divorce were that:

- The woman was poor and looked for a man who could support/sustain her and look after her daily needs.
- She was scared so she looked for a man who could give her protection in such a society that shows suspicion of women living without men.
- She attempted to escape from the miserable reality that she lived in with her extended family.
- She had low self-confidence, or self-esteem which drove her to make wrong decisions and selecting the wrong marriage partner.

Divorced woman 7: "I have had two teenagers (14, 16) and our income support is not enough. I was exhausted from everything that had to be done daily such as shopping; refilling and carrying the heavy gas cylinders and big water bottles and dealing with the problems of the two boys in school and the neighbourhood. I usually hired a taxi to go here and there because I faced much harassment from people because I was a lone woman. My children needed a father to look after them and attend the parent's days that I could not do because it is a male school, therefore I married, but unfortunately with the wrong man who instead looking after me, wanted me to look after him. He was a lazy man and did nothing to provide for us. I rejected him and got a divorce."

Divorced woman 8: "I got married and then divorced three times. I got divorced from my first husband because of a genetic disease preventing us from having healthy children, then I married again and after 17 years and 5 children I got divorced after a painful experience because of his affairs with other women. Two years later I married my third husband because I was scared to live alone, so when I learned that he was a religious person, I expected him to treat me well but he was the opposite after marriage. He had a first wife and he did not respect me; he treated me cruelly and was very stingy. He deceived me by his religious appearance so I ask for a divorce."

Divorced woman 9: "My first husband divorced me after 15 years because he married again and his new wife did not want me in his life. He kept the children with him and I returned to my brother's house. This experience broke my heart and made me feel down, so when another man proposed to me I felt happy and I accepted to marry again. That man was worse than the first one; he wanted to keep our marriage a secret because he had another wife. I refused that, then he divorced me. On returning to my brother's house again, his wife and children treated me as a maid. They were not happy for me to stay with them. My friend organized another marriage for me with one of her relatives and I accepted because I wanted to escape from the pressure surrounding me. My further bad luck was that the man was a drug addict and he treated me badly and always beat me. I could not bear it any more so I filed for a divorce through the court. I now live with my baby in a charitable flat."

6.2.2.4 The needs of divorced women's families

The divorced women emphasized in their interviews the following needs:

- Clear laws and legislations that deal more fairly with their cases to ensure their rights in the property of their ex-husbands to ensure a dignified and decent life for themselves and their children after divorce.
- A review of the procedures and protocols of the courts and the judicial system, especially in divorce cases. They stressed and demanded justice and equity for divorced women and a clear agenda for laws to set clear and fair rules on personal status issues, especially for divorce, child custody and inheritance.
- Those courts provide females with their own sections and specialist female staff to deal with women's issues, especially in the cases of divorce where women need to understand more clearly the legal issues relevant to their cases.
- An increase in the official income support and monthly allowance of divorced women provided by the SSD.
- A solution to the housing problem with secure and free public housing or the provision of housing benefits.
- The provision of training and decent job opportunities for them to be able to increase their income.

6.2.3. The case of abandoned women's families (a horny life/ or complexity of life)

This chapter is focused on hearing the women's stories which will in turn provide indicators of how the women and their families fell into poverty and how they were forced to assume the role of head of household, despite a range of unforeseen barriers.

6.2.3.1 The stories of the heads of abandoned women's families

Abandoned woman 1: Fozyah M., 38, illiterate with 7 children. Her husband has been absent for 9 years.

"I have lived alone with my Mother and 7 children since my husband disappeared 9 years ago. I was forced by my divorced mother into an early marriage when I was 12 years old - he was 32 and poor with a low paid job. His irregular income was barely enough to cover the necessities. I lived in poor conditions with my 7 children; our life was difficult but my mother and our neighbours helped us. My husband was sick and over time, his situation became worse. The doctor diagnosed him as being mentally ill. He was aggressive and stayed indoors without speaking to anyone. Sometimes it seemed as though he did not know his family. I thought he was possessed by the jinn. I had a difficult time looking after him and the children. One day he went out and did not return. I searched everywhere: hospital, police stations and all over the neighbourhood but I did not find him, he just disappeared. I was very sad but thought it was God's will and our destiny. Life continued but was hard. I went to the Imam of the local mosque and asked him to help me. He was a good man and supported me with some *zakat* money and he told me of some helpful charities. A few months later I was able to get a charitable house from and some regular income with food vouchers every month. I had to force my oldest child to find a job after school as a street seller of bottles of water and boxes of tissue. I also tried to make money by making Arabic perfume and selling it to the women in the local area. Some friends recommended that I apply for SSD income support. I tried this, but they required an official document from the court explaining my situation as an abandoned woman. I could not go to the court at that time because it required time, money and someone to help me to understand everything. After a while I felt that I needed the official document to be able to get ID cards for me and the children. After getting the official document, I could apply for SSD income support but I have not yet received anything."

Abandoned woman 2: Nawal D., 39, 4 children

"I am the second wife of my husband who works as a social worker in the public educational sector and has a good salary. I have been married more than 12 years and my marriage was an unhappy experience. My husband was always nervous, shouting at me and sometimes beating me, especially when I asked for money for shopping or for the children. It would make him angry and he would go out, spending several weeks at his first wife's house with his mobile switched off to prevent me from calling him. I lived for many years suffering in silence without enough money for food, rent or the children's needs. I have not seen my husband now for more than a year and when my children ask where he is I tell them he is outside the country. I sold all my gold jewellery piece by piece to cover the necessities. I also borrow money from my friends to pay the rent. I talked to my brother several months ago and asked him to speak with my husband officially about choosing to either take his responsibilities or give me a divorce. He replied that he will pay the rent on the house with some costs of living; he does not want a divorce. I still have not received any money from him. I applied several months ago to the Women's Association and to the SSD for support and assistance. Both organizations required approval documents from the court that show my current marital status as an abandoned woman. It took time and effort to satisfy the court's conditions but I got the document a month ago. I am waiting now for the SSD support. I would rather be divorced but I am scared that it will be more complicated than my current situation. All I want now is to live with my children in peace without worrying about the rent, food or school requirements I am sure their father could offer that, but he does not want to - so what should I do?"

Abandoned woman 3: Fatimah A., 40, educated with 6 children. Her husband disappeared 6 years ago.

"My husband disappeared six years ago; he went to work and simply did not return home, so I searched in everywhere: his workplace, his friends, his family and finally I informed the police who investigated the hospitals and jails but they did not find anything so at present, I do not know whether he is alive or dead [she cries]. He had a well paid job at SAUDI ARAMCO [the biggest National

Company of Petroleum in Saudi] and he had a savings account at the Bank, We had our own house but my husband rented it out and made us live in another house near his parents. After his disappearance, I was shocked to discover that my husband had withdrawn all our money from the bank; he had sold our rented house and had left a large mortgage to be paid. I had no idea about my husband's world. Afterwards I lost everything: my husband, my house, the salary after 22 years at ARAMCO. We were suddenly poor. The worst thing was that ARAMCO froze everything relevant to my husband's salary and his financial rights that should've been given to us - his family. ARAMCO's response was that the situation of my husband was not officially clear so officially he was not dead therefore they would not pay anything to me. I sold all our valuables and borrowed money to be able to hire a lawyer. I thought this might help to arrive at a satisfactory solution with ARAMCO but the company insisted on an official certificate from the court on my husband's main cause of death. When I asked the judge to provide me with a certificate that stated that my husband's status is considered dead, the judge said that I should wait until my husband's estimated age would be around 99, then the court could provide me the approval certificate. I thought he was joking. I was shocked - my husband was 38 years old when he disappeared so after 61 years, his estimated age will be 99. The judge threw me out of the court session[41] Because of this I have not received anything but I am very grateful to my husband's friends who supported me during the first three years by providing me and my children with

---

[41] - I sought advice from an *Aulma* (a specialist in Islamic religious issues) who worked as a court judge. Usually these persons have knowledge in such issues known in Saudi as "*Fatwa*". Fatwa is a religious term which means a religious decision or a religious opinion that could clarify a specific case. Fatwa is supposed to be released by a specific religious person who represents the official religious institution in the country, so mostly fatwas depend on *Madhab* or the official religious school of the 'Hanbali Madhab' which prevails in Saudi society. Islamic schools or Madhabs have different opinions, especially regarding controversial issues. In the case of this woman, she wanted the judge to give her a *Fatwa* on her husband's absence. Opinions can differ and can fluctuate. The flexible opinion is that after four years, the absent man would be considered dead so that his wife could pass into the *Iddah period* for 4 months and 10 days, after which she would be considered a widow. In Saudi Arabia, according to the Hanbali School, the judge seemed to adopt the inflexible opinion by stating that the woman should wait a specific period of time until her husband could be considered a dead person and she could be considered a widow.

a small monthly allowance. They also helped me to apply for SSD by providing me with documents that the SSD required. I now live with my husband's parents in their home but I am looking forward to getting my own home and living a better life with my children, therefore I hope I win the case against ARAMCO and get my full financial rights."

Abandoned woman 4: Hassenah A., 55, 3 children
"Actually I did not want my husband because he was a drug addict and he always caused problems at home. Rather than spend the money on his family, he spent it on these illegal things so I believed that his being at home was not safe for my children. I have teenage children - two boys and one girl - so they could imitate him. We argued over this issue and I tried to get a solution that would keep our family safe, but unfortunately the result was a broken marriage. I asked him to leave the home and to hurt me, he took my children and left. After a while the children ran away and returned home because he beat them. I talked to him to get an acceptable agreement on my divorce and custody of the children but he shouted at me saying he would not give me a divorce and threatened to take the children by law. I therefore raised a divorce case in the court, explaining everything to the judge and asking the court to give me custody of my children. After many months the judge told me that firstly, because my husband refused the divorce, the court would not be able to force him unless I changed my claim to another kind of divorce called *Kuluh* where I would have to pay for the divorce. Secondly, in terms of the children's custody, because the children were over 7 years old, the court, which follows the *Hanbili Madhabs school,* would only give the two boys the right of choice to be with whom they wanted. The court would not give the girl the same right because the *Hanbili School* gives the custody of the girl (who is over 7 years) to the father. I cried because I felt that it was not fair, that even after all the problems with that man, I still had to pay to get my divorce and he will take my 14 year old daughter which will put her in a dangerous situation, with him being a drug addict. My case is still in the court and I have nothing to live on so I applied for SSD income support and I'm still waiting for a reply."

Abandoned woman 5: Salha A., 41, 4 children

"My husband left me and his children three years ago. He had his own business and I did not know about his world. He used to travel abroad and would spend the money on his own pleasures. His business in the country is under a different name and because of that, he could deceive the SSD and register himself and his family on income support. He received our monthly allowance without covering our daily needs. I was fed up with everything and argued with him, asking him to give me enough money or I will complain to the SSD. He went out and did not return. I spent a month searching for him and informed the police but all my efforts were useless. I lived in extreme poverty with my children, so I applied to the Women's Association for help with the rent. I sold my gold jewellery to feed my children. After two years I went to the SSD to apply for income support but I was surprised to find out that my husband still received our allowance and he had just renewed the card several months before. I tried to explain to the manager that we had not had anything for three years but he said this was my problem and I would have to go to the court and get official approval on my current situation as an abandoned woman."

6.2.3.2 Analysis of the stories of abandoned women's families

The abandoned woman is an increasing social problem in Saudi society. Abandoned women are classified as '*Mahjorah*' according to the local vernacular. Abandoned women can be categorized into the following:

1. The woman whose husband has left and given up his responsibilities towards the family and the children, which could be the result of a remarriage to another woman, mental illness, debts problems etc.
2. The woman asked the husband to leave the house or she left with the children to live in her family home. In most cases like this, the man would not participate in a divorce and he would often suspend his financial responsibilities towards the children as a sort of punishment for his wife.
3. The woman whose husband is missing and his whereabouts are unknown, leaving the woman with the responsibility for the welfare of the family. This

situation is more complex than the other categories of abandoned women because the husband technically exists, with no evidence of his death.

4- The man left his Saudi wife and his children because he could not satisfy the conditions of the Home Office to stay in the country so he could no longer remain the husband of a Saudi woman

The term '*Mahjorah*' is used by support organizations such as the SSD and the Charitable Women's Association particularly when dealing with those women in categories 1 and 2. The women of category 3 are faced with many barriers because the man's absence is ambiguous.

Within this study, the number of abandoned women was 16 which constitutes about 14% of the sample. Saudi society views the problem of abandoned women as a significant threat to the stability of the family. Much more problematic is the lack of civil laws or legislative policies that protect the rights of women and children. It is a difficult research area due to the sensitivity of the problem and therefore there is a lack of accurate statistics and data.

The social reality of abandoned women's families: how the family became poor and how abandoned women became the breadwinners and heads of the family

The problems of the abandoned woman's family multiplies due to poverty and the loss of the breadwinner and also because of the ambiguity and lack of clarity on the current marital status of the woman who is not widowed, divorced or even married. The pressure of the socio-cultural context, the lack of relevant data and statistics and the lack of policies and regulations that deal with such family problems increase the complexity of the circumstances surrounding those women and their families and accordingly increase their poverty.

Referring to the categories listed in (6.2.3.2), the studies below will highlight how the abandoned women became breadwinners and heads of their families.

1- The first category of women, whose husbands are still visible in society but have abandoned all responsibility, are left without any male sponsor and therefore no protection and fall into poverty.

Abandoned woman 10[42]; 4 children
"I did not know what was wrong with him; he always quarrelled over trivial things and complained of boredom. One day he went out and did not return. I did not know where he was. My brother searched for him everywhere - at police stations and hospitals but he didn't find anything. Then after about a month his friends told my brother that he had left the country. After many months, we knew he was in the country but he did not want to contact us. I did not know what to do but my family advised me to stay in my house and they would support me as much as they could so I did. I have been in this situation for two years since he left the home left the children without anything. Life is difficult [she cries] and I am struggling to provide the necessities for the children. My relatives supported me and I applied 4 months ago for SSD to get a monthly allowance but I am still waiting."

Abandoned woman 5 " He told me that he would marry another woman and that he would not be able to pay for two houses; so he will no longer pay for me and my children. I argued with him saying that the children are his responsibility. He simply left the house and married a second wife and he rarely comes to see the children and give them money. He paid rent for several months but after that I have not heard from him. I have been living without him for 3 years. My brother supported me but not for long because he has a family responsibility. I applied to the Charitable Women's Association and SSD but they required official approval stamped by the court regarding my marital situation. My case is still with the court and I am wondering if the court will treat me fairly or not! What I want is to get a monthly allowance that covers the necessities for my children, or for the court to force their father by the law to sponsor his children."

---

[42] - This number and other similar numbers mention to the cases's number or her file's number in the analysis record.

2- The second category of women left their husbands because they could no longer feasibly live with them for reasons such as: some husbands were addicted to alcohol or drugs or some committed acts that were contrary – from the women's point of view - to religious or moral ethics. The interviews showed that this category of women asked their husbands to leave home, or the women left home, taking the children usually to their parents' or relatives' home. The common reaction of the husband in such cases was to give up his financial responsibility towards the family and children as a kind of punishment for his wife. According to the interviews, the wives of those men who gave up their financial obligations towards the children responded in one of the following ways:

- To be patient and silent and to manage the financial and other problems without reference to the husband.
- Raise a lawsuit against the husband claiming divorce, child maintenance and custody.

Abandoned woman 9: "My husband was drinking alcohol and I was sad because he was not a good Muslim. I was patient for many years for the sake of my children, but when he started to bring his friends home to drink I felt very scared because it put me and my children in great danger because I was worried that next door could inform the police. I asked him to stop the shameful act but he refused, so I took my children to my father's house. He ignored us and did not send any money for the children. I have now been two years in my family home. My father is retired and he will not be able to cover my children's maintenance forever so I applied for SSD income support but was rejected because I am still married. A few weeks ago I raised a divorce case in the court but this takes a long time and I am worried about covering the cost of living for my children."

Abandoned woman 11: "We were originally a poor family living on SSD income support which transferred directly to my husband's account as the head of the family. The money was supposed to be for the family but my husband took everything and only paid a little to me which was not enough for our food. I argued many times with him and one day he went out and did not return. He disappeared and as a result, we no loner get income support. I complained to the SSD and told them that my husband had disappeared and taken our income support, but their reply was that my husband is still the head of the family so they cannot change the situation unless I provide them with legal approval from the court on my situation as an abandoned woman. Only then will they decide whether they will support me or not. I do not know what this procedure means. Also I do not know where the court is. I really do not have any money to pay the cost of it all. Today I have just borrowed the cost of the Taxi from my neighbour to come here to the SSD."

3- The category of women whose husbands were missing for unknown reasons meant that the women found themselves in a twofold dilemma: 1- the dilemma of taking the responsibility for the home and children; 2- the dilemma of searching for her missing husband. As a researcher, I met such cases but there is not enough data on them because the women generally are taciturn and reserved due to cultural considerations relevant to their status. Examples of this are abandoned woman 1 (Fozyah M.) whose husband has been missing for 9 years and abandoned woman 3 (Fatimah A.) whose husband has been missing for 6 years. These cases could be representative of many more similar cases, where husbands suddenly disappear and leave his wife without protection and without any evidence of his whereabouts and more importantly, knowledge of whether he is dead or alive. The woman will inevitably encounter many obstacles such as the lack of clear civil law to deal with the case and the chance of being deprived of social support until their problem is 'solved' even though the solution remains out of the reach and is essentially with the husband. The families and other unknown similar families are at the mercy of decision-makers who work to unstated, unwritten laws, whilst trying to protect their homes, their income and their families.

4- The category of families abandoned by a man against his will due to reasons relating to the laws of immigration, residence, work and nationality (where the husband is non-Saudi) comprises 10% of the interview sample (see Table 5.16). Most women in this category expressed that their husbands were prevented from working and living in the country particularly after the main changes to regulations on work policies that occurred as a result of the Gulf War in 1990[43]. Some of the Saudi wives had Yemeni husbands and expressed how their men were forced to return to their country as a result of their failure to satisfy the conditions of work. Because Yemen is a poor country, the women preferred to stay with their children in Saudi rather than go to Yemen with their husbands. Thus by selecting this choice, these women became the heads of their families.

Further case studies highlight variations of the problems:

> Bahryah, 75, 10 children. Her husband left her 20 years ago, so she worked in the fodder market as a fodder seller: "I am Saudi, from Jazan and my husband was Yemeni. I was 17 years old when I married and I lived with him for about 39 years, we had 10 children. My husband had a good job because he was Yemeni, so he enjoyed many advantages from working in Saudi without an *Iqamah* [a permit for residence and work]. Everything was good, but after the First Gulf War, life changed and became complicated, so my husband lost his work and he had to get a permit in order to stay and work. In our case, it was very difficult and we needed a lot of money. He decided to return to his country but I couldn't go with him, so he took five children and the others remained with me. The family was spilt up and I became responsible for my children here, so I worked in the fodder market. The money was not enough but I was able to seek help from a charity. My children are grown up but they do not have ID cards and they have not been able to work or receive benefits in this country. The other part of my family has settled in their life in Yemen. My life was and still is difficult; I do not blame my husband, but the unfair regulations."

> Skekah B. 44, educated, 3 children: "My husband is a non Saudi and he worked in a company with a good salary. We were happy until he became ill which had

---

[43] - After the First Gulf War in 1990, in Saudi Arabia and other gulf countries, many regulations and laws were changed for security purposes, focusing on labour, immigration and residency. In Saudi Arabia, many Arabic minority groups no longer had the same residential benefits that they had before the war, so many couldn't satisfy the new conditions of the Saudi Home Office and therefore had to return to their countries.

an impact on his job performance. He was then dismissed from the job and became unemployed. As a good wife, I tried my best to support him, but he is proud and his self-esteem pushed him to seek another job despite his illness. He did not find any work and he could not get support from the government bodies because he was a non Saudi. Because of this, he decided to return to his homeland (Syria). I could not go with him because it is very hard for me to live in another place with a different culture and far from my parents. I therefore kept the children with me, despite being faced with many difficulties and not being able to cover all necessities. The SSD provided me with income support but excluded my children. I am a Saudi woman, but the system did not help my husband to remain with his family. The same system did not support my children and include them in the SSD allowance so I have to face the responsibility and difficulties alone."

The research provides evidence that all categories of abandoned women find themselves in a cycle of barriers and difficulties whilst trying to take responsibility for their children. Some of them had to follow lawsuits against their husbands where there was clearly a lack of policies and institutional support in such cases. The abandoned women referred to the following sources of support:

1- The extended family and the kinship network (relatives), who provided the women with support according to their ability and financial status.
2- The court and the judicial system, where these abandoned women found themselves in some stage of their life referred to - or had to refer themselves - to the court to find a solution for their situation. Mostly, the women asked court to either force the husband to take full responsibility towards his wife and family, or to legally leave and consent to a divorce in order for the woman to be able to manage her life as a divorced woman.
3- The police and the local authority, where some of the abandoned women found themselves in a specific situation and had to ask for help from official government bodies, especially with the issue of an 'absent husband'. Some of the

women had to inform the police and contact the local authority (called *Immarah*).[44]

4- Neighbours, Mosque and the Mayor of the local area; abandoned women contacted these recourses regarding getting various forms of support.

5- Social security department (SSD) and the Charitable Women's Associations: the women were recommended by friends or neighbours to contact these organizations for social support.

Although the abandoned women referred to theses various social institutions to get support, the interviews with those women showed that they had not got what they expected. For example, the evidence showed that most extended families and relatives were also poor with their own problems. In terms of the court and judicial system, as previously explained in the section about widows and divorced women, the systems did not support women's issues; therefore the women faced many difficulties and complications regarding their cases. Moreover, evidence from the interviews reflected that the judicial system seemed to be biased against women's issues in favour of customs, traditions, and the patriarchal culture. With regards to some government and non-governmental bodies such as the SSD and Charitable Women's Associations, the abandoned women expressed their disappointment towards the reaction of these institutions that did not provide them with effective help or support. The main problem has been a lack of clear civil law to guide the women and have their rights protected. The interviews also showed that the SSD and Women's Associations were not independent of the social context of society and as such, demanded that the women, in order to satisfy the social conditions; get legal approval from the court as a condition for obtaining help, despite this making the women's situation worse. The neighbourhood, the local Mayor and the local Mosque appeared to be the most effective sources of support.

6.2.3.3. Barriers and difficulties faced by the abandoned women's families

---

[44] - The KSA has 13 provinces or Immarah, each one officially ruled by a prince of the royal family (Amier) who has to manage the local issues of that province and its citizens. The Immarah and Amier are subordinated to the central authority in the capital Riyadh.

Abandoned women's families faced economic and social problems because of the female head having a specific position based on her unclear marital status which hindered access to many social support systems. These abandoned women have a serious problem in terms of how they are regarded and assessed socially and legally by the community where they tend to be treated as married women whose options for support are closed or limited. The reality is that the women have no husbands but cannot be treated as widows or divorced unless a legal and legitimate decision is made through the court and the judicial system. For more clarification, one of the informants called 'Sheikh Ahmed' who works as judge and is a specialist in Shari'a Law in the 'general court of Jeddah' was interviewed. Sheikh Ahmed told that theoretically no woman, according to Islamic law, should find herself without a sponsor, her sponsor officially being a male guardian such as a father, a brother, a husband or even a son. If a woman has none of these, then another close male relative should sponsor her. In the instance of a woman having no relatives or poor relatives, then the main responsibility lies with the state. In terms of the abandoned women, Sheikh Ahmed considered that the court/judicial system should play a significant role to force the husband who abandoned the family to take either responsibility towards the woman, home and children or give the woman a divorce to be free to re-organize her life. Islamic Law disagrees with leaving women in such an unclear position because it causes problems for women, families and society.

- **The woman's legal identity and her problematic marital status**

An abandoned woman faces problems with her legal status (or legal identity) based on the assumption that she is still married and therefore her husband is supposed to be her representative before governmental and social institutions. Interviews with those abandoned women reflected that because of the social barriers, they were recommended by friends, neighbours and support institutions to resolve problems by first identifying their marital status through legal action via the court. Only at this point can the judicial system help abandoned women by either forcing the husband to adhere to his family responsibilities or adopt strict legal action by forcing him to give an official divorce although the women complained of the bureaucracy and lack of clear and accurate law on such family issues.

Abandoned woman: "I am bored of this situation; I have been abandoned for three years now. I have spent the last two years in court following my divorce case. I could not get any benefits because I have to provide official approval of my situation and the court proceedings are very slow and complicated so until now, they have not been able to help me get divorced and they could not force him to pay the cost of living for the children. My case looks hopeless and only God can help [she cries]."

- **Abandoned women, court, and the judicial system**

Abandoned women face difficulties regarding how the court and judicial system deals with their cases in the light of a lack of law that organizes family issues. From the interviews with abandoned women, it was clear that when the women raised such lawsuits against their husbands who have given up family responsibilities, the court process took a long time with complicated procedures to conclude any outcome if at all.. Even after a judgment, the court does not have the power to make these judgments applicable. For example, as some cases reflected, the court could make a judgement that the man has to pay the cost of living for his children, but there is no follow up and many men did not pay anything, forcing the women to return to the court to complain.

It is also apparent from interviews with the abandoned women that the judicial system seems biased in favour of the man. Many women reflected that in their cases, the judge did not make it easy for the woman to divorce, although all the evidence supported her claim. Most of these cases were transferred by the judge to a 'Kuluh divorce' – which meant that the women were financially disadvantaged. Abandoned women expressed that they had no choice but to accept the Kuluh divorce because the judge recommended by them to in order to finish their case quickly and get an official letter from the court that would enable income support.

The women expressed concern and often anger at lengthy court processes which ended up disadvantaging them by not granting divorce or approval required by some institutions that the women had to deal with. As a result, the women could not get any social support and were unable to re-marry someone who could look after the family (see for example the stories of abandoned women 1 and 3).

Abandoned woman 3 "All the official institutions asked me to provide them with an approval from the court to get social support and to receive my husband's financial rights from the company where he works. Instead the judge informed me that I would have to wait 59 years to get that approval."

- **Children, fathers, and nafaqah (The cost of living or obligation maintenance by relative)**

The main problem that abandoned women faced was when their husbands stopped paying their financial obligations towards the children (called *nafaqah* or cost of living). Most husbands did this as an act of punishment towards their wives; therefore the women became the main or sole sponsors of the family. Many cases showed that when abandoned women sought the help of the court to claim financial rights for their children, the court's judgment of *nafaqah* did not apply. This meant that not only did the father not pay, there was no legal action taken by the court to force that father to pay the cost of living for his children.

Abandoned woman15 ".He left me and his children. I do not care about myself but I do care about my children and how I can sponsor them. I tried to talk with him but he did not listen. I went to the court to complain and after many months, the judge ruled in the favour of the children, but my husband did not pay anything. I returned to the court but the judge did nothing for me, so what is the use of the court if the judgments aren't applied?"

- **Social support organizations**

Abandoned women discussed the difficulties they faced in order to get social support when the SSD and the Charitable Women's Associations required official approval from the court to identify their position as an abandoned woman. The women had to endure a complicated process at the court and other related governmental bodies. During the interviews, the abandoned women were wondering why there was not any kind of coordination between the social support institutions and other governmental bodies in terms of the abandoned women's issues.

Abandoned woman 14 "My husband left me five years ago and the court did not help me to get a divorce. The SSD and charities asked for official letters from the court in order to get social support. I returned to the court and I am still waiting for their answer. I honestly feel that I am wasting time and effort."

Abandoned woman 13 "Why did the SSD ask the women to get approval from the court if things were clear? They could check the documents that she provides or the local Mayor could give her an approval. Going to the court costs the woman a lot of time, money and effort and at the end it might not even be worth it. You can look around and ask women what is happening in the courts, then you will know how much this is a nightmare for these women."

- **Civil laws, policies, and relevant governmental bodies**

From the details of the cases of abandoned women, it is important to provide an accurate law that can justify or identify the issues of the abandoned women's families, especially regarding problems such as:

I. Those that occur between the family and some formal organizations such as 'the General Organisation for Social Insurance' and its reaction in the case of the absent employee as in the story of abandoned woman 3. In such a case, the protection of the family's rights is at risk if there is no law to inform this issue.

II. Those caused because the man gave up his duties and financial obligations towards his family, despite having a well paid job. The women suggested that it is necessary for there to be a law that could force a man to sponsor his children or to have the cost of their living taken directly from his salary or bank account.

III. Those caused because of the implications of existing laws such as labour, immigration and naturalization when a Saudi woman has a non-Saudi husband. The non-Saudi husband will not experience the same advantages as a Saudi national, therefore the law, in continuing to treat this man as a non-Saudi, despite his family status, deprives him and his family of many rights such as fair work opportunities, health, educational and social care services. This position has affected the stability of family life, particularly when the husband took the decision to return to his home country and the Saudi wife mostly stayed in her country alone and poor with children to be responsible for.

6.2.3.4 The needs of the abandoned women's families' category

1. Abandoned women and their families need a fundamental solution for the basic problems relevant to abandonment caused by their husbands. The women need urgent and clear laws that protect their rights and constrain the husbands to adhere to his responsibilities towards his wife and children, or give his wife a formal divorce with strict commitments to look after and sponsor his children.

2. Abandoned women need the judicial system to deal more fairly and justly with their issues. Most women, during the interviews, expressed their displeasure and dissatisfaction with the application of the current judicial system where they found it biased in the favour of men and the women dealt with in a strict and inflexible way. In other words such women's issues need to be reformed within the judicial system and its regulations reviewed in light of emerging problems of contemporary Saudi families.

3. Abandoned women's families need a family policy that protects the family members in the case of emergency events / incidences like the sudden absence of the male provider.

4. Abandoned women's families need a reform of the social security system's regulations that deal with their issues. These regulations need to be more flexible and broad-minded in order to understand the controversial factors of abandoned women's circumstances. The SSD should create a supportive environment of mutual cooperation with other governmental bodies relevant to these women's issues such as the police, the court and the local authority. Such coordination between these official bodies would make it easy for these women and their families to understand and satisfy the conditions of income support.

5. Some abandoned women expressed their urgent need for the revision and reformation of some policies, regulations and laws of labour, emigration and naturalization. These women need this reform to take into account the position of Saudi women who are or were married to a non-Saudi man and to enable her husband and her children to live and work in the country with rights to health,

education and social services, as other Saudi citizens. This will resolve most problems of this category of abandoned women who are FHHs. This in turn would ease the pressure on social services and social support organizations.

6.2.4. The case of the prisoners' wives families (families in the wind)

6.2.4.1 The stories of the female heads of the prisoners' families

Prisoner's wife 1: Fayka A., 39, illiterate, 5 children. Her husband is in jail charged with possession of drugs.

"My husband was arrested and sent to prison when he was trying to buy drugs. He has been in prison for six months now. When I visited him the first time he gave me a letter and told me to take it to the social security department (SSD) and when I did, they registered my family as a prisoner's family and gave us a monthly allowance. I married my husband, who is also my cousin 20 years ago, when we were living in Jazzan and he was a soldier in the army. He then left the army and worked in a hospital as a receptionist. After a while, he was dismissed from this work. He could not get a good job because he was not well educated. He hated Jazzan so we moved to Jeddah City, but he could not find a job. My family helped us because of the children. My husband's situation changed dramatically for the worse: he was spending most of the time with his friends and became a drug user. He started to beat me and the children and took valuables from the house (even the air conditioning machines) and sold them to get drugs. Everything got worse when my children dropped out of school. My neighbours helped and charitable food was provided for me and my children. I was honestly very happy when the police caught him because I could be safer and we could eat good food based on the SSD allowance. My problem now is that my children are teenagers and without school or work so they spend most of their time on the streets. I also have a disabled child who needs more support and I hope my husband stays in prison because our status as a family is better than before and we can eat normal food like other people."

Prisoner's wife 2: Safinaz, 40, educated with 4 children. Her second husband is in prison because of debt problems related to his business.

"I divorced my first husband 4 years ago because he was unemployed. I have 3 children so I worked as a female photographer for wedding parties to be able to cover the cost of living for my children. As a divorced woman, I faced many problems because of the social negative attitude of society towards divorced women; therefore I accepted marriage to an older man who is older than me by 20 years. He also was married and has children. This man was generous, kind and compassionate towards my children and he allowed them to live with me after marriage. I lived in happiness with him and had a baby boy but then my husband experienced some financial problems that make him bankrupt. This was two years ago: his work partner took everything and left my husband in trouble with big debts to the banks. My husband was charged and put in prison. His sons tried their best to release their father but they couldn't reach an agreement with the creditors. He has been in prison for two years now and I do not know when he will get out, so we just pray that he will be included in the list of debt prisoners who are released each year by the King who pays their debts. I have faced a lot of problems since my husband was jailed. The SSD only give us a monthly allowance that has to be divided between the two families: me and his first wife and it is not enough for both of us. I also have debts to the landlord because I haven't been able to pay the rent for two years and I have received a legal a warning to pay or get out of the property. In this society, when a woman lives alone for some reason, she is under supervision. This is what happened in my case when the administration office of the building where my flat is located sent me a letter asking for clarification about the identities of some men who were seen visiting me. When I read that, I cried a lot because I was under suspicion as a bad woman. I talked with the administration, explaining that the men were my husband's sons who visited me and looked after me by bringing my shopping and paying my bills. I want my husband to return home and I do not want anything else like income support or other assistance which I think is for the real poor people - but I am not poor, I am in this situation because my husband is in a prison."

Prisoner's wife 3: Tajah B., 52, educated with 3 children. Her husband is in prison because of his debts:

"My husband had a cargo office at the port, but during the last few years, his business was affected negatively, so he faced financial difficulties and became bankrupt with huge debts. When the creditors demanded their financial rights, my husband couldn't oblige, so he was put in prison. He has been in prison for 4 years and according to the law, he will not be able to get out until he pays all the creditors or until the King releases him along with other debt prisoners (the King usually pays their debts every year in the holy month of Ramadan – the fasting month of Muslims). My husband also has another wife and children and because I am the first wife I have to look after them. Because of that, I have had to ask my eldest son (23) to suspend his academic studies and look for work to be able to cover our cost of living. What we get from the SSD is not enough, because we are two families living in two houses and having to pay the rent, bills and cost of living. I do not know how long my husband is supposed to be in the prison and I can not visit him because I can not bear seeing him in there. He is an old man now with many health problems. Recently I sent a telegram to the Royal Office of the King, explaining the problem and requesting my husband to be released."

Prisoner's wife 4: Zabebah M., 55, illiterate with 8 children. Her husband is in prison because of a charge of using and dealing drugs and alcohol:

"My husband had a previous prison record. I married him 25 years ago and during that period, he was jailed several times for many reasons, mostly because of drug and alcohol use. He was unemployed and could not find a job because of his addiction situation. I struggled a lot in my life with him and I have 8 children and I can barely offer them the necessities. My relatives, neighbours and the charity provided us with food and some clothes. We were living in the house of my husband's father; an old house with broken windows and damaged doors. He died several years ago and he left the house to my children, otherwise we would have found ourselves living on the street. The electricity company cut the service several months ago because we have huge bills that we have not paid yet; therefore we lived in the dark intil my next-door neighbour provided us with an extension lead for the electricity. It is illegal, but what should I do - there is no other choice?. My life was miserable because of my husband, who was the biggest mistake in my life - a drunk who always beat me and my children and he prevented my three eldest daughters from going to school, so they have no education. I registered the other children but they are hardly in school because they have not got the same things that the other school children have. I tried my best to offer them school requirements from the charity. My husband is in prison and I hope he stays there forever. The local Women's Charitable Association has provided me with support and they recommend that I go to the SSD but I honestly do not know where it is or what I should do or say. I do not have any identity documents for me and my children because everything was in my husband's name. Sometimes when we could not find food, I used to go to the mall centre near our living area and sit down in a specific place and beg. A shopkeeper noticed me many times and asked me if I were Saudi and why I was begging. I told him my story and he asked me to go to his shop once a week to collect some money that he collected as donations from the shopkeepers of the mall centre. What I want now is to get a suitable life for my children: food, school requirements and to be able to pay my bills so that we can have electricity. I would also like to repair the windows and doors: I do not want anything else apart from my husband remaining in prison - that is better for us and for him."

Prisoner's wife 5: Emaiss S., 50, has 3 children. Her husband is in prison because of an accident causing somebody's death:

"My husband worked as a taxi driver and a year ago, when he was driving on the highway outside the city, a traffic accident occurred and damaged his car completely while the other car's driver died. My husband was injured and went into hospital for treatment. According to the traffic police's record, the major fault was with my husband, so the court judged that my husband had to pay what is called in Islam '*Fedyah*' which means compensation for a killing caused by an accident (it is 100,000 Saudi Real - about £18,000). This is a large amount of money, so when my husband couldn't pay, he was put in prison until the compensation is paid to the family of the man killed or until they can waiver it. Since then, I have lived with my children in bad conditions where we just have SSD income support and this is not enough for our daily needs. I do not have relatives here in Saudi; I am Indonesian and married this man long ago, so he is all my family [she cries]. Me and my children look forward to hearing from someone as a donor who could help and pay that money to enable my husband to get out of prison and return to his family."

6.2.4.2 Analysis of the stories of the prisoners' families.

The prisoners' families faced many problems in their daily life due to the imprisonment of the male breadwinner of the family. The wife would commonly find herself in the middle of a dramatic scenario, having to support her husband and taking full responsibility for the house and the children.

The prisoners' families category constitutes 21 families, which comprises 11% of the study sample. The interviews with the prisoners' wives showed that their husbands have been jailed for reasons such as: possession of drugs or alcohol for personal use or for dealing; debts; fighting; smuggling Kat or hashish; smuggling weapons; theft; fraud or suspicion of terrorism. Each case depends on why the husband was arrested, charged, and jailed.

From the interviews with the prisoners' wives who head their families, it appeared that those families are considered socially in different terms, in other words some of them can be classified as poor class whereas others can be classified as middle-class families falling onto hard times as a result of the pressures the breadwinner faced or because of his desire to get rich quick and or increase the family income. Thus, evidence from the interviews showed how poverty, need or greed was linked to committing certain crimes or illegal actions by some male breadwinners

In general, the interviews reflected that the imprisonment of the head of the family was a painful shock and changed the reality of family life and losing the breadwinner put the burden of responsibility on the woman who found herself in a position of responsibility for the home and the children as well as following the case of her jailed husband.

The social reality of the prisoners' wives families: how the family became poor and how abandoned women became the breadwinner and head of the family

The problem for the prisoner's wife started from the time when her husband was arrested then taken to jail. That incident changed family life and the woman had to look after her family and manage the details of everyday life. Such issues in Saudi society are a difficult matter for a woman. The experience for a Saudi housewife could induce fear and panic because the woman customarily does not have to deal with the outdoor world to manage her family issues; she is used to being served by her husband and playing her roles as wife and mother inside the household unit and her husband is the representative of his family. Saudi culture and society is formed to deal specifically with the man so when women find themselves heads of their families, as for example the prisoners' wives, the surrounding circumstances are strange and difficult. The women had to contact official organizations relevant to their husbands' cases in addition to following up the legal progress of the cases. This would be happening in the Saudi social context where the issues are complicated and the women were usually illiterate or only basically educated and had to deal with everything alone.

The interviews showed that the women first knew about their husband's arrest via the police when they turned up at the home to arrest the husband, or when the police called to inform the wife that the husband was in custody. Some women still did not know where their absent husbands were. The first thing those women did was to ask support from their relatives or neighbours to find their husbands who were later found at the jail or in custody of the police because he had been arrested. The women might then have the right to visit their jailed husbands in prison or custody, then the husband can provide an official letter to take to the SSD to be able to get income support. This type of income support is guaranteed by law for all Saudi prisoners' families regardless of the type of charge on the head of the family.

The state protects prisoners' families by transferring them officially to SSD so they can get a monthly allowance. The women reported that this procedure eased the impact of the disaster of losing the head of the family to prison; therefore these families expressed their gratitude to the state for this right.

Prisoner's wife 6: "My husband is in jail on charge of possession and drug dealing. His friends dragged him to this source of income when he was unemployed and could not find any work, so what could he do to feed his family of wife, mother and his seven children? I visited him in jail two months later and he gave me a letter, emphasizing that I had to take it as soon as possible to the SSD to get our monthly allowance. This actually solved a big problem and I felt very comfortable because the SSD will sponsor me and my seven children. Imagine without this, how we could eat?"

So, the transfer of the prisoner's families to the social security department's services reduced dramatically the negative impact of the crisis experienced by the families due to the imprisonment of their breadwinners. Although these families received income support from the state, they mentioned how inadequate that support was in dealing with covering their necessities such as rent, bills, cost of living, children and school requirements. The female heads faced the problems of dealing with issues of poverty as well as the need to pursue the legal development of the cases of their husbands.

6.2.4.3 Barriers and difficulties faced by the prisoners' families

The interviews with the prisoners' wives reflected that those women suffered the implications of their husbands' imprisonment and in general the women's lives and the social context of how and where theses families live. Beside all these difficulties there was the problem of organizations such as the police, court, prison, the association for care of the prisoners' families and the SSD.

It is hard for a family to face the imprisonment of the male breadwinner. At the beginning is the initial shock of the arrest and imprisonment, then the family and its female head are faced with daily difficulties. The interviews with prisoners' wives showed how the female head was full of fear at this stage because she had to think about how to manage family life and deal with her husband's legal problems and how best to support him. The evidence showed that the most difficult thing the prisoner's wife faced at this stage was the lack of legal support and assistance in enabling the woman to understand what has happened to her husband and how to deal with the legal issues relevant to her husband's problems.

Prisoner's wife 7: "It was a huge shock for me when the police came home and arrested my husband. I was crying and my children were screaming. I could not understand why they took him and what I should do, I called my brother who investigated the police stations but we could not find him. It took two weeks until my brother found him in custody where he was charged with possession of drugs. It was a difficult time; I couldn't eat or sleep; I was just thinking about how I could look after my seven children and how I can feed them".

- **The prisoners' families and social stigma**

Social stigma is one of the problems faced by prisoners' families, where the family is often embarrassed and ashamed as well as blamed, directly or indirectly. Such social reactions usually happen in Arab societies, including Saudi society, where people are socially and culturally observed and where the reputation of individuals and family is subject to the social and cultural norms.

Saudi society still conducts social interventions of the family by relatives, as dictated by the cultural norms and religious values that promote interest in family relationships and supporting them in emergency situations. The interviews with prisoners' wives showed that the behaviour of the now imprisoned husband is unacceptable to relatives because it places a burden on the family. When these families deal with social institutions as prisoners' families or wives, they found themselves treated differently. The children tended to find difficulties in school and their friends because of their new label as prisoners' children. All of these implications of being prisoner's families are increased when being judge socially and culturally according to the charges against their breadwinner.

Prisoner's wife 8: "My husband is in the prison because the police found him in possession of unlicensed guns. We are Bedouin and weapons are a normal part of our life. People like gossip and I heard people describe my husband as a dangerous man and a weapons smuggler; therefore I isolated myself in the house. My children fought with the local children because they said bad things about their father. I wish I could move from the house but I can not because I have not found a cheaper one."

Prisoner's wife: "When a man goes into a prison for whatever reason, there will be a black mark against him. My husband is in jail because he issued no-credit cheques as result of a huge debt on his business. He got out of prison and tried to work, but everybody would avoid him because of his status as an ex prisoner. People do not look at individual cases, so even if the person were innocent, people will continue to believe that he is guilty. Prison therefore remains a stigma and a shame in the history of that person, whether or not he is innocent or guilty."

- **Lack of a legal support system or legal advice and guidance system**

The prisoners' wives expressed that there was no guidance or advice system to advise them or lead them to what they should do when their husbands are arrested and sent to prison. If such a system exists, it would ease a lot of the suffering of the families and the women. Generally, when their husbands were arrested by the police and put in prison, the women had no idea about what they had to do or where to go because the experience was new to them. No official system could support the family in such a situation or advise them of the right course of action. There is no official organization to act as a bridge between the prisoner's family and the institutions related to the prisoner's case. The women normally ask support from relatives or neighbours and go to the legal services departments of the police or court to investigate the legal status of their arrested husbands. Those women who do not have male relatives will find it difficult to understand their husband's legal situation.

Prisoner's wife 9: "My husband was a drug addict and last year he disappeared for a month and I could not find him. After two months, my cousin found him in prison where he had been charged with drug possession. During that time I was not informed from any official body where my husband was. When I visited him later for the first time, I was crying because me and my 5 children were in a horrible situation. He gave me an official letter and explained that I had to go directly to the SSD to register my family as a prisoner's family and be provided with a monthly allowance. I was comforted by this but I was also confused and angry, thinking that if the state guaranteed a monthly allowance why did they not inform me officially of this? I also wondered why I was left trying to find my husband whilst trying to feed my children."

Prisoner's wife 10: "I do not know how long my husband will stay in jail. He had a cargo office in the port but his business did not do well so he became bankrupt with large debts. He was taken to prison because he couldn't pay his debt. The King each year releases many prisoners after repaying their debts, therefore for three years we looked forward to hearing the name of my husband on this list. I appreciate what the SSD pays for us monthly but honestly, it is not enough to cover the cost of living that goes up gradually."

- **Cost of living**

Although the SSD supports the prisoners' families, the interviews with the female heads showed that this income support was not enough because it did not cover house rent, bills and school requirements. The prisoners' families faced difficulties with the cost of living, especially if the family included children or other vulnerable categories such as the elderly or the disabled. There is an exception in the prisoner's family who is already poor so when the breadwinner is imprisoned, the family considers this to be God's mercy because they become entitled to SSD income support: a great advantage, providing the family with at least the basic life requirements of which they were deprived before. This type of prisoner's family has less to fear at the loss of their male head.

Prisoner's wife 11: "My husband was a drug addict and he was jailed several times. After a while he became a drug dealer. I completely disagreed with his actions and we argued a lot but his answer was that he needed an income to feed his family because he could not find a job. When the police arrested him, as much as I was sad I felt a sort of comfort because he would be safe in prison and my family would benefit from the monthly allowance and I could therefore could manage to look after my 6 children. I fear when he comes out of prison how we will manage, especially with the loss of our income support."

- **Problems with the social support organizations**

Prisoners' families have to contact official and unofficial organizations such as the Social Security Department (SSD), the Association of Prisoners' Families and the Charitable Women's Association. In terms of the SSD, although it is not difficult for the prisoners' families to access it, the monthly allowance does not cover all of their daily requirements. Regarding the Association of Prisoners' Families and the Charitable Women 's Association, the women reflected on difficulties of bureaucracy and routine that affected the efficiency of these organizations, as well as the lack of professional staff who dealing inefficiently with women and their families.

Prisoner's wife 12: "..the Association of Prisoners' Families was no benefit to me and my family. When I visited this association asking for support, they just took my data and contact number but I haven heard from them. I read in the newspaper about their positive role but I saw none of this."

Prisoner's wife 13: "The Association of Prisoner's Families is just a name without actions. Me and the other prisoners' wives who I know went to this association asking for support, but unfortunately, we have not got anything yet so we went to the Women's Charitable Association, asking for support, but they informed us that their support was just for widows and divorced women. They told us to contact the Prisoners' Families Association but we complained because they know that the association has problems."

6.2.4.4 The needs of prisoners' families category

The interview with prisoner's families showed that this category has many basic needs such as the following:

1- Prisoners' families need more understanding from the local authorities to deal with their special position and needs and they need their income support allowance to be increased. According to the women's interviews, income support was not enough for their family's daily requirements therefore they need an increase for the basic life requirements such as rent and the children's needs.

2- Prisoners' families need guidance and a system that could guide the families and their female heads to the correct procedures necessary for contacting the right governmental bodies depending on their legal situation. This advice system is necessary and important for those families headed by a female who has to contact official institutions, which in Saudi society is controlled and administrated by male staff. These women need more information and awareness regarding their cases.

3- Prisoners' wives need some official institutions to be more effective and offer more help regarding the families' issues, in particular the Association of Prisoners' Families. The prisoners' wives criticized the inefficiency of the association and suggested that it become more active in their issues.

4- Prisoners' families mentioned their need for more social and cultural understanding of their situations. For example, they need the media and press to focus on their issues and they need more social awareness of society towards prisoners' families' problems, such as the risk of social stigma and social prejudice that those families and their jailed heads face even after their release. Many prisoners could not find jobs or be socially integrated into society in a way that could solve their problems and relieve their poverty.

5- Prisoners' families need social and legal advisers and specialists to provide them with a variety of services. They also need to be supported more in their living via for example training and retraining programmes and opportunities and the provision of work opportunities to improve their income.

6- It is necessary, from the point of view of the prisoners' families, for there to be a specific official body (governmental or non-governmental), for example lawyers, social workers, psychologists and sociologists who could look after those families and deal with their issues, basically being a bridge between the families and the societal organizations.

6.2.5. The case of the married women's families (shadow of a man is better than a shadow of the wall)

6.2.5.1 The stories of the heads of married women's' families category
Married woman 1: Kadejh A., 55, illiterate with 12 children. Her husband is 60 years old and works as a security guard for a female school.

"My husband works as a security guard (doorkeeper) for a secondary female school; he has been in this work now for 20 years and he is expected to retire next year. He receives a low salary - just 3565 Saudi Riyal per month (about £594); this is not enough for our needs. Fortunately our house is free because it is an attached house specifically for the doorkeeper of the school. It has three bedrooms: one for me and my husband, the second for the five boys and the third for the five girls. They are crowded within those rooms; we miss a lot of things that the children need: we need a larger house, more food and clothes, but there is nothing we can do. My husband became ill because of the pressure and because of that I tried to help him by taking on some responsibilities. I went to some local charities and registered my family for social support and also because my husband works in this female school, I explained to the headmistress of the school our situation and she suggested that I worked some hours as a cleaner in the school. This provided me with some money so I did. I also sometimes bring women's goods and cosmetics from the city centre and sell them to women in the neighbourhood, just adding a small profit because they are poor like me. All of these means and alternatives I did to increase our income and help my husband. I also suggested to him that he should give me his monthly salary and I will manage the family budget very carefully. We now live better but nevertheless we still need many things. What I am worried about now is that when my husband retires next year, we will lose this free house, so how can we afford to rent another house? My children are still in school – only my oldest daughter has graduated from University last year, but she has not yet found a job so I think we will face a more difficult time."

Married woman 2: Munerah A., 70, illiterate. Married to a non-Saudi man (Yemeni) who is 80 years old, ill and disabled due to aging. She has 8 children; all are married except two who live with her.

"I fell in love with this Yemeni man when he was working as a farmer at my father's farm in the southern part of the country. He was a good man from a good family background, therefore when he proposed to me, my father agreed and blessed this marriage. We have been married now about 50 years. We lived a happy life and have 8 children. He was a good responsible husband who offered me all life's requirements. He worked outdoors and I looked after my house and children. Then all my children married except two sons who still live with me and my husband. My husband worked in different jobs as a sales man, a broker in the housing sector, then a taxi driver, but 15 years ago, he started to suffer from aging illnesses and he had a stroke, so he could not walk or talk for a while. He also had blood pressure, diabetic and heart problems, so since then I became responsible for him and for our family's issues. His extended family in Yemen wanted him to return but I am not giving him away, he is my life partner and I have to support him in this difficult time as the good Muslim wife should do. I am now responsible for my family. My children have supported me as much as they can by giving me some money monthly. My brothers also did. I registered with a Charitable Women's Association for social support and it provided me with some food every six months. Some friends recommended that I apply for income support (SSD) so I applied, but unfortunately the SSD refused my application replying that because I am married to a non-Saudi man, I am not eligible for income support. I applied again and again and fought for many years to show and prove that my husband is elderly and I am a Saudi citizen. I will not give him up and I need my rights and my husband's rights to income support. After three years of struggling with the procedures of SSD, they agreed recently to give me income support (not my husband, even though I presented them with his health reports). So I am now in receipt of income support and I have to look after my husband and my two children who live with me because they can not find work although they graduated from the university. My husband needs health care and medication. The National Health Service has apologised to him because he is non-Saudi and cannot use it, so I have to pay for private health services and this costs a lot of money. I share with this man the sweet and sour of this life and I will not leave him under any circumstances. I am not satisfied with the injustice from the systems when they deal so unfairly with a woman and her family. In my situation I need free health care for my husband and we need housing and an increase in my monthly allowance which should also include my husband and I should be able, as a Saudi woman, to live with my family in dignity."

Married woman 3: Mutebah A., 63, illiterate, married to a retired solder who is 75 years old. She has 2 boys from this husband and 4 daughters from her ex- husband (her story is also discussed in the widow's section).

"I was a widow with 4 daughters, then my brother-in-law asked to marry me to look after the four girls who are the daughters of his dead brother. I accepted marriage to him, although he was married to another woman and has children because he was a good man and seemed serious in his desire to protect me and my four children. He raised my daughters and became better than their real father and later I had two children (boys). He sponsored two houses with two wives and many children. He was retired from the military sector and his salary was not quite enough, therefore he worked as a taxi driver. He continued working until he got too old then he stopped because of his health situation. Then I became responsible for our large family. Some of our children work and are married. His first wife died. All my daughters are getting married to their cousins so there is just one son and one daughter livig with us. They graduated from the university, but they have not found a job. I suggested to my husband that I will take responsibility for the family and manage our household, therefore I took his monthly pension which was 2000 Rail (about £333) and tried to manage but everything nowadays is getting so expensive. The pension is very low and it is not enough for all of our requirements. I have had cancer for several months and when I could not find an appointment at the Royal Hospital (public health sector), I had to go to a private doctor and this cost me a lot of money and still costs now for treatment and other relevant tests and medications. Within all of these responsibilities, I try my best to manage my family life by getting support from charities and the SSD but the SSD replied that pensioners are not eligible to get income support. I am very sad but although all is difficult, I am still in control of our situation. The circumstances are getting worse day by day and there seems to be no specific body who could provide help or advice - what can we do?"

Married woman 4: Fatemah A., 39, educated with 4 children. Her husband is uneducated and on low paid work.

"My husband had a very simple education; he can barely read and he could not write. He worked in the port in a very low paid job and although the monthly salary is very low, he continued for many years because he could not find another good job. We have been married for 15 years and have 4 children. From the beginning of our married life we could not manage the cost of living which was high and our income was low and limited. We faced the problem of house rent, so we left many houses because we could not pay the landlord. To solve this problem, my husband took a debt from the bank to pay the late rent and accordingly the bank reserved half of his salary so we couldn't manage anything else. When my husband needed money to fix his broken car, he borrowed that from his brother and some friends. We have now reached a stage where our salary just goes to the creditors so there is no money left for our life. I am now responsible for managing our life. I try to get support from my relatives and also from the charities. I went with my husband to the SSD asking for support but they have not accepted our application and they also informed us that debtors could not be on the list for SSD. My family is in trouble now and my husband's health has gone worse because he feels as though he has worked just for debt and we cannot get out of this problem without real help. But who can help us? The rent for the house, food and the children's requirement are our urgent need and we can barely find money for them."

Married woman 5: Am-nujood, 40, educated with 8 daughters. Her husband is unemployed and a drug addict.
"What can I do! This is my destiny to be married to the wrong man. We have been married for more than 20 years. He was working in a garage repairing cars but he did not continue work because of his bad friends who dragged him into alcohol and drugs. We spent years of our marriage fighting and getting divorced, then returning to our life because of the children. My patience and staying with him was a big mistake that cost me and my 8 daughters the chance of a decent life. I did not want more children but this was God's willing. I lived a miserable life with this man; he stole and sold all my gold jewellery that my family gave me at my wedding party. Most times we do not have food, but my family and close neighbours who know our story help us as well as the *Imam* (religious man) of the mosque who sends us seasonally money from some donators in benefit of the 8th girl. Many times, the landlords ask us to evacuate the

house because of non-payment of rent. When the last landlord threw our things into the street two years ago, I left it with next door and took my children in two Taxis to the Holy Mosque in Mecca. It is the house of God so no one asked us to go out. To be honest, I felt embarrassed to return to my brother's house; he only has a small flat. My family searched for me for a long time until I called them and informed them where we were. During the three days that we spent in Mecca, we easily found food from those generous people who divided out food for the poor and we drank Zamzam (the Holy water of the Holy Mosque). My brother came with a big car and collected us from the Holy Mosque and called my husband's family to solve the problem. They collected some money to rent a small flat for me and the girls. After that, I went to the Women's Association and told them my story. They sympathised with me and provided me with support; they put me on the list of urgent support and recommend that I go to the SSD to get monthly income support, but the SSD informed me that because I am a married woman and my husband is living, we have no entitlement for SSD income support. I now live in that small flat where the rent was paid for six months and after that - where can I go? How can I live with 8 children without any official support? The condition of SSD to get income support is to get a divorce, but that means I have to endure another long and painful experience with the court system and with that addict! He has disappeared now and left us with nothing. Now we are barely alive with support from my family, my neighbours and the local charity who supports us because I have 8 girls without a father. The girls are similar to orphans and this means a large wage from God to whom supporting women with orphans, according to Islam, would protect them from hell and lead them to heaven."

6.2.5.2 Analysis of the married women's families category

The married women's families' category is the fifth sub-category of the sample of this research. In this category, the woman is married and she heads the family despite her husband existing in the family. The wife in this case is responsible entirely or partly for the family's well-being because her husband can not because of reasons such as: he is unemployed, elderly, ill (mentally or physically), disabled etc. In Saudi society, as mentioned earlier, the husband is the official breadwinner who is responsible for his family socially, legally and financially. However, in emergency situations, when the social role of the man (husband) is affected, his wife would generally take on responsibility for the family. As the interviews reflected, many Saudi women found themselves in a position where they had to support their husbands and take either total or partial responsibility towards their families. This behaviour was also motivated by religious and social values as well as the social ethics that motivate the woman to support her husband in the event of family crises. In this research, the number of married women's families interviewed was 27 which constituted 24% of the sample. This percentage was actually the second largest sub-category of the sample, the largest one being divorced women's families who numbered 34 cases, comprising 30% of the sample.

The social reality of the married women's families' category: how the family became poor and how the married woman became the breadwinner and head of the family

In Saudi society, any woman, as mentioned earlier, is supposed to be sponsored by her male guardian, but the interviews with some married women showed that those women were not necessarily being sponsored by their husbands. The evidence underpinning this situation was that the family suffered problems that affected in some way the social role of the man towards his family. Thus the man (the husband) was for some reason unable to look after his family, or even cover the cost of their living expenses. In such a situation, the woman (wife) would take responsibility for looking after her family by being the family head, especially when the religious values and the general social principles and ethics of the traditional society supported this role and stressed the importance of supporting women in such situations.

There are several reasons that could affect the social role of the man / breadwinner and force the woman to take responsibility for her family. These reasons include: unemployment, illness, disability, the income limitation due to being on low pay or being retired and the financial implications of debts. All of these reasons were reflected through the women's interviews and showed how the family became poor and how the married woman became the breadwinner and head of her family. Below are some explanations according to evidence from the interviews.

- **Unemployment**

Some interviews with married women reflected how unemployment was a big problem in Saudi society and how it dramatically affected family life. These women were married to men who suffered from temporary or chronic unemployment, where those men have not found work despite having qualifications and skills compatible with the labour market. The women explained how they found themselves in the position of head of the family and supporting their husbands by looking after family issues and managing everyday life. In such cases, this woman could not leave the husband and family to struggle alone so she would ask for support from her family or neighbours and the Women's Charitable Associations. Some women also relied on their own savings or by selling their gold jewellery to cover the cost of living. Some other women tried to work from their homes by cooking and selling food, sweets and cookies to increase their income.

Huda, 38, is a married woman with 4 children. Her husband is unemployed.

"My husband did not find a good job because he has no qualifications, therefore he accepted low paid work such as a security man at a supermarket, or a monitor of construction workers but all these jobs were very low paid, with long hours. He gave up work and tried to start a small business, but he had no money. Last year he went to the Offices of the Ministry of Labour asking for help and advice but nobody could help him. Now he works sometimes as a private car taxi driver but he is scared to be caught by the police who will fine and jailed him because he has no licence to drive a taxi. He would need money and to go through a long official process to obtain the licence and even a replacement car. When I saw my husband in this situation, I felt sorry and sad, so I tried my best to help and take more responsibility, therefore I went to the charity and registered our family with them. I also tried to find a job but I could not with 4 children and no qualifications A few months ago I went to the SSD to ask for support or advice but they rejected my application, saying that my husband needs to find work!"

- **Limited income**

The interviews with married women's families showed that there was a situation where the husband had a low or limited income that was not compatible with the daily needs of the family. The limitation of their income was due to one of the following reasons:

1- The husband is retired and his state retirement pension is low. This was a common situation for most retirees, especially those who were retired from the military sector, who make up a noticeable proportion. This agreed with the study of the Saudi Pension Department (please refer the Literature review) that indicated the poor economic position of the military pensioners (see Albaaz, 2005).
2- The husbands work in low paid jobs and therefore have low or limited income.

Thus according to the interviews, the married women in such cases preferred to take responsibility for their families and become the heads of their families, trying to manage the daily needs whilst supporting their husbands through that difficult time. The women who have been interviewed mentioned that when they found their husbands in a situation such as illness, old age or retirement with a low pension, they supported their husbands by trying to take on all or part of the family's responsibilities. Therefore the woman (wife) perceived that she had to satisfy her life / destiny as predestined by God. This means that she had to be a patient wife and prove herself a good Muslim woman by supporting her husband as much as she can. The wife is therefore trying to bridge the gap in her family life by seeking support from relatives or charities or the social security department, or otherwise she would work to increase the family's income.

With regards to the situation of the low pension of some retirees / or state pensioners, the interviews with married women highlighted the problem, especially among the retirees of public sector and some military sectors. This is considered a significant problem which the media and press highlight in any discussion on poverty. The retirees / pensioners are considered to be in one of those categories who could face poverty because of their low state pension which does not cover their needs. A previous study has been conducted by the Saudi Pension Department (the study cited in Albaaz, 2005) investigated the military pensioners showed how 60% of their monthly income was less than (3000 SR- about £500) and how 58% lived in old and small flats. The evidence from this study shows that there is a serious poverty problem among this category of the population.

Mutebah A, 75, her husband is 85 and retired from the military sector.

> "My husband retired from the military sector a long time ago. At that time he was relatively healthy and strong, so he worked as a taxi driver in his private car to increase his income, but after getting old and ill, he left his taxi work and then we had to rely only on his pension, which was very low and not enough for our daily requirements. My sons, who were married, tried to help us, but they could not provide too much because they had their own family responsibilities. Although I am old and ill, I try my best to help my husband because it is my duty to do that. I therefore manage our life as much as I can, without letting him feel bothered about our family financial difficulties. I asked my brothers to help me and I registered with a local charity to get a share of the seasonal support for the poor. I heard about SSD so I went to the general office asking for support, but they told me that because of my husband being on the state pension, we are not entitled for SSD income support. I argued with the manager because I heard the King on TV saying that the state guaranteed a monthly income to support the poor, so I think my family deserves income support and also I think these governmental bodies do not perform their work properly in supporting the poor. It is true that we have a state pension, but it is just pennies, not enough for our daily food, so we still need help."

In terms of the families whose breadwinners are on low pay, this could be considered another real problem that causes and increases poverty, because the family income is not enough to cover the cost of living. The interviews with women from this category showed that these wives did not blame their husbands, but on the contrary, they appreciated the work and effort of their husband and they did their best to support them. The married women took several routes to support their husbands and families in such circumstances which included the following: they sold their valuable things such as their gold jewellery, they spent from their savings, they asked support from relatives or neighbours, or they asked for formal support from local charities or the SSD. All of these efforts were made by these married women to bridge the gap between the actual family's income and the real requirements of their daily lives.

Kadejh A. (see the story number 1 in this section) said:

"As you have seen, my husband works as a security guard (doorkeeper) in a female school; nonetheless his salary is not enough for the cost of living of our big family. The good thing about his work is the free house where we live. The pressure affected my husband's health, he is always sad, so I decided to support him by taking part of our family responsibility. In the meantime I take his monthly salary and manage our budget and I try to get support from the charity as well as work as a cleaner here in the school to get some money."

- **Debt / or debt trap**

The interviews reflected that some families experienced difficulties because of the man who is the breadwinner of the family falling into the debt trap. The woman (his wife) found herself in a situation where she had to support her husband and look after the family by taking part or whole responsibility for the family, as demonstrated in the Fatimah A story (story No. 4 in this section):

"I could not leave my husband alone with this cycle of problems caused by debt. Nobody could support him, so I had to do that, it is my duty. The real problem is that his job is low paid, so his monthly income is now reserved for the debts, therefore there is nothing left for our food and the cost of living. I had to think how I could manage this to enable the family to survive. I sold my gold jewellery a long time ago and I asked my brothers to help me monthly by giving anything they could. I registered my family with many charities for social support. I worked as a cleaner in some houses in the local area. All that was difficult, but by the will of God, our life is going on. I went with my husband to the SSD, asking them for help for our family to get out this debt trap, or at least some advice as to what we can do, but their answer was that there is no help for debtors."

- **Difficulties because of the different nationality of the husband**

Some cases, for example Munerah A., (story number 2 in this section) reflected that the family faced problems and then fell into poverty because of the difference in the nationality of the husband. For example, if the breadwinner of the family (the husband) was non-Saudi, there is much evidence from the interviews to show that this man is not able to find fair employment opportunities or to establish his own business, the way a Saudi man can. The Saudi woman who is married to a non-Saudi said that her husband faced many difficulties: he could not enjoy the free health care system and he had to manage his legal stay and his permit for work which meant that he had to be guaranteed by his wife or someone else, according to the Saudi law of residence and work.

In this case, and other similar cases, the Saudi wife usually did not give up her duty and responsibilities towards her husband and she behaved as Munerah A. did, trying her best to look after her husband and her family, especially if her husband was old and ill. The most painful experience, as expressed by these women in the interviews, was when the women experienced the realty of the laws and regulations that dealt unfairly with their non-Saudi husbands and prevented them from enjoying important services such as the free National Health Service and SSD benefits, even though they are poor and their wives are Saudis. The Saudi wives expressed how they suffered a lot from this situation and how they felt that their families were deprived of services enjoyed by other citizens. Despite these barriers, the Saudi poor women fought to keep their families safe and protected under these circumstances.

> Munerah A,: "When I married my husband many years ago, he was a young and strong man and during our marriage, he offered me a good and comfortable life, although he was non-Saudi and his work was low paid. Now my husband is old and ill and our life's standard has changed so we are faced with many financial difficulties. Although it is impossible to leave him or let him return to his country, as he used to say when he felt bored of everything around him, this religiously and ethically is unacceptable behaviour.. I will not let him down whatever difficulties we face, he will stay with me here in my country and I am

responsible for him and our life. I felt shame when the SSD refused to support him because he is a non-Saudi, any way it does not matter, no one dies of hunger. We will live together and God will support us."

- **Other complicated and interrelated issues**

Evidence from the interviews showed that some married women were forced by some complicated and overlapping issues to be the heads of their families, then to take entire or part responsibility for looking after their family and children, as happened with Am-nujood (story number 5 in this section). The woman in such a case could find herself surrounded by painful events caused by accumulated, complicated and overlapping factors. In terms of that Am-nujood and other similar cases, it appeared that she tried to deal with and overcome these complicated events surrounding her family life in order to maintain the family. Such a scenario was evident in some cases of married women's families with problems such as the husband's addiction to drugs or alcohol, the psychological disorders or mental health of the husband and being part of a big family that involved many children or other family members. All these factors and circumstances constituted a stressful environment that created pressures on the woman accompanied by a sense that these women existed in a continuum of problems with no clear solutions.

Am-nujood: "What I can do? I have 8 daughters and their father is ill and an addict. I experienced a painful time with him. I could not get divorced so my problems with him continued and developed. He came home to eat and sleep and he shouted and fought to get money or anything from the home. Me and the girls were living in constant fear. I was unable to do anything to solve the problem or escape from these conditions. Currently he is absent and we do not know where he is and I do not want him to come back. To feel safe is better than getting food, so I feel safe because that man is not in the house. The biggest issue for me is to care for my eight daughters."

Another woman (39) with 3 children is married to a man who has psychological problems:

"My husband is psychologically ill. Most of the time he experiences depression and anxiety and stays in his room alone, closing the door and crying like a child. He is supported by a lot of medication to make him stable and calm. I could not abandon him in this difficult time; he is the father of my children. Moral and religious values emphasize on the importance of looking after him, so I have a big responsibility towards him and my children as well. The big problem is that my abilities are limited and I do not have enough resources to manage the life of my husband and my family. There is not enough money and social or health facilities to care for my husband's needs. As the head of my family, I also need a lot of things but in reality, there is nothing so I try to live and manage life according to what is found or received from relatives or charities. The SSD gave us income support but it is not quite enough. My husband needs more than just money: he needs good health care and specialist help and his family need help to cope with his situation."

Thus, it can be seen that many married women find themselves facing life alone because they lack their husband's support for various reasons. They find themselves in a position of had to bear part or all of the family responsibility because of circumstances or barriers that have hampered the husband's ability to fulfil his responsibilities towards his family. In such cases, the woman has to play the role of wife, mother and head of the family in order to look after her husband, her children and the family well-being. Added to this is the ordeal of negotiating carefully with the social, cultural and economic conditions, as well as the problem of poverty itself that can negatively affect the well-being of the family unit. Therefore there are many difficulties and problems created in poor married women's families and some of these difficulties will be explored next.

6.2.5.3 Barriers and difficulties faced by the married women' families

There are overlapping problems that hinder the role of man (the husband) and push the woman (the wife) to take responsibility for her family. Some of these problems are discussed below.

1- The problem of little or no family income due to difficulties suffered by the male head of the family, such as unemployment, lack of work and low income because of the lack of his state pension or his low paid work. All these problems overlap and place a heavy burden on the woman who then becomes the head of her family.

2- Problems relating to the physical or mental ability of one or more family member such as a spouse or children. In such cases, the female head faces more complicated problems if her husband or another family member were sick, disabled or mentally ill. The problems increase with the presence of vulnerable groups within the family such as children and / or elderly, as well as teenagers and young people who need more resources. Married women who head their family usually face other specific problems such as gender, age and the social needs of the family members beside the basic problem of poverty that affects the whole family.

3- Problems relevant to regulations and civil laws such as the 'Saudi nationality law' and its implications towards the naturalization of a woman's non-Saudi spouse or children. Immigration laws and residence and work regulations do not facilitate or support the position and issues of Saudi women who are married to foreigners, thus there I no availability of social, heath or economic facilities and services for the other family members of that Saudi woman who is now regarded by official governmental bodies as a non-Saudi citizen. These circumstances come together to increase the burden on the Saudi wife who has become a head and breadwinner for her family.

4- Problems are experienced by married women when they deal with the social support institutions such as the social security department (SSD) and / or the Charitable Women's Associations. For example, at the SSD, the issues of the married women's families can be complicated in comparison with other categories of FHHs. Some evidence from the interviews suggests that the clearest reason for the complexity of this type of FHH was due to the presence of the man (husband). For example, when a married woman applies for SSD or to the Charitable Women's Associations she faces more difficulties than other categories such as widows or divorced women. The reason behind these difficulties seems to be the fact that these social institutions reflect the prevalent culture of Saudi society and the social context for the married woman's is that of having a male breadwinner, regardless of that breadwinner's personal circumstances, therefore they are less of a priority for social support than other families who do not have a male breadwinner (widows, divorced women's families). It is therefore clear to see why those married women who need support for their family found themselves forced to take another direction in order to convince the social institutions of their real need for support. Unfortunately, there is no clear and official regulation, especially in the SSD, to provide support for women in these circumstances. There is no category of support that covers people who are on low paid work or pensions or in debt. Therefore, the married women's families were unable to obtain assistance consistent with their current circumstances: unemployment, low pension, low paid work etc.

In terms of the satisfaction with the SSD's conditions of acceptance, married women's families struggled to convince the institutions of their needs and eligibility for social support. This process was surrounded by difficulties and took time and effort from the women to convince the final decision-maker (according to the women and the informants this is the Minister or the Deputy of the Minister) to sign the application form so that the family gets an 'acceptance' or a 'non-acceptance'. In the case of Saudi women married to non-Saudi men, the situation becomes more complicated, particularly if she needs to apply for SSD income support or support from the Charitable Women's Associations. The complexity is caused by: 1- she has a husband therefore he is supposed to be the provider for his wife and his family; 2- if her husband has a specific problem preventing him from sponsoring his family, the SSD could look through her application but the basic obstacle will remain that this man is not a holder of Saudi citizenship, therefore he is not eligible for social assistance, even though his wife is Saudi. Thus, the poor 'married women's families' in this case where the husband is a non Saudi and is ill, disabled, elderly and / or unemployed will not be treated equal to other Saudi families. The difference in nationality in this case affects the eligibility of that family and its female head to receive their rightful social support. In addition, married women's families are prevented from benefiting from other social services that are available to Saudi citizens.

Further to this, this category of married women's family, as expressed in their own words, felt excluded and marginalized socially, culturally and economically from many social, health and educational services that other Saudi families enjoy.

All the economic, legal, and social problems faced by the married women's families under the current social support regime reflect that this regime lacks the holistic and comprehensive approach to dealing with family problems, thus these problems and difficulties will remain intertwined and overlapping in their effects on the daily life of individuals, families and society.

6.2.5.4 The needs of the married women's families' category

The married women's families' category needs comprehensive and integrated solutions to deal with the overlapping factors that lead to poverty. Some of their needs are described below:

1- There is an urgent need in Saudi society to solve the problem of unemployment or to reduce its social effects in several ways such as, for example, by helping unemployed people to receive training and work opportunities and to improve social security regulations by including 'unemployment benefits' or similar to benefits offered in the UK, for example 'Job Seeker's Allowance' (see Child Poverty Action Group 2011: chapters 16 and 17).

2- Significant consideration should be given to the problem of people on 'limited or low income' whether in retirement or on low paid work; it is important to support them by bridging the gap between the real income level and the real cost of living.

3- The families need to be able to access welfare services, especially for particular groups and family members such as the sick, elderly, disabled and mentally ill.

4- Social security regulations need an urgent and fundamental change in order to include the 'non-Saudi husband' to his wife's entitlement for income support, especially if her husband is elderly, ill or disabled. This could somewhat ease the pressure experienced by those women who head their families and try to provide them with the basic requirements.

5- The Social Security System needs further modification to take into account and be consistent with real social circumstances and current living conditions.

6- This category of families need help in establishing, promoting and instigating financial institutions that specialize in helping debtors to find real and effective solutions for their problems and to secure help with their problematic debt trap in order to improve their standard of living.

Thus, the married women's families, as with the other FHHs categories, need social policies that are integrated into a coherent framework which supports the development process of the Arab Human Development Report in the literature review (see UNDP; 2002, 2003,2005,2006,2009, also ESCWA 2005, 2004, and 2009).

Conclusion

This chapter presented rich and detailed evidence of the daily life of the subcategories of the research sample and how they deal with their social reality. These details provided an honest and close picture of the lives of these FHHs and showed the interpenetrated realms of those families and their heads that were: 1- public realms (society, culture, state, welfare system and social support institutions); 2- private realms (women's worlds, specific stories and experiences that have led women to head their families such as divorce, widowhood, abandonment or the imprisonment of the head of the family). The chapter showed how these subcategories and their female heads have a similar experience in some aspects of the public realms but they experience quite different private realms.

The chapter also showed how the details of everyday life reflected common features of basic needs which can be classified as: housing, health, income, education and work. There are specific requirements for each category based on their own experiences which interact with the two factors of: 1- loss of the man (male breadwinner) from family life which caused poverty and 2- gender (being women). The result of that interaction between these conditions formed a different experience for each subgroup in terms of their social conditions, problems and social needs.

Chapter seven
Social Policy in Practice

Introduction

This chapter presents social policy in practice: in other words, how FHHs and their breadwinners experience social policy and the social support organizations represented by the Social Security Department (SSD) and the Women's Charitable Associations. The aim is to explore and highlight the pros and cons of the social policies' application as reflected through the interviews with the FHHs and with the informants (elite) who either work in the social support institutions or have an interest in the subject of poverty in general and female poverty in particular in Saudi society.

In addition, because of the importance of designing and building effective social policies relevant to the reality of FHHs and their daily needs and requirements, which is an important target for this study, the researcher has developed a set of general and detailed recommendations in the final section of this chapter. The researcher considers these recommendations to be important and essential outcomes.

This chapter is divided into the following sections:

1. Analysis of the interviews with the FHHs to explore Saudi social policy in practice.
2. Analysis of the results of the interviews with the informants (elite) to establish their views regarding important issues relevant to the poor FHHs.
3. General and detailed recommendations for reforming, improving and formulating effective policies for the eradication of poverty among FHHs.

7.1 Analysis of the interviews with FHHs to explore social policy in practice.

One of the goals of this study has been to explore the relationship between FHHs and the social policy and welfare systems as represented by the SSD and Women's Charitable Associations. The interviews with the FHHs therefore included questions about the practices and applications of these systems in the daily lives of the women and their families. The interviews were based on the following questions:

1. The reasons for their visits to the social support institution.
2. What support and aid had they received from the social support institution?
3. What they were expecting from the social support institution?
4. What was their impression of the services, programmes and support of these social support institutions?

Next, a summary of the women's answers will be presented in a way that gives a picture of the real practice of social policies in the daily lives of Saudi's poor FHHs.

7.1.1 Why are you coming today to this social support institution? What do you want?

The women who were interviewed answered that they came to these institutions, whether the SSD or the Women's Charitable Association, because of the following reasons:

1. They needed financial and/or in-kind assistance provided by the institutions.
2. To request or apply to get a residence (free house) or at least to apply for rent allowance.
3. To complete the application form of the SSD or the Women's Charitable Association and submits the necessary documents to register in the support system.
4. To renew the current ID card or update personal data for getting a new ID card.
5. To make a request to include one or more family members and complete the official process to get income support.
6. To make a request or inquire about an additional service offered by the institution.
7. To make a request to increase the amount of 'income support' because it was not enough for their demands and cost of living.
8. To make a request to get aid or funds for school requirements of the children that cost a lot of money in terms of clothing, shoes, books and stationery.
9. To request support for bill payments for services such as electricity, water, telephone etc.

10. To inquire about the services' fund for poverty and benefits for help in the payment of debts, or to make a loan request for health services: chronic disease drugs (blood pressure and blood sugar levels), medicines for serious diseases (heart and cancer), and other medicines.
11. To inquire about a fund or loan that could help the poor families to pay their debts.
12. An inquiry about some health services such as treatment or obtaining urgent medicine, especially for those who were suffering chronic disease and/or serious diseases such as heart, kidney and cancer where the public health services were crowded and gave long-term appointments to see a doctor or for surgery. In the case of necessary medicine, it is not always offered free of charge at the public hospitals even for the poor, where most of the time the patient has to buy the medicine and accordingly the poor cannot afford it.
13. A request for support with basic needs and requirements for babies and young children such as milk and diapers which are very important for the children but cost a lot of money, therefore the poor cannot afford to buy them.
14. To ask for support and assistance for an eye check for themselves or for their children and for the glasses they will need after that.
15. To request important services for vulnerable family members such as the disabled or elderly, to request a hearing aid for the deaf or a wheelchair for elderly or disabled persons because such things are costly.
16. A request to involve some family member in the support system such as the non-Saudi husband of the Saudi woman, or the divorced woman's children.
17. A request for support or advice to find a job for the woman or for her qualified child who could not find a job.
18. To ask for support to get equal opportunity for their children to be involved in the academic educational system (university education) or to get funding for professional training courses.
19. To ask for funds to pay the current university tuition for their children who could not get acceptance for free educational services.

20. To ask for support or advice regarding issues that prevents them from getting income support. Maybe they need support to get some official document from problematic bodies such as the civil issues department, the pensions department, court or the prison authorities.
21. To make a complaint against a family member who is representing the family in the SSD because he takes all the benefit from the family and usually this person is the husband.
22. To ask for support to help women to get an official stay and work permit for her children who are officially non-Saudi citizens.
23. To ask for advice about how to deal with governmental bodies that make problematic issues for the family or deny them their rights to income support such as the department of pensions, the social insurance department and other bodies that create complicated issues for these women and their families during their applications for income support.
24. To find accurate information about jailed husbands and their official charges, and how long they are supposed to remain in jail.
25. To help some friends or neighbours who want to apply for income support for the first time.

7.1.2 What did you get as support and assistance from the social support institutions?

The sample was asked about the kinds of support that they had been receiving, and their answers can be summarised as follows:

1- We received a monthly allowance from the SSD that was transferred directly to our bank account.
2- Financial support as Social Subsidy (SSUB).
3- Seasonal food aid every three or six months from the Women's Charitable Association.
4- Transfer to a local optician to get a free eye test and glasses.
5- Vouchers from the Women's Charitable Association for free food products from the local supermarket.

6- Transfer to a privet clinic to get health care services paid for by the Women's Charitable Association.
7- Obtaining annual clothing as well as used or new furniture to furnish the house.
8- Money or donations distributed by the Women's Charitable Association to its beneficiaries as alms/charity (sadaqah or zakah) during a religious session such as Ramadan and Eid.
9- Free house or apartment in charitable housing for women: 'Ribat' supervised by the Women's Charitable Association.
10- Free training courses paid for by the Women's Charitable Association to benefit women and/or their qualified children in English language, computers and Microsoft Office, health and beauty, sewing and designing clothes, and typing and secretarial work.

7.1.3 What they were expecting from the social support institutions.

The female heads were asked in the interviews what they expected to get from the social support institutions and their answers can be summarized as follows.

1- To get enough money for monthly income support from the SSD.
2- To receive from the Women's Charitable Association a good amount of money that represents the full zakah rather than a small and useless amount of zakah/zakat.
3- To be offered an effective solution to a housing problem by, for example, an offer of free accommodation, or half rent, and if that could not be found then at least support by providing housing benefit (as cash) that could help to pay house rent.
4- Getting an exemption to utility bills or a reduction in the price of facilities such as electricity, water and phone.
5- An annual increase in income support to cover inflation and the increase in the cost of living, where the purchasing power parity (PPP) is decreasing and the SSD income support does not cover the basic demands of everyday life for the poor.
6- To include all family members in SSD income support with a full portion for each person.

7- For there to be more coordination between the SSD and other relevant organizations in a way that makes it easier for poor women to overcome the difficulties and barriers that prevent them from getting their right to income support.
8- To improve the buildings and facilities of the current SSD and Women's Charitable Association where the women and families come to apply for social support; also it is expected that female staff could deal with the women's issues in a more understanding way.
9- To be provided with better services and more quality food products and more funds for the beneficiaries of the Women's Charitable Association.
10- It was hoped that family members (husbands and children) who could not get Saudi nationality could be treated more fairly and equitably and integrated into the system of income support.
11- It was hoped that family members with urgent health care or surgery needs might obtain early treatment by transferring them to the public or private health sectors, and making quick arrangements to solve their problems.
12- It was hoped that the support institution could provide free medication for people with serious or chronic diseases who needed medication but could not obtain it for some reason.
13- It was hoped that an effective relationship could develop between social support organizations and the other governmental and nongovernmental bodies involved in poor women's issues such as the courts, the civil issues department, the national poverty fund etc.
14- It was hoped that clear information would be provided about programmes and services such as the National Poverty Reduction Strategy (NPRS) and/or the National Charity Fund (NCF) that clients had heard about from TV and thought that they might be available via the SSD and/or Women's Charitable Associations.
15- To find a suitable training course for children to help them to find work.
16- It was hoped that financial or in-kind assistance could be secured, and also advice regarding planning for income-generating family projects (or the productive family project).

17- It was hoped that women staff in the SSD might work as advisors to guide poor women as regards what they should do when they visit for the first time, which section to go to, the right application form to fill in, and the procedures they should follow etc.

18- It was hoped that the SSD and Women's Charitable Associations would introduce something like a front desk or reception that could help the FHHs and direct them and answer their queries. It was also hoped that help would be provided in the form of guidebooks, brochures, leaflets and publications that would give the beneficiaries some information about the organization, its services and conditions, when and how to apply, and some useful contact telephone numbers.

19- It was hoped that a specific section would follow-up applications and give the women updated information about their social support applications, or if there was anything else that should be completed or checked.

So it is apparent that many who visited the social institutions could be described as missing important things that they expected to find during their visits, but unfortunately their expectations were not met.

7.1.4 Opinions and impressions of the services, programmes and support from the social support institutions?

As regards the SSD

1- The level of income support from the SSD is not enough to cover the cost of living for FHHs taking into account the cost of house rent and utility costs.

2- The procedures to apply for income support are complicated and take a long time.

3- Applicants often do not receive any additional aid from the SSD that could help with housing rent, health care, utility costs and school costs. The SSD gives financial support with tough requirements and long processing times, and it makes offers to some categories only, so not all of the poor can be guaranteed support.

4- The regulations of this institution sometimes seem unfair, especially when regulations exclude – for some reason - various categories from the support system such as, for example, the husband and children of poor Saudi women who are married to a non-Saudi man, even though they are poor and the woman is a Saudi citizen.
5- There is no comfortable environment for women at the SSD where all staff are male and there are no female sections or female staff to guide poor women to the right procedures for applying for income support.
6- The SSD does not help all categories of FHHs on the same level. Some can obtain income support easily. This applies to widows and divorced women. In contrast, abandoned women, married women and prisoners' wives face lots of difficulty and complexity.

As regards Women's Charitable Associations:
1- There is pressure and high demand from poor FHHs on the services of Women's Charitable Associations. A result is that it becomes a matter of selecting beneficiaries, while the conditions for receiving support become difficult, and the application form is complicated.
2- The services are few and scarce compared to previous years, and the quality of food products provided for the poor seem to be of poor quality compared to what the normal Saudi family consumes regularly.
3- The amount of money that is distributed during religious seasons as alms or zakah from the rich to benefit the poor is small and currently is almost non-existent and therefore not available. So FHHs rarely receive cash assistance compared with the situation a few years ago.
4- There is no guidance or consultation system in these institutions that could help poor women to understand what they have to do or which other organizations could help them, and how.
5- The conditions for social support become more difficult and complicated with time. For example some Women's Charitable Associations ask for more official proof in particular cases such as from abandoned women. Also, it has become necessary for the FHHs to provide the support organization with 'the house lease contract' to prove that they are living close to the Women's Charitable

Association so they are within the scope of its services, otherwise they will not be able to join the support system.

6- These organizations facilitate the process for some categories such as divorced women and widows, whereas they make it more complicated for other categories such as prisoners' families, abandoned women and married women's families.

7- The buildings are old, small and inadequate. Processing social support claims can take a long time. So the FHHs apply and then have to wait for the decision as to whether or not the case deserves support. Female officials and social workers are few and they are not unable to cover all cases, especially at peak times such as the distribution of seasonal aid.

8- The associations have no clear criteria for assessing all situations, so some FHHs are given social support whereas some are refused although they seem very poor and deserving.

The answers of these women create a realistic picture of how the families deal and interact with the social support institutions. We can understand why they went to these institutions, what they have received as social support and what they were expecting to receive, which reveals the differences between their expectations and what was available in reality. Finally, this evidence discloses the women's judgments and evaluations of the services of these institutions.

7.2 Analysis and results of the interviews with elite informants.

As previously seen, a number of elite informants were interviewed (18 in total). In this section these interviews will be analyzed in order to highlight and clarify issues relevant to social policy practices from the viewpoints of these informants. These interviews proved useful because they highlighted matters relating to differences between the regulations and the actual practices of these institutions vis-à-vis poor FHHs.

The informants were experts, officials and professionals, mostly working in the social support institutions (SSD and the Women's Charitable Associations in Jeddah City). The interviews focused on poverty in general and female poverty in particular, besides some other issues relevant to the relationship between FHHs with the current social welfare system. The interviews have been analysed, and the results are presented in this section under the following themes and questions:

1- The current services and programmes provided by the social support institutions for poor FHHs.
2- Future services and programmes for FHHs.
3- The difficulties and barriers faced by these social support institutions during the process of support.
4- Suggestions and recommendations suggested by the informants relevant to female poverty and the policies of these institutions.

7.2.1 The current services and programmes provided by the social support institutions for the poor FHHs

The social security department (SSD)

The SSD generally offers cash benefits. There are two types of income support: the Social Security Pension (SSP) and the Social Security Subsidy (SSUB). SSP is a monthly allowance paid to the beneficiary who is ineligible for support according to other SSD regulations. The SSUB is another type of income support paid once to the eligible beneficiary; it can be described as temporary support for cases that satisfy the regulations and conditions of SSD (see more details of these two types in chapter 3). We noted that the SSD's budget has been increasing dramatically, especially in the last few years, and that zakah provides the main financial resource for the SSD and also for the other state fund.

The SSD is the only support institution that has an electronic database and computer system to store and deal with its beneficiaries' data. All SSD offices across the country are connected through the same electronic information system, and because of this the information is more accurate via the SSD than in the cases of the Women's Charitable Associations. The SSD, via its local offices around the country, reports regularly to the SSD main office the important problems and difficulties that face the offices during daily work with beneficiaries. These reports are taken into account by the decision-makers as a basis for each review, reforming and updating the SSD to suit the requirements of the institution and its beneficiaries.

Women's Charitable Associations

The interviews with the informants, who worked in different positions in the Women's Charitable Associations, showed that the charitable associations were offering the following services to beneficiaries:

~ They provide basic food commodities such as rice, sugar, milk, cooking oil, laundry powder, hand and body soap and shampoo. These products are placed in boxes according to the portion identified for each poor family. This is based mainly on the number of family members but the food products can also be provided according to weekly or seasonal timetables whereby families are informed officially in advance of their turn to check the timetable and given other necessary information to pick-up their portions of food assistance. The main condition for receiving such in-kind assistance for any poor family is to be registered officially with the local Women's Charitable Association, which means being able to satisfy the conditions and regulations of that charity such as being a Saudi national, being poor or a poor FHH, and satisfying any other conditions, and the family must always be resident in the local area of the charitable association.

The Women's Charitable Associations also offer clothing (whether new or used) along with furniture and home appliances etc.

These benefits are available only according to the quantity and quality of donor contributions. It was noted that donations to the Women's Charitable Association varied according to the seasons so they could be higher in the religious seasons of Ramadan and al-hajj. According to the directors of certain charities, the donation process in Saudi society, especially for charities, had been affected negatively by the consequences of September 11th (2001) which was followed by a dramatic decrease in the rate of donations. This was explained as a result of the increase in social and political awareness of the problem of terrorism. This awareness resulted in important changes such as new efforts by the state to monitor and supervise the flow of financial transactions including donations to charitable or religious organizations. Moreover, according to some informants, another important change that had negatively affected funding and donation procedures was when the local authorities adopted a course of action to prevent local voluntary funds flowing to local mosques and some religious associations, which also stemmed the flow that benefitted the local poor and charity work. All these procedures were adopted by local authorities to help the political system supervise the flow of money. However, this affected social attitudes, and support and donations to charities shrank significantly.

Another economic factor that seemed to have affected charitable giving was the global economic crisis and its impact in the Kingdom. This was clear from the increased unemployment rate and inflation, resulting in a drop in the standard of living for a significant category of people who could be described as belonging to the middle class. Therefore, this category of population was poorer, so their current financial capacity would not allow them to donate to charity as they had done in the past.

An important service provided by the Women's Charitable Associations is offering opportunities for poor FHHs to apply for and obtain free housing in one of the charitable developments known as 'waqif' (see more detail in chapter 2), if housing is available and if the families satisfy the conditions of both the Women's Charitable Associations and 'waqif'. In Jeddah City, some of the charitable housing is established by rich people for the benefit of the poor. Some of this charitable housing is administered by the Women's Charitable Associations under the legal umbrella of the Ministry of Social Affairs (MSA). The Women's Charitable Associations were running such charitable projects in a way that could assist their beneficiaries; so the poor could apply to be on the list for free housing. In general, most of the poor could not obtain charitable housing simply because none was available: priority was given to the poorest from the category of women and FHHs.

The Women's Charitable Associations also organized charitable bazaars or what are known in the local language as 'charitable Souk' or 'charitable Bazzar'. These encourage the women to present and sell their own products, especially in the case of productive families' projects. The Women's Charitable Associations organize and sponsor many opportunities for training courses (short and long courses) for the women and/or their family members; the aim being to encourage them to develop their skills and knowledge so as to be able to obtain suitable jobs and increase their incomes (see Alsreaha S. 2001 and 2007 for jobs and Saudi youth attitudes). The idea is to help individuals and families to escape from their current situation as receivers of income support and dependence on the SSD system. Most short courses for women include how to use the computer, English language, crafts, drawing, designing and sewing clothes, health and beauty, secretarial and office administration and cooking. Most these courses were supported by financial and business organizations such as banks (in particular Islamic banks) and private sector companies where financial aid was a manifestation of social responsibility towards society and local communities.

7.2.2. The future services, programmes and plans of the social support institutions

What future services are social support institutions planning for poor FHHs? The interviews with informants from the SSD and Women's Charitable Associations discussed plans that were expected to make positive changes.

SSD

1- The Social Security Department had ambitious plans to develop what are called supplementary aid programmes (see chapter three for more detail) that aim to extend non-cash assistance to cover some aspects of daily life for the poor such as assistance with school requirements and uniforms, home furnishings, support with electricity bills, prescriptions for medication etc. These provisions should enable the poor to cover some of their basic needs outside the scope of their SSD monthly allowances, which means that the poor may be able to save some of the monthly allowance for other purposes.

2- The SSD plans to develop its own electronic information system and database and make it accessible to all sections of the Ministry of Social Affairs (MSA) and to all SSD offices around the Kingdom.

3- The SDD has its own ambitious plan to revise and reform its regulations in order to be more coherent and consistent with the current conditions of the poor and the social reality of their communities. The SSD also plans to overcome and resolve fairly the problem that has emerged through applications concerning, for example, retired people who have limited income but are excluded from income support, the various nationalities among couples that prevent them from receiving income support, the need for an unemployment or jobseeker allowance, and other controversial issues. All these issues are currently the subject of deep discussions among the decision-makers at the main SSD office in Riyadh and it is expected that significant modifications to the SSD's regulations will happen soon.

4- There is increased coordination and co-operation between the SSD and other government projects such as the National Charity Fund (NCF) and the King Abdullah Ben Abdul-Aziz Foundation for Housing. The aim of this co-operation is to activate programmes for poor people such as housing programmes, and to overcome the difficulties that prevent the poor from benefiting from housing projects, especially poor women and FHHs.

5- The SSD has a plan to develop effective programmes for helping FHHs to be more active, independent, and have a positive attitude to work rather than depend on SSD support. This plan includes initiatives such as 'productive families' and 'micro-finance' projects. There is concern within the SSD about how to attract the relevant categories of women and FHHs to such projects.

6- The SSD has plans to expand women's participation in the SSD offices by opening women's sections and providing these sections with female staff rather than having exclusively male staff as currently in all SSD offices. The female staff will deal with other female administrators, researchers and social workers. This is an important step and will result in positive consequences in the work environment of the SSD. 1- It will ease the pressures of work on the main SSD bodies that are administered exclusively by male staff. 2- The poor women and FHHs will find it more useful and convenient to deal with female staff who should be more understanding of women's issues than the male staff and they should appreciate the special problems of the Saudi women who are not, according to their cultural context, used to dealing with men in the public domain.

7- The SSD proposes to study and develop health care services for its beneficiaries. This will be via a sort of health insurance programme that would include all those on SSD and their families in a comprehensive health service.

Women's Charitable Associations

The Women's Charitable Association was looking to develop partnership programmes with governmental and other non-governmental organizations in order to raise the level of poor FHHs: for example, partnership programmes with the Islamic Bank, Al-Ahli Saudi Bank, the National Charity Fund (NCF), Abdul Latif Jameel Community Service Programme (ALJCSP), the Centennial Fund and the Human Resources Development Fund (HRDF). The ultimate goal of these partnership programmes would be to promote social responsibility on the part of the organizations towards the poor. This meant that the organizations should become more responsible and committed to their social obligations towards society by providing, for example, more funding and support for the programmes, plans and courses that aimed to raise the social and economic status of poor FHHs by providing them with education, training and career opportunities.

7.2.3 The difficulties and barriers faced by the social support institutions.

Difficulties faced by the Social Security Department

- **Financial difficulties.** The interviews with the informants reflected two points of view on this matter. 1- Some informants thought that the SSD did not have any financial problems related to the sources of its budget that basically relied on money collected from alms, zakah and the state fund. The money did not seem to be the main problem of the SSD. Rather, the main problem was how the SSD could assess and find the really needy to be included within the support system. The SSD needed to be able to filter out of the social support system those deceptive people who claimed poverty and prevented the genuinely poor claiming income support. 2- The other point of view was that financial difficulties were the real problem for the SSD because the number of poor people had increased dramatically for overlapping reasons including the shrinking of the Saudi middle class that occurred after the collapse of the Saudi stock market in 2006 as well as the impact of the global financial crisis of 2007. Therefore the poor in Saudi society had significantly increased in number and the voices of the poor became louder.

- **Buildings and human resources.** Most informants reported that the SSD needed improved offices all around the Kingdom. The value of improvements was clear in the case of Jeddah, where there were big and modern buildings equipped with the modern equipment necessary for the level and complexity of the work. Also, the SSD offices required more qualified human resource specialists in sociology, management, social policy and social work in accordance with the work requirements.

- **The centralization of decision-making.** Centralization of decision-making is a common factor in many sectors, especially in governmental organizations where nearly all decisions should be taken by the central authorities. According to some informants, the SSD offices around the Kingdom would transfer many applications and problematic cases to the higher authority in Riyadh - to the main office of the Minister of Social Affairs or the Deputy of the Social Security System where the decisions would be made regarding acceptance or rejection or any other procedure. This process actually hindered the work of the SSD office and encouraged bureaucracy within the governmental organizations, as well as making the beneficiary wait for a decision.

- The current SSD offices were a totally masculine work environment; there were no female staff to help deal with female beneficiaries.

- There was no effective coordination between the SSD and other governmental and non-governmental organizations concerned with poverty eradication issues.

- The governmental programmes and policies for poverty eradication still had shortcomings and defects. Therefore it seemed that they were inadequate to address the current poverty problem.

- Housing programmes were considered the most important and urgent requirement for poor women and FHHs, but until the current time, according to some informants from the SSD, the SSD had not yet provided anything that could help or answer the FHHs' inquiries regarding this issue.

- Child poverty seemed to be neglected by the SSD. Therefore there was no clear concern for this within the regulations, programmes and services of the SSD.

Difficulties that faced the Women's Charitable Associations

1. The lack of equipment and material sources that women's association need where there were just small and old buildings, also a small number of staff as opposed to a large number of beneficiaries. In addition to that, the budget of the charity would not allow for employing a sufficient number to cover all the charity's work. Also there was lack of social consciousness of members of the community about the importance of voluntary work.

2. Women's' charitable associations face problems related to the organization of work in so far as there are no updated regulations, or accurate and clear information systems to enable them to manage and deal with beneficiaries' data. Also there are no clear and accurate mechanisms for communicating and exchanging information between relevant institutions that deal with poverty and FHHs.

3. Women's Charitable Associations face some kinds of fraud where beneficiaries apply and register their documents with more than one association so that they can receive multiplied aid, which was happening as a result of the lack of precise information systems enabling the women's chartable association to check the validity of the beneficiaries' data and whether or not the family was registered in another place.

4. Women's Charitable Associations face a trend away from voluntary work, and this is a problem that requires research to determine the causes of the problem and how it might be resolved.

7.2.4 Suggestions and recommendations by the informants from these institutions relevant to female poverty and policies (a vision for the future)

All informants agreed on the need for there to be a clear vision for the future that could combine the work of all the social support institutions within an integrated social support system and an integrated social policy aiming to reduce poverty among women and FHHs. The informants emphasised the leading role of the state in producing a comprehensive policy to protect the Saudi family against emergencies that might affect levels of economic, social and living conditions, driving them into the cycle of poverty and need. They also suggested that the social conditions of poor FHHs should be part of a comprehensive approach/vision that would include not only improved services provided by social support organizations to the poor FHHs, but also improved general social conditions and social environments where these FHHs live and interact. There was particular emphasis on changes regarding women such as: evaluation, amendment and reform of current legislation, especially of the judicial system and those parts relevant to the family and women's issues so as to improve the status of women in society by their empowerment and increasing their opportunities for participation in the public domain. Further recommendations focused on reducing gender differences as much as possible and trying to achieve a kind of gender justice for Saudi women that would accord with an Islamic framework, and curtail the power and severity of certain cultural traditions and customs that impede women. Finally, everyone agreed on the need to achieve, or enable women to obtain equal opportunities in education, training and employment.

7.3 Recommendations for reforming, improving and formulating effective social policies for the eradication of poverty among FHHs

This section presents the author's recommendations that could be taken into account by decision-makers in their plans for the eradication of poverty among FHHs in Saudi society. The researcher believes that these recommendations and suggestions form core principles on how the governmental bodies and decision-makers who are working in the areas of poverty and FHHs, could improve, develop, reform and formulate effective and integrated policies for combating and eradicating poverty in Saudi society in general and among FFHs in Jeddah City in particular.

The previous two sections presented the findings from the interviews with female heads of households as well as elite informants who mostly worked in the social support institutions or had concerns with poverty and FHH issues. It was important to obtain specialists' and officials' points of view as well as the views of the female beneficiaries. This section will take into account what has been presented previously and will present the researcher's recommendations for the improvement and reformation of the social support system. In this section, the researcher will build on her recommendations based on her experiences and what she found during the fieldwork, along with what the female heads and the informants mentioned during the interviews.

This section presents the recommendations divided into three parts:

1- Strategic recommendations: concerned with the macro-level relevant to poverty and FHH issues, which must be viewed in a comprehensive and coherent way which is open to radical solutions.

2- General recommendations relevant to the general needs that were identified during the interviews with the female heads; these general needs concern housing, health care, income, education and work.

3- Specialized recommendations: relevant to the specific needs of each subgroup according to what was raised during the in-depth interviews about their problems and needs. For example, there are recommendations for widows' families, divorced women's families, abandoned women's families, prisoners' wives families, and married women's families.

7.3.1 Strategic recommendations

1. The Islamic and cultural heritages of Saudi society need to be embedded in its efforts, plans and mechanisms for fighting poverty. Examples of this are working to activate the Islamic perspective and policy framework for the eradication of poverty and the cultural and traditional principles of social solidarity and social cohesion supposed to lie within families, kinship and neighbourhood relationships. In Saudi society, religious and traditional values have a strong impact on people's lives and it would be useful if they were more deeply drawn upon to achieve the goals of strengthening social responsibility towards the poor and vulnerable. In such a case, the religious and cultural mechanisms such as zakah, waqif and social solidarity via

sadaqa and nafaqah would be both practical and acceptable tools for poverty reduction.
2. A National Agenda or Project for Poverty Reduction needs to be formulated on the basis of: 1- a clear conceptual framework including clear definitions of poverty, methods of poverty measurement and a national poverty line; 2- clear and precise statistics and data on the numbers of poor, poverty pockets, and poverty lines for each province, the distribution of poverty according to variables such as the geographical area, gender and age, and data on the workforce and the rates of unemployment among males and females; 3- an ambitious and continually updated plan with short and long term goals and with a comprehensive vision of poverty as a multi-dimensional problem.
3. Expansion and facilitation of participation by the private sector, encouraging businesses to play a more effective role and recognise their social responsibilities by sharing in the project of poverty reduction.
4. Expansion and facilitation of participation by civil society and voluntary organizations in poverty reduction.
5. Increased and improved levels and quality of communication and coordination between the SSD and other governmental and societal organizations that address the issues of poor women and FHHs. This applies to ministries and governmental bodies such as the Ministry of Social Affairs, the Ministry of Labour, the National Civil Department, the Ministry of Justice, and the Ministry of Waqif and Islamic Issues. All these official bodies were mentioned by the female heads during the interviews when they talked about their experiences and the difficulties and barriers that they faced during the process of seeking SSD income support. The female heads have to complete many official documents from these governmental bodies, but they had no idea where they had to go and what they had to do. The recommendation in this respect is for all these bodies to be integrated at one centre to represent each ministry or each official department. This will help the FHHs who will be able to return to each section if they have any queries or requests, and they should then be able to receive correct information on the procedures they have to follow. This centre with its various sections may be best located in the same building as the SSD, the city council building, the municipal building or '*Immarah*'. The aim of this

centre should be to serve poor women and FHHs who traditionally have difficulties in obtaining income support, and these difficulties need to be addressed by reforming some official procedures. These different sections should provide the FHHs with consultation, advice and guidance on how to process their claims, applications and requests to the official bodies.

6. The Saudi development plan should identify and include all the tools, techniques and operational plans required to implement the state agenda for poverty eradication among FHHs. The development plan should engage with issues of women's empowerment and their participation in projects of social development. In addition, it will be essential to confront all of the difficulties that hinder women and to reduce, as much as possible, gender differences, and to monitor and evaluate progress.

7. The contributions and efforts of international and regional organizations that specialize in poverty eradication and poverty reduction such as the UN, UNDP, ESCWA etc. must be taken into account.

8. There must be an accurate national database that should include the vital data about the entire population from sources such as the National Population Census, statistics on the workforce and employment data amongst others. In Saudi society, such information does not appear to exist or is not available in an organized format that would enable researchers, specialists and social commentators to observe and monitor the growth, movement or decline of poverty and other social phenomena. If this kind of data and information was organized electronically this would provide a firm base that could be used by professionals, researchers and specialists to develop important quantitative and qualitative evidence resulting in accurate reports on, for example, poverty indicators, poverty lines and poverty pockets.

9. To activate and promote funding of research on poverty in general and female poverty in particular.

10. To guarantee the sustainability of projects for poverty reduction and for all development projects that have relevance to combating poverty or promoting women's empowerment. These projects for poverty eradication must have the stability and sustainability to be able to achieve their goals.

11. To evaluate current projects for poverty reduction in Saudi society such as the National Poverty Reduction Strategy (NPRS) and the National Charity Fund (FCF)

which have been mentioned previously in chapter 4. The aim of this evaluation should be to address the following issue: have the projects worked and to what extent have the projects achieve their goals? It is essential in this respect to assess and evaluate the practice and the applications of these projects so as to understand the extent that the poor and FHHs benefit from the projects at the level of their daily lives. In other words, what differences to their lives have these projects made? It would be useful if there was official documentation from the state for such projects through, for example, an official guidebook or official website to enable people to see more details about the projects, their targets and achievements.

12. To establish a 'National Family Policy' based on Saudi religious, social and cultural contexts. The Saudi family policy could aim to achieve the following: 1) - to improve and promote the standard of living of the Saudi family at social, educational and economic levels; 2)- to promote family values and focus on the family as an important unit for development, taking account of special issues of members, especially the vulnerable such as women, children, the elderly and the disabled, and paying attention to youth issues; 3) – to expand and promote women's participation in the labour market with guarantees of gender justice in employment and wages, to give women the same rights as men; 4) - to empower the family by providing support and help that enables the family to adapt and cope with the rapid changes in social and economic life and to seek the right ways to avoid poverty and conditions of need.

13. To establish and promote an appropriate 'safety net' that should involve programmes such as the social security insurance programmes, the centres and programmes of maternity and child care, the care centres for disabled people, care centres for the elderly and other programmes targeting vulnerable groups who cannot work or otherwise generate enough income.

14. To establish an information base on female poverty which should be concerned with all data and statistics on female poverty, the family and FHHs on dimensions such as: 1- real numbers within these categories and the proportions of the residents and the total of the female population; 2- their distribution according to geographical areas and the social support institutions from which they get support and benefit along with the kinds of benefit they get. It is also a recommendation that the

proposed information base on female poverty should collect, organize and control the national data, information and statistics on female poverty, poor families and FHHs in terms of the positions of women in education and employment. It is also recommended that the proposed policy scrutinizes the status of women regarding unemployment, the divorced and other women's issues raised in the courts, and all other specific women's issues that could highlight and explain the social and public contexts surrounding Saudi women and their development and empowerment.

15. There are some important recommendations for the Social Security System (the SSD) which is the official government body responsible for supporting the poor and FHHs via the distribution of alms and zakat taken from the rich and given to the poor according to Islamic law.

    a. The evidence showed that the SSD in Saudi works as a charity system whereby it distributes cash support to beneficiaries as a monthly allowance, in accordance with quotas, granted to the head of the family and then to the rest of the family members. So allocations vary from one family to another depending on the family size. However, it appears that this procedure is not sufficient to meet the growing needs of family life. Therefore the researcher proposes a strategy to estimate the real needs of the individuals and families and assess those needs in a way that would produce a balance between the 'real need' and the 'monthly allowance'. It is important for the Saudi SSD to change the distribution policy from just giving income support as a charity to an approach of giving it according to an assessment of needs. This suggested method needs to be adopted by the government with serious and basic changes in the approach and structure of the current social security department, assisted by consultant specialists and professionals with expertise on social policy and welfare state issues.

    b. The SSD needs to establish, build and activate an advisory and guidance system that includes professionals of both genders to direct and guide the poor and FHHs in the appropriate ways for applying and following-up on their applications. The recommendation is to pay more attention to the process where FHHs, as the evidence shows, need a lot of advice and guidance so as to understand, first of all, the process, then to understand whether or not they have satisfied the conditions of the SSD and what they should do to overcome any barriers. The researcher recommends a guidebook issued by the SSD which includes everything about the system: the regulation of social support, the conditions of eligibility and the timetable for applying along with the difficulties that applicants might face during an application for income support. This guidebook would also be useful for specialists, researchers and social workers who need to attend the SSD or other social support institutions.

c. The centralization in decision-making that prevails in all governmental departments, and is also found at the SSD, is not useful. To transfer the applications of many cases to the main office in the capital Riyadh is not necessary: the manger of each SSD could deal with many of these cases and take suitable actions according to available resources and regulations. Centralisation in decision-making disrupts and hinders SSD procedures. It is therefore suggested that each regional SSD office should be given the power and authority for decision-making, particularly in urgent and emergency cases. Thus there will be more flexibility and less disruption to the lives of the poor and FHHs.

7.3.2 General recommendations

This section relates to the main and basic needs of poor FHHS such as housing, health care, income, employment and education, these needs being the most common among all subgroups of FHHs.

- **Housing**

The 'housing problem' in Saudi society has become a great social problem that has gained formal and informal interest via the media, press, decision-makers and the public. This problem has to be resolved in a way that enables citizens to own their houses or at least to be involved in real estate schemes such as the rental of property that results in ownership of the houses, or other programmes that could save the family from destitution, especially when the family is faced with an emergency that could impact on their income rendering them unable to pay their house rent. It is essential to co-ordinate housing policies to enable all citizens, at a minimum, to pay the house rent. This section will present recommendations for resolving the housing problem with regard to poor families:

1- Establish a specific department such as The Administration of Housing Services for SSD Beneficiaries. This department should be a part of the Social Security Department (SSD) or the Ministry of Social Affairs (MSA) and its aim should be to produce housing policies for the poor, and in particular the poor on SSD, especially poor FHHs.
2- Establishing this department would allow data and information about SSD beneficiaries who are eligible for housing support to be transferred to the housing department where their eligibility would be assessed.
3- Establishing such a department would ensure that housing services were provided to the poor and FHHs via SSD as a right guaranteed to them by law or by the regulation of social welfare and their rights as citizens. Based on that, the poor and FHHs on SSD should get one of the following housing services as a right guaranteed for them:
   a) A free housing unit should be offered to beneficiaries whether they are individuals or families. This housing unit could be located at one of the 'state public housing charities'.
   b) A specific amount of 'housing benefit' should be available to enable the beneficiary to pay his/her house rent. The housing benefit could be paid by the housing department directly to the account of the beneficiary or to the property owner if the beneficiary met all the conditions of eligibility and if the property was satisfactory measured against conditions required by the housing department.
   c) To be given a flat or house located in one of the residential/housing projects that could be rented by the housing department to distribute to the beneficiaries as free housing, so in this case the property owner would be the housing department itself.
4- The government should be further involved in resolving the housing problems of citizens and poor beneficiaries of SSD. Some suggestions are:
   - The planning and implementation of medium-cost public housing projects and the distribution of these housing units to citizens, especially poor people and FHHs on SSD. This distribution could be free or

implemented with a 'reduced rent system' according to the status of the beneficiaries and their ability to satisfy the conditions.

- The government could rent appropriate tracts of residential housing according to need. The housing department or any other governmental body could distribute these housing units to the needy through support mechanisms such as free housing or reduced rental.
- Groups who do not satisfy the free housing requirements could be given a housing allowance, which means a certain amount of monthly income, calculated according to the average rent and the number of family members and their needs. The housing allowance could be paid into the beneficiary's bank account or to the property owner.
- The government could take advantage of the mechanism of Islamic Endowments (Islamic waqif) which has enabled many charitable housing projects to be built by the rich for the benefit of the poor and FHHs. In Jeddah, for example, there are many of these charitable houses (waqif), but unfortunately most of them are empty because they are old buildings and need a lot of renovation and maintenance to be suitable and safe for residence. Therefore it is recommended that the government renovate these houses and transfer them to the SSD or the housing department for distribution to the poor and FHHs.

5- Housing projects for the poor are suggested as part of the objectives of the country's development plans. It is also suggested that the housing problems of each city, town or province of the Kingdom be dealt with separately in accordance with the area's needs, the population categories and their sub-cultures and lifestyles; for example Bedouins, rural or urban. Another suggestion is that the MAS or SSD be responsible for the budgets of the charitable housing projects for each region according to its needs and the number of poor and their style of living.

- **Health care**

The suggestions and recommendations in this respect can be summarized as follows.

1. Improve the quality of public health care and to ensure that there is justice in the health care system, especially in the case of the poor and FHHs whose daily lives reflect aspects of injustice in the public health system. It is suggested that the poor and FHHS should be given priority, especially when dealing with patients with special circumstances and those who need help with their appointments, prescriptions or medication. In the case of the poor or FHHs who cannot obtain appointments because of increased demands on the health care services, the recommendation is that the poor patient should automatically be placed by the system in a private health service at the expense of the Ministry of Health or the Ministry of Social Affairs.
2. Develop and improve the services of local health centres and also develop a system of family doctors in every neighbourhood to ensure that families get appropriate primary health care.
3. Develop the home health-care system to provide health services to the poor, elderly and disabled and those who are unable to visit the hospital and who have no carers.
4. Establish a carer system based on eligible people who have the ability and skills to provide home care services to people in need, especially for the poor who are elderly, incapacitated or disabled. It was noted among the SSD beneficiaries that some poor women and FHHs heads are elderly, disabled, or need a carer to look after them inside and outside of the home. They were usually persons who did not have any close relatives or family members. The solution will be to provide such services to these categories of poor and vulnerable people via the social support institutions (SSD or the MSA). The UK has a benefit called 'carer allowance' and a similar benefit should be provided either by the SSD for the beneficiaries themselves, in which case they could hire carers and pay for them directly, or the SSD would provide the carer to the beneficiary, taking responsibility for their employment, monitoring and payment.
5. Establish a programme of 'health insurance', widely available to the public, with a specific mechanism that would ensure inclusion of the poor and FHHs on SSD. This is needed especially in view of the increasing complaints against the public health services where there are gaps and non-coverage of the poor. In the

case of the poor not being able to afford private health care, if other services are not available, then the appropriate and best solution is health insurance provided by the Ministry of Health or the Ministry of Social Affairs.

6. Formulate a system of free prescriptions and medication for the poor and FHHs from the local pharmacy. It is suggested that each prescription be recorded electronically in the pharmacy according to the patient's social security number and should be signed by the patient on income support. Another solution will be to identify specific pharmacies where the poor and SSD beneficiaries could obtain their medication or other medical requirements for free.

7. Provision of other medical requirements such as glasses, hearing aids and wheelchairs for the disabled or elderly, which must be available for the poor and FHHs free of charge or at a discount. The SSD or the health insurance system could pay.

8. The Islamic endowment should be directed towards medical and health care for charitable health endowment buildings. It is recommended that people be encouraged to direct endowments to hospitals and health centres that serve the poor. This will amount to a revival of the tradition of the Muslim waqif.

9. For children and family members of poor FHHs to register at local institutions for special needs such as the Saudi Institute for the Deaf and Mute, the Institute of Comprehensive Rehabilitation of Severe Disabilities, and the Al-Noor Institute for the Blind. These institutions have to cover the needs of all citizens, and in particular the poor and FHHs on SSD, but some people cannot get a place. Therefore the Ministry of Social Affairs (MSA) should pay for a private and specialist institute to look after them and cover the costs of their care. Thus no-one will be left outside the framework of care.

- **Income**

1. It is proposed that the financial benefits of SSD (SSP & SSUB) should be increased and paid to the beneficiaries according to an assessment based on the actual needs of the beneficiary. The estimating process should be through a committee that should investigate each case and decide how much each needs.

2. Increase financial allocations annually after calculating and including an annual increase in the cost of living, because many other factors affect the lives of the poor. Inflation and the high cost of living will damage the interests of the poor and increase their poverty and suffering.
3. The poor and FHHs should be given a facility for procuring food and children's products. These facilities could be a 'reduction card' or an 'SSD discount card' that would enable the poor and FHHs to get what they wanted at an affordable price. This would help them to save the rest of their income support for other needs.
4. Resolve or at least reduce the negative impact of unemployment especially on the poor and FHHs. It is important for there to be ways to create job opportunities for all citizens, especially for the poor and FHHs on SSD; job opportunities that suit their abilities and appropriate training, so as to obtain additional sources of income, are priorities.
5. It is important to take into account the problem of female unemployment in general and among the heads of FHHs in particular. One suggestion to deal with this problem is for there to be a specific jobcentre aimed at attracting poor women and FHHs that would provide them with advice and consultation, as well as connecting them with other bodies and organizations that could offer jobs or training opportunities.
6. Introduce, explain and facilitate projects that could help poor women and FHHs. Examples include the 'productive families' project' and the 'microfinance project'. Such projects can help poor women in Saudi society, but the social contexts, including what will be appropriate for the non-Saudi community must be carefully examined. It would be helpful if the SSD or MSA started a partnership with the FHHs until they were able to lead themselves to success.
7. Support for the purchase of children's items like clothes, milk and diapers as well as children's medicines. This should be available to poor and non-poor, Saudis and non-Saudis.
8. Introduce control of the prices of consumer goods, especially basic foodstuffs. This control should be by a government body such as the Ministry of Commerce (MC) and reviewed whenever salaries are increased or when the King increases

the level of income support for those on SSD. Prices will increase dramatically without any control. Purchasing power will be affected negatively for the entire society, but in particular the poor and FHHs. It is suggested that strict laws and regulations should prevent traders from increasing the prices of consumer goods and this task should be the responsibility of official bodies.

- **Work**

1. Establish 'jobcentres' in all districts of the cities under the supervision of ministries such as the Ministry of Labour and the Ministry of Social Affairs, with partnerships with other government and non-governmental organizations that are interested in such issues: for example, the SSD, Chambers of Commerce, charitable sectors and other institutions that have an interest in the labour market and reducing unemployment. The main aims of such jobcentres would be to help people find jobs. The centres could operate as links between job seekers and employers. The job seeker would attend the nearest jobcentre and ask for job opportunities. Then he/she would see what was available and complete an application form for any suitable jobs. If the person did not meet the job requirements he or she could seek opportunities for training to improve his/her chances of securing employment.
2. Encourage female heads to join the labour force, even for low-paid work as this will be a good strategy for encouraging poor people to begin to alleviate their low income status. This should be facilitated by the SSD as another type of financial support for people on low incomes. The SSD should support poor women and FHHs to find job opportunities, perhaps working as a link between poor women//FHH job-seekers and employers from the public, private and charitable sectors.
3. Organize and offer training opportunities for female heads and other poor women who wish to join the labour market.
4. Children of FHHs who are qualified and eligible for work but who cannot secure employment could be provided with income support called 'jobseeker's allowance' or 'unemployment social support' if they satisfy the conditions of the

SSD which could be: 1) - they have to be serious in searching for a job; 2) - they have to be registered at the local jobcentre as jobseekers and, if there are jobs available, they have to demonstrate their seriousness by applying, even for low paid jobs which would be supported with another allowance from the SSD that could top-up earnings from low paid work.

- **Recommendations regarding vulnerable categories**

The following recommendations are concerned with particularly vulnerable categories such as the elderly, the disabled and children, who make up significant numbers among poor FHHs.

Women, society, and legislation

Saudi society needs the overall status of women to be improved. The suggestions are as follows.

1. Change and improve the image of women in the public domain and highlight the positive aspects of Saudi women within and outside the Kingdom. It is important to improve Saudi women's image to prevent the negative attitudes and behaviour that stand against the empowerment of women. Women need to increase their participation in the public sphere because they are usually, according to public opinion and as reflected in the Saudi media and in this research with evidence from the interviews with female heads, official informants and decision makers, represented by religious doctrines, a traditional culture, and a patriarchal ideology in ways that do not reflect the real spirit of Islam and are in conflict with the core principles of Islam. The traditional culture has a strong impact on and control over many aspects of social life, and because it is supported by a particular religious trend, this gives the traditional culture the power and influence to stand against any attempt to improve or empower women or promote their participation (see in this respect Bashatah, 2009). The suggestions for changing this are as follows.

- Top decision-makers in government bodies that represent the state could support women's issues by making critical decisions that support women and development programmes that aim to empower women by increasing their participation in the public field as well as in the labour market. This would improve Saudi women's status and living conditions.
- The media and press have to change the stereotype of Saudi women from the distorted image created and reinforced by the strict traditional culture.
- The educational system should include materials in its curricula to demonstrate and clarify issues such as gender, women's rights, their position in Islam and the importance of women's participation in development which does not contradict the spirit and values of Islam.

2. It is important for there to be an assessment and modification of the prevailing judicial system and legislation as this applies currently to women's issues and personal status cases in the Saudi courts. There are many criticisms of the legislation applied in the courts, especially in cases of the family and women, where the legislators have been accused of being misogynist and not reflecting the spirit of Islam.

3. There must be a legal framework that protects the identity of women and their civil rights, and also guarantees them the same legal and civil rights as men. This is necessary in order to protect women and their families. The legal system should assess and change all practices and laws that disrupt the affairs and interests of women and their families. This includes the Civil Status Law, the Nationality Law, the Labour Law, and other laws that seem to increase the suffering of FHHs.

4. Provide equal opportunities for women in the labour market with special attention to the promotion of poor women and female heads of their families by giving them priority in some of the services and opportunities for training and employment.

5. Pay more attention to women's legitimate rights (religious rights, guaranteed by Islamic law) and legal rights (which are guaranteed by Saudi law), and civil rights (guaranteed in accordance with the prevailing system of citizenship in Saudi Arabia). This awareness should be spread through the media, mosque and

neighbourhood, educational institutions such as schools and universities, and the family and local community. It would be useful to establish social activity centres to educate women in their rights and provide them with advice and guidance about a range of issues.

The elderly and disabled

1- Establish specific policies for the elderly and other categories such as the disabled by creating services such as the 'carer system'. This system could provide each elderly, disabled or incapacitated person with the right to have a carer provided by the office of the SSD or MSA. Another model would be the provision of 'carer benefits' whereby the responsibility for selecting and paying for his/her carer rested with the beneficiary. This would benefit poor FHHs if they fell into any of these categories.

2 - Provide adequate health care to needy, elderly and disabled people at public hospitals and, in the case of a shortage of available appointments, attention must be given to transferring them to private health care at the expense of the Ministry of Health or the Ministry of Social Affairs. It should be their right as citizens to be guaranteed full health care.

Children and childhood

It is important to include the issue of 'child poverty' in the operational agenda for national poverty reduction, and this should be included in any effort to deal with the poverty issues of FHHs. Child poverty is a major issue for many of these families since a large proportion have children and face problems in terms of their multiple deprivation of life and school requirements. Therefore it is recommended that child poverty should be considered as part of family poverty and all efforts to eradicate FHH poverty should take into account what should be done to reduce child poverty. Children's rights need a strict law and severe sanctions against those who harm the interests of the child, especially in cases of divorce or conflicts in child custody following divorce or abandonment. Some parents, especially fathers, give up responsibility for the physical and financial care of children, behaviour that is often calculated to hurt the woman. Therefore it is essential to protect by law the rights of the child and guarantee children a stable upbringing. The law should protect the rights of the child by enforcing parental responsibility towards children. There should be legislation and mechanisms to protect children from homelessness. Many children escape school and home to live on the street, so children's circumstances need to be understood and the integrity of the family needs to be promoted, especially families headed by women that lack a male sponsor and protector of the children.

7.3.3 Specialized recommendations

These are relevant to the special needs and requirements of each category of FHHs according to their social circumstances and social conditions of their everyday lives.

Recommendation for widows' families

1- These families need urgent assistance for the widows to complete the ceremony of mourning and the funeral. Also, there is a need for assistance for bereaved children in the grieving period for the loss of their father, and the new widows (the mothers) who face difficulties in managing everything.

2- Widows' families need acceleration of the legal issues of inheritance, custody, etc. It is suggested that widows need legal support, especially in problems faced in court. Therefore it is important to guarantee by law the Islamic rights of these widows, particularly the legal custody of her children, and widows should have the right to formal representation before the official authorities.

3- Husbands and fathers should be required by law to comply with the official procedures of the national civil department by including all family members on the official family card and ensuring that individuals are identified and registered according to his/her civil number. These procedures will guarantee the rights of individuals in the event of the death of the male breadwinner of the family and will protect the rights of the widow and her children, especially the right to income support. This suggestion will save time and make the current struggles of widows unnecessary.

1- Provide widows' families immediately with their rights to assistance and support, especially in the absence of people who could help and specifically if the widow is elderly, or her family has vulnerable members such as disabled, ill or elderly people, in which case the family will be faced with many layers of suffering. A carer or carer benefit will enable a widow to overcome immediate problems after the death of her husband.

Recommendations regarding divorced women

1- Review, check, and reform most of the legislation that courts rely on for cases of the family and children, and in particular in the cases of divorce, custody, alimony and claims for alimony on behalf of children. All these suggestions will provide a good structure and will decrease suffering among currently silent women who face many barriers in the courts and who lose their right to social support because of complicated and outdated legislation.

2- Re-issue the 'document on the personal status of the family' which contains the legal framework that organizes aspects of family life and the relationships between family members. The document should be in the Arabic language wherein it is called *Moudaouna*. This document will act as the foundation for reforming the judicial system and court proceedings.

3- Women need to be educated and guided about their legal rights, especially on the issues of divorced women where their ignorance of their rights makes it easier for them to be exploited. They have been deprived of rights guaranteed by Islamic law because they have no knowledge and because there is no clear and accurate legal system to protect their rights.

4- Review the courts' rules and procedures, and listen to women's voices against unfair judicial rulings, especially on the issues of divorce and the protection of women's rights.

5- Provide the courts with advisers and counsellors who could advice women on legal issues, especially custody and divorce documentation.

Guaranteeing social justice in all issues relevant to women and avoiding the disadvantages and struggles that poor families headed by divorced women face will take time, but this is necessary in a fair society. Strong legal action must be taken against any person or institution that attempts to undermine the regulations and laws, especially with regard to women's issues and legal rights. There have to be specific and effective ways to deal with men who divorce their wives then abandon their responsibilities towards their children.

Recommendations for the abandoned women's families

1- Review and reform the laws relating to abandoned women, especially in the cases of families with children. These laws should be re-evaluated to protect the rights of women and their children and to grant them freedom by providing for divorce within Islamic law regardless of the existence or non-existence of the deserting husband.

2 - Formulate laws that address problematic cases; for example, the dilemma of the abandoned woman who has been left by her husband for many years. In such cases the decision should always benefit the woman and her children.

Recommendations for prisoners' wives' families

1- There needs to be a clear way of clarifying and explaining to the families, in particular the prisoner's wife, the legal implications of her husband's situation and of helping the family cope with this problem.

2- The prisoners' wives need a guarantee from the local authority of their right to know about their husband's situation, and to maintain a connection between the family, the prison and the local authority.

3- The families need government and non-governmental organizations to look after their issues and raise their specific requests and concerns.

4- The families need urgent financial support, especially at the beginning of their crisis to help them cope and pass a difficult time that has a huge impact on their lives.

5- The prisoners' wives need to be informed and kept updated about issues relevant to the cases of their husbands.

6- The prisoners' families need more understandings about the prisoners' issues and alongside this, the prisoner 'stereotype' needs to be challenged in order to reduce stigma and facilitate greater social acceptance regardless of the charge, in order to enable the prisoner to integrate more easily into society on release and avoid marginalization. The media, press, mosque and education will have significant roles to play in these important changes.

Recommendations for married women's families

1– Reform aspects of the citizenship, immigration and work laws to ensure justice for Saudi women who are married to non-Saudis, and to give full rights to the family of a Saudi man who is married to a non-Saudi woman. The Saudi woman should be able to include her children and her husband in her rights as a Saudi national. This will guarantee for her the right to live in dignity, in particular in the event of poverty, and poor FHHs who are married or were married to non-Saudis will be able to receive income support for their families.

2 - Amend and modify the social security laws and guarantee social justice, especially for members of poor FHHs, where regulations are biased against women and against their husbands and children when they are non-Saudis.

Recommendations regarding youth issues

The youth category, male and female, form a significant number within poor FHHs. Some of them have a high level of academic education but unfortunately cannot find work. The following recommendations are to improve the situation within these poor FHHs:

1- Provide the youth with opportunities for training and employment by connecting them with job providers.
2- Provide financial support (an allowance) for those who are jobseekers.
3- Find solutions to the increasing unemployment problem, maybe by involving the youth in official organizations, and expanding public, private and voluntary job creation. Even simple, low paid work, supported financially by the state, will be beneficial. This could be one of the projects on the national agenda for poverty reduction because the problem of unemployment is part of the problem of poverty, leading to increased criminal activity among young people.

Chapter eight
Conclusions

Introduction

This research has been an exploratory study of social policies and programmes for the eradication of poverty among poor female-headed households in Saudi society (Jeddah City). The main aim of the research has been to study female poverty and social policy by investigating a sample of poor FHHs in Jeddah City and how they dealt with their poverty in their everyday lives, as well as their experiences with the social welfare system, represented by two organizations - the Social Security Department (SSD) and Charitable Women's Associations. The thesis has covered four sets of issues: 1- poverty profile, which entailed studying the social, cultural and demographic characteristics of poor FHHs in Jeddah City. 2- the daily lives of FHHs and how they interacted with their social reality within and outside of the household unit. 3- policy in practice and the relationship between FHHs, social policies and the welfare systems. 4- recommendations and suggestions to reform the social policy and welfare systems.

The fieldwork has been primarily qualitative, investigating a sample of 112 poor female-headed households who were accessing two types of social support: the Social Security Department (SSD) and the Charitable Women's Associations. Another sample of informants (elites) - officials, experts and decision-makers whose work was relevant to poverty eradication and social support institutions – was also researched.

This section presents conclusions from the research divided into the following:

1. Summary of thesis content;
2. Summary of the main findings in the light of the research objectives and the research questions;
3. Implications for policy, briefly, because these implications were presented in chapter 7;
4. Recommendations for further study.

8.1. Summary of thesis content

The research was part theoretical, part analytical and part empirical. The theoretical part (chapters one to four) outlined a conceptual framework; the first three chapters reviewed previous studies of poverty globally, then at the Islamic level, the Arab regional level and finally the Saudi level, and Jeddah City in particular. The methodology chapter clarified the research subject and the specific methodology and tools that were designed to achieve the research goals.

4- **Chapter One** provided a theoretical background and global literature review. This included poverty definitions, measurements and poverty and gender issues. This chapter aimed to build a fundamental understanding of poverty concepts and their implications, and explored the overlap and inter-penetration of poverty and gender issues and how these are mirrored in international studies. **Chapter two** focused on poverty in Islam and Islamic countries to present an alternative framework of how poverty and, in particular, female poverty can be conceptualized. The chapter considered poverty in the Islamic context, poverty in contemporary Islamic societies and finally women and poverty from the Islamic perspective. **Chapter three** looked at poverty within Saudi and other Arabic societies, presenting the socio-cultural context of female poverty and FHHs within these contexts. **Chapter four** described the methodology for investigating the research subject, presenting the research goals, objectives and questions, and suggesting a qualitative approach as the most appropriate empirical research method, based on in-depth interviews. Additionally, further details of the research design and data collection and selection of the main sample (112 FHHs selected from the SSD and Charitable Women's Associations in Jeddah City) were presented. **Chapter five** presented the socio-cultural and demographic characteristics of poor FHHs in Jeddah City and provided more detail on Jeddah City in terms of the place, the culture and the people of Jeddah. **Chapter six** presented a description of the lives of all categories of poor FHHs (the study sample) with a number of representative stories from each category, analysed according to how the female heads became the breadwinners of their families, the problems they faced and their family requirements. **Chapter seven** looked at social policies in practice, highlighting the benefits and disadvantages of the policies in application as reflected through the interviews with the FHHs and with the elite informants. This chapter provided strategic and detailed recommendations for reforming, improving and formulating effective policies for the eradication of poverty among FHHs in Saudi Society. **Chapter eight** concludes with a summary of the research, the main findings, policy considerations and recommendations for further studies.

8.2. Summary of the main findings in the light of the objectives and the research questions.

The main findings are summarised below, as relevant to the research goals. Questions were derived from the goals, then the analysis of the data answered the questions and achieved the goals, as shown below,

Goal one: (poverty profile) - studying the social, cultural and demographic characteristics of poor FHHs in Jeddah City.

The research found that the FHHs in Jeddah City represented by the study sample were characterized by the following socio-cultural and demographic characteristics:

1. The male head (the man/husband) was missing from family life so the family was headed by the female. The majority of the heads of families were single mothers through widowhood, divorce, abandonment, the husband being in prison or suffering sickness, old age, or unemployment.

2. These female heads were mostly uneducated or had a low or basic level of education. According to the evidence from fieldwork, their children had a high level of school dropout.

3. The FHHs were mostly heading large families – approximately 73% of the sample lived in families with between 4-9 members.

4. The families had no regular earned incomes because the heads had no jobs; about 93% of the sample were housewives.

5. The Social Security Department (SSD) was the main income source for 43% of the FHHs.

6. Sixty-one percent of the sample were living in southern and eastern Jeddah and 39% were living in northern Jeddah.
7. The majority of the FHHs (63%) were tenants and lived in small flats (most with 2 or 3 bedrooms) and about 29% of the FHHs lived in old traditional houses that lacked good, modern living conditions.
8. A significant number of FHHs were deprived of both official support from the SSD (33%) and from Charitable Women's Associations (53%) for reasons beyond their control that prevented them from satisfying the terms and conditions of social assistance such as incomplete documentation for the substantiation of marital status or a shortage of personal documents if the husband or children were classed as non-Saudis.
9. Seventy percent of the FHHs relied entirely on social security for financial assistance.
10. The quantitative and qualitative evidence showed that that the poor FHHs in Jeddah City were not regarded as in the same category as other poor sections of society; they were treated differently because of their origins and family backgrounds as well as the reason for their poverty. So although the poor FHHs shared similar circumstances and poverty conditions with other poor households, they were regarded as culturally and socially different. The qualitative evidence showed that the poor FHHs could be divided into the following categories :

- Families who had always been poor, who had more than likely inherited poverty from their poor families. They lived mostly in the slums and had lifestyles that could be described as a 'culture of poverty', especially those who were migrants from the other poor regions in Saudi, the southern regions of the country for example.

- The women's family backgrounds were not poor originally, living acceptable lifestyles, but for various reasons the women had become poor. In other words, these families could be considered and could be assessed socially as lower middle class, on the margin between the poor and the middle class category of Saudi society. Their original families were not poor but neither were they typical middle class families because the typical Saudi middle class family can provide at least the minimum life requirements such as decent housing, education, food, clothing, school requirements, the cost of utility bills for electricity, telephone, and water, a car, the ability to go on holiday at home or abroad, and access to technology for entertainment at home such as TV, satellite channels, computer, telephone and mobiles. This category had experienced social and economic changes that had affected their social position as lower middle class, causing them to fall into poverty and join the beneficiaries at social support institutions. This category of poor people was growing due to the lack of effective safety nets and social services, and therefore they grew poorer with time. This is leading to the erosion of the middle class that is gradually shrinking within Saudi society.

- Families were classified as middle class according to Saudi society's understanding, but as a result of circumstances beyond their control they could be called 'the new poor', emerging due to changes in the economy that had increased the unemployment rate, mixed with the collapse of the Saudi stock market in 2006–2007. This collapse led to the loss of many Saudi citizens' money and property that was held by a bank as collateral for loans, leading to poverty and debt.

- Families had their own social status according to their family name or their tribal origin but these families were not necessarily rich. There were families regarded as having high social status but in reality they had a low economic status: they may have lost their money or property or were the poorest branch of a status family; they might not receive any support from relatives and relied on the state income support system.

Goal two: (daily life) - studying how poor FHHs experience everyday life and how they interact with their social reality inside and outside the household unit.

1. The female heads of households became breadwinners for their families due to reasons such as the male breadwinner of the family being absent through death, divorce, abandonment, imprisonment, or other reasons such as being old and retired or ill, or any other reason that could impede exercising his full responsibility towards his family, therefore the woman had to step into that role.

2. The FHHs faced difficulties relevant to how they could offer basic life requirements to their families. All FHHs agreed that the most important needs were food, housing, enough income to offer a decent life for their families, school requirements for the children, health care and medication, and the needs of vulnerable people within the families such as the elderly, disabled, babies and children.

3. The details of the social reality of the everyday lives of these FHHs revealed the inter-penetrated realms of the families and their heads that were: 1- public realms (society, culture, state, welfare system and social support institutions); 2- private realms (women's worlds, specific stories and experiences that had led women to head their families such as divorce, widowhood, abandonment or the imprisonment of the head of the family). The evidence presented showed how these sub-categories and their female heads had similar experiences in some respects in the public realm but they experienced quite different private realms.

4. The women's stories reflected two types of social framework:
   - A general framework in which the women lived and shared the same social and cultural contexts with other women who had similar experiences. For instance, divorced women, whether or not they were heads of household, faced similar problems and difficulties related to society's attitudes, judicial system and legislation that were often loaded against women in divorce cases.
   - A specific framework that reflected the particular social and cultural context relevant to each individual's experience. This means each woman had her own unique story, reflecting diverse circumstances and different scenarios.

5. The analysis of the everyday lives of the poor FHHs of Jeddah City reflected common features of basic needs, which can be classified as housing, health, income, education and work. There were also specific requirements for each category based on their own experiences, which interacted with the two factors of: 1- loss of the man (male breadwinner) from family life, which caused poverty and 2- gender (being women). The results of the interaction between these conditions created a different experience for each sub-group in terms of social conditions, problems and social needs.

6. It seemed that poverty among FHHs in Jeddah City had a feminized aspect according to the stories of the female heads. There appeared to be a relationship between the social conditions of their poverty, problems and needs, and the factors summarized below.

Gender difference

The female heads faced difficulties related to how society and culture treated them; they had to take on the role of breadwinner and be responsible for their families, but society and culture, as evidenced in the female heads' stories, presented the women with social and cultural barriers that hindered their efforts, and this was intensifying their poverty.

Legislation, laws and justice with respect to women's issues

The legislation, which in this context means the rules and regulations of Sharia law as understood and applied in the Saudi judicial system, had relevance to many central problems of the female heads and their families, especially in the case of family issues and personal cases raised in the courts. According to the evidence, many women found themselves losing many of their rights, especially in divorce and abandonment cases, where it appeared that the legislation was unfavourable towards women. The legislation insisted on controlling women and maintaining traditions and religious teachings which kept women within a specific social space. Keeping women within a specific and limited social space reduced their participation in the public domain. The women and FHHs had therefore been affected by the many complex socio-cultural interactions that worked to increase the problem of their poverty.

Civil law in Saudi Arabia and under Islam is supposed to deal with all citizens equally and to be neutral as regards gender. Unfortunately, the evidence from the interviews showed that this was not the case, especially in respect of 'naturalization law' and 'labour law' for Saudi women who married non-Saudi men. These problems are highlighted in chapter six: the application of such laws had a negative impact on the lives of the poor FHHs who were prevented from accessing their rights as citizens of services such as work, public health care, education, social services and SSD income support. The laws and civil regulations worked against the women, increasing the female heads' problematic issues of poverty and need.

Women, social support institutions and social welfare systems

As the stories showed, there was much evidence of the women complaining and seeking more justice, access to services and fairer regulations, whether at the SSD or the Charitable Women's Associations. Many female heads believed that there was a blatant 'gender injustice' in the distribution of income support between men and women through SSD regulations and that there was unnecessary complexity in dealing with women's applications because they had to provide many official documents - officially signed documents from their guardians, and official letters from the court. The woman could also suffer exclusion from the income support system if her husband and children were non-Saudi. Therefore, the social support institutions mirrored the traditional culture regarding women's issues.

Goal three: how social policy operates in practice by examining the relationship between FHHs and social support institutions.

1. The results showed that only 67% of the sample received official support from the SSD; 33% of the sample did not receive any support from the SSD despite being poor.

2. The FHHs appreciated the financial support from the SSD but were not happy with the amount of income support, which was not enough to cover the cost of living for them and their children.

3. About 48% of the sample were in receipt of benefits and support from charitable associations, whereas almost 52% did not receive any benefits or support from charities, despite their status as poor and needy.

4. The FHHs were not happy with the services of the Charitable Women's Associations whose support had declined dramatically over the last few years in quantity and quality.

5. The FHHs expected more financial and in-kind support from the SSD and Charitable Women's Associations but their expectations were not met.
6. The FHHs needed an increase in their state income support to match the increase in the cost of living.
7. FHHs needed a more feminine environment to deal with their issues in the SSD; they emphasized the need for female staff to be installed.
8. FHHs asked for an increase in social services and health care services, especially for vulnerable family members such as the elderly and disabled.
9. The FHHs emphasized their need to be given free housing and accommodation or at least housing benefit.
10. The FHHs complained about the complicated procedures when applying for social support, often involving other official processes such as the courts. They requested help desks or offices in the SSD to help them complete their applications.

Goal four: (recommendations for social policy) - guidelines for formulating effective social policies for combating poverty among women and poor FHHs in Saudi society.

Important recommendations have been made based on this research towards improving and formulating effective social policies for the eradication of poverty among FHHs. These recommendations cover three main sets of issues, as follows:

6- Strategic recommendations: these focus on the macro-level of poverty and FHH issues. At this level there needs to be a coherent strategy to deal with poverty. These recommendations have taken into account the lack of precise data and information on poverty and the necessity for there to be a strong link between the state's projects and policies for poverty eradications as well as the importance of establishing supportive policies such as a 'national family policy', and a 'poverty information policy'. These strategic recommendations are addressed to decision-makers, and to national and local authorities that could influence decision-makers to apply the recommendations.

7- General recommendations relevant to the daily needs that were clear from the interviews with the female heads and through the researcher's observations of the social environment of Saudi society. These general needs concern housing, health care, income, education and work.

8- Specialized recommendations: relevant to the specific needs of each sub-group according to what was raised during the in-depth interviews about their problems and needs.

8.3. Implications for policy

As mentioned in goal 4, the research has produced important recommendations for formulating and implementing effective policies for the eradication of poverty among FHHs.

At the strategic level: there should be plans to set goals, timetables and an evaluation in place in the light of the findings.

At the public level: integrated policies are needed to improve the quality of life of FHHs by developing and improving provisions in housing, health care, income and work, and addressing the needs of vulnerable categories such as the elderly, children and the disabled.

Specialized recommendations: the problems and needs of each category of FHHs should be dealt with according to their special circumstances. The sub-categories of FHHs are the same as within the sample group: widows' families, divorced women's families, abandoned women's families, prisoners' wives' families and married women's families, also taking into account young people's issues.

8.4. Recommendations for further study

This research has been an exploratory study of female poverty through an enquiry among FHHs in Jeddah City and the implications of their relationship with social policies and the social support institutions. The research has highlighted many issues relevant to women, poverty and the welfare systems, plus the paucity of research on these important issues. Recommendations for future studies follow, based on what seems most important in Saudi society regarding women and poverty issues.

Poverty in general

- More research is needed on poverty in Saudi society in order to identify a satisfactory conceptual framework including a poverty definition, poverty types, a poverty line and poverty measurements suitable for Saudi society. There also needs to be more knowledge about pockets of poverty - the numbers and the distribution of poor people in the Saudi provinces, cities and towns, as well as the reasons for poverty in each type of place.

- More detailed studies of the various categories of poor in Saudi society are needed. This research studied FHHs yet there are other poor categories in which the problems are not necessarily the same. The study of poor categories will lead to more understanding of their situations and to strategies that are more effective for eradicating their poverty.

- More concern should be given to the issue of social exclusion and the groups in Saudi society who are marginalized because of their race, ethnicity or gender. As yet, little is known about them.

- More concern should be given to studying categories of migrants, especially those from the southern part of country, for example Jazan. Those people make up a significant and noticeable category of beneficiaries of the SSD and the Charitable Women's Associations, and we need to know more about why they left their home areas and why they have to rely on SSD income support. In other words, do they reflect a culture of poverty?

Women and poverty or female poverty

- There need to be deeper analytical studies of the status of poor FHHs to examine each category in terms of their problems, needs and the most suitable framework to adopt to deal with their poverty.

- The feminine aspect of poverty needs more analysis to investigate the relationships between social and cultural values, legislation and the social conditions of poor females in order to discover if there has been a feminization of poverty in Saudi society.

- The concept of the 'feminization of poverty' needs a comparative study that could produce a framework applicable to both FHHs and MHHs in Saudi society.

- There need to be further studies of the justice system and gender in Saudi society, especially in the case of labour and naturalization laws.

- There needs to be further analysis and comparative studies on race, immigration and ethnicity, and their relationship to poverty and social exclusion in general and female poverty and exclusion in particular.

Social policy and the welfare system

- There is a need for more in-depth studies of the relationship between women and the social welfare system, in particular the SSD.

- Policy analysis of SSD regulations could be the first step towards reform of the social support system; especially the SSD's income allocation system that takes into account a basic standard of living and a national poverty line.

- There need to be evaluation studies of current social policies and the welfare system in terms of regulations, programmes and services.

- More studies should be conducted to investigate housing projects and how these projects can fulfil the requirements of those in need of assistance, as well as how they can be made available in the short-term in cases of urgent need.

- More studies should be conducted on the role of waqif (endowment) in the eradication of poverty, especially in the case of offering free houses and accommodation for the poor and, in particular, poor FHHs.

- More studies should be conducted on integrated social policies and how they can be used to support development and increase women's public participation.

- Evaluation studies need to be conducted on the NPRS and other poverty projects and their role in reducing poverty in general and female poverty in particular.

- There need to be more studies on the poverty of vulnerable categories such as the elderly, children, disabled people and young people.

BIBLIOGRAPHY

Abdul-Gafaar, A. (2007) Poverty: definition, indicators and measurement methods in GCC countries (A case study of Bahrain). In Forum on the Millennium Development Goals (MDG) and their implementation in social policies, *13–15 May 2007*, Riyadh, Ministry of Social Affairs (In Arabic).

Abdul-Kaleg, G. (2007) Macro-economic Policies for Poverty Reduction and achieving the MDG in Syria, *Poverty, Institutions and Development in the Arab World: The Eighth Annual Conference of the Arab Society for Economic Research (ASFER)*, ASFER, Cairo (In Arabic).

Ab-Lyail, M. & Sultan-Ulma, M. (2004) State Authority to Impose Social Security Taxes and its Role in Poverty Reduction, *Conference on the Problem of Poverty in the Islamic World,* International Institution for Muslim Unity (IIMU), Malaysia (In Arabic).

Abramovitz, M. (2006) 'Welfare Reform in the United States: gender, race, and class matter', *Critical Social Policy*, 26. 2, pp. 336-364.

Abu-Shikah, A. M. (1990) *Women's Liberation in the Era of the Prophet*, Dar al-Kalam, Cairo (In Arabic).

Abu-Yarab, A. (2004) Causes of Economic Underdevelopment of Muslims according to Ibn Khaldun, *Conference on the Problem of Poverty in the Islamic World,* International Institution for Muslim Unity (IIMU), Malaysia (In Arabic).

AGFUND (2006) *Arab Gulf Programme for United Nations Development* [Online], AGFUND, Available from: http://www.agfund.org/. (Accessed: 12 January 2007).

Ahmad, Z. (1991) *Islam, Poverty and Income Distribution*, The Islamic Foundation, Leicester.

Ahmed, L. (1992) *Women and Gender in Islam: Historical Roots of a Modern Debate*, Yale University Press, New Haven.

Akinsola, H.A. & Popovich, J.M. (2002) 'The Quality of Life of Families of Female-Headed Households in Botswana: A Secondary Analysis of Case Studies' *Health Care for Women International*, 23, pp. 761-772.

Al-Bir Welfare Society (BWS) Records (2007), Jeddah (unpublished).

Al-Bir Welfare Society (BWS) Records (2008), Jeddah (unpublished).

Al-Daruti, A. (2004) Social and Cultural Dimensions of Poverty in the Islamic World, *Conference on the Problem of Poverty in the Islamic World,* International Institution for Muslim Unity (IIMU), Malaysia, (In Arabic).

Alfaris, A. (2003) *Poverty and Income Distribution in the Arab World*, Beirut, Centre for Arab Unity Studies (In Arabic).

Al-Fasylaya Women's Welfare Society (FWWS) Records (2007), Jeddah (unpublished).

Al-Fasylaya Women's Welfare Society (FWWS) Records (2008), Jeddah (unpublished).

Algarib, A.A. (2005) Poverty in Saudi Arabia: reading in the adopted procedures, *Arab Future Journal*, 311, January, pp. 40–62.

Al-Gyzani, K. (2007) *Proposal for Poverty Reduction in the light of the Orientations of Islamic Education*, PhD Thesis, Um al-Qura University, Saudi Arabia (In Arabic).

Alhabshi, S.O. (n.d.) Poverty Eradication from Islamic Perspectives, [Online]. Available from: http://elib.unitar.edu.my/staff-publications/datuk/JOURNAL.pdf. (Accessed: 12 September 2009)

Alhemish, M. (2007) 'The Impact of Recessional Fiscal Policy on Poverty levels in Syria', *Poverty, Institutions and Development in the Arab World: The Eighth Annual Conference of the Arab Society for Economic Research (ASFER)*, ASFER, Cairo (In Arabic).

Al-Hibri, A. (1982) 'A study of Islamic herstory: or how did we ever get into this mess?: To the memory of my mother, Yusra Midani, who was an active, independent, and capable Muslim woman', *Women's Studies International Forum,* 5, pp. 207-219.

Ali, K. (2008) Marriage in Classical Islamic Jurisprudence: A Survey of Doctrines, in Quraishi, A. & Vogel, F. (eds), *The Islamic Marriage Contract: Case Studies in Islamic Family Law,* Harvard University Press, Cambridge, MA, pp. 11–45.

Ali, M.M. (2004) The Role of Productive Education in Poverty Elimination in Islamic World, *Conference on the Problem of Poverty in the Islamic World,* International Institution for Muslim Unity (IIMU), Malaysia (In Arabic).

Al-Kalili, A. (2004) The Political Dimension of Poverty in the Islamic World, *Conference on the Problem of Poverty in the Islamic World,* International Institution for Muslim Unity (IIMU), Malaysia (In Arabic).

Al-Najaar, A.-M. (2004) The Dogmatic Dimension of Poverty in the Islamic World, *Conference on the Problem of Poverty in the Islamic World,* International Institution for Muslim Unity (IIMU), Malaysia (In Arabic).

Alneim, A. (2004) *Urban poverty and its association with internal migration*, PhD Thesis, King Saud University, Saudi Arabia (In Arabic).

Al-Omir, A. S. (2004) The Ethical Dimension of Poverty in the Islamic World, *Conference on the Problem of Poverty in the Islamic World,* International Institution for Muslim Unity (IIMU), Malaysia (In Arabic).

Al-Rabie, I. (2004) Causes of Poverty in the Islamic World Today, *Conference on the Problem of Poverty in the Islamic World,* International Institution for Muslim Unity (IIMU), Malaysia (In Arabic).

Al-Refaie, H. (2004) The Economic Dimension of Poverty and its solutions in the Islamic World, *Conference on the Problem of Poverty in the Islamic World,* International Institution for Muslim Unity (IIMU), Malaysia (In Arabic).

Al-Shubiki, A. (2005) *Poverty line estimated for social benefits recipients under social security system in Riyadh City*, PhD Thesis, King Saud University, Saudi Arabia.

Al-Shubiki, A. (n.d) *Social problems of the poor woman in Saudi society* [Online], Available from: http://www.islamonline.net/arabic/in_depth/women/articles/wordfiles/11.doc. (Accessed: 30 November 2006).

Alsreaha, S. (2007) A*voidance of Some Jobs in Saudi Society: A Social Study on Reasons of Youth Occupational Avoidance of Customer Related Market in Jeddah*, PhD Thesis, King Abdul-Aziz University, Saudi Arabia (In Arabic).

Alsreaha, S. (2001) *The Social Prestige of Jobs and The Fundamentals of Occupation Choice: Factors Leading Saudi Youth to Avoid Simple Craft Jobs: A Case Study in Jeddah'*. Masters research, King Abdul-Aziz University, Saudi Arabia (In Arabic).

Al-Turky, S. &. El-Solh, C. (Eds) (1998) *Arab Women in the Field: Studying Your Own Society*, Syracuse University Press, New York.

Assaaf, G. et al. (eds.) (2003) *Poverty and Development in Lebanon*, Lebanese Centre for Policy Studies (LCPS), Beirut.

Ath'aliby (d. *c.* 1037 CE) *Fiqh al-Lugha*, Almamoon, Jeddah (In Arabic).

Ba-Gader, A. & Alturki, S. (2006) *Jeddah: Mother of comfort and intensity*, Dar El-Shorouk, Cairo.

Ba-Gader, A. (2004) Zakah from the Perspective of Sociology: the Role of Zakah in the Poverty Eradication, *Conference on the Problem of Poverty in the Islamic World*, International Institution for Muslim Unity (IIMU), Malaysia (In Arabic).

Ba-Gader, A. (2008) *Poverty: the Social Effects, and Anti-Poverty Programmes In Gulf Cooperation Council (GCC) countries*, Council of Ministers of Labour and Social Affairs, Gulf Cooperation Council for the Arab Gulf States, Al-Manamah (In Arabic).

Barlas, A. (2006) *Does the Qu'ran Support Gender Equality? Or, do I have the autonomy to answer this question?*[Online], University of Groningen, Netherlands, Available from: http://asmabarlas.com/PAPERS/Groningen_Keynote.pdf. (Accessed: 12 September 2008).

Bashatah, F.S. (2009) *Some Social Dimensions for Woman's Imagined Roles in Saudi Society Through Al-Nawazil: An applied Study on a Sample of Fatwa From The Committee of Supreme Ulama in Saudi Arabia*, PhD Thesis, King Abdul-Aziz University, Saudi Arabia (In Arabic).

Berthoud, R. (2004) *Patterns of poverty across Europe*, Policy Press, University of Bristol, Bristol.

Bill, J.A. (1972) 'Class Analysis and the Dialectics of Modernization in the Middle East', *International Journal of Middle East Studies*, 3, pp. 417-434.

Bonner, M. (2003) Poverty and Charity in the Rise of Islam in Bonner, M., Ener, M. & Singer, A. (eds), *Poverty and Charity in Middle Eastern Contexts*, State University of New York Press, Albany, pp. 13-30.

Bonner, M., Ener, M. & Singer, A. (eds) (2003) *Poverty and Charity in Middle Eastern Contexts*, State University of New York Press, Albany.

Booth, C. (1902) *Life and Labour of the People in London, First series: Poverty, vol 1*, Macmillan, London.

Brady, D. & Kall, D. (2008) 'Nearly universal, but somewhat distinct: the feminization of poverty in affluent western democracies, 1969-2000', *Social Science Research*, 37, pp. 976-1007.

British Sociological Association (2006) *Statement of Ethical Practice,* [Online], [Online], British Sociological Association, Available from: http://www.visualsociology.org.uk/BSA_VS_ethical_statement.pdf (Accessed: 10 November 2008).

Brown, U., Scott, G., Mooney, G., & Duncan, B. (eds) (2002) *Poverty in Scotland 2002: People, Places and Policies*, CPAG/Scottish Poverty Information Unit, London/Glasgow.

Bisharah, A. (2007) *The Rentier State and the Disabled Democracy*, Centre for Arab Unity Studies, Beirut.

Child Poverty Action Group (CPAG) (2011), *Welfare Benefits and Tax Credits Handbook*, CPAG, London.

Cohen, M. (1994) 'Impact of poverty on women's health', *Canadian Family Physician*, 40, pp. 949-58.

Combat Poverty Agency & Equality Authority (2003) *Poverty and Inequality: Applying an Equality Dimensions to Poverty Proofing* [Online], Bridgewater Centre, Dublin, Available from: http://www.cpa.ie/publications/PovertyAndInequality_2003.pdf (Accessed 2 January 2006).

Corden, A., Hirst, M. & Nice, K. (2008) *'Financial Implications of Death of a Partner'*, Research Works, 2009-1

Coudouel, A., Hentschel, J.S. & Wodon, Q.T. (2002) *Poverty Measurement and Analysis*, in PRSP Sourcebook, World Bank, Washington D.C [Online]. Available from: http://siteresources.worldbank.org/INTPRS1/Resources/383606-1205334112622/5467_chap1.pdf (Accessed: 12 September 2007).

Cramer, J. (1974) 'Births, Expected Family Size and Poverty' in Morgan, J.N., Dickinson, K., Dickinson, J., Benus, J.M., & Duncan, G. (eds), *Five Thousand American Families: Pattern of Economic Progress*, vol. (7), University of Michigan, Institute for Social Research, Ann Arbor, pp. 279-318.

Davies, L, McMullin, J.A., Avison, W.R., & Cassidy, G.L. (2001) *Social policy, gender inequality and poverty,* [Online], Canadian Cataloguing in Publication Data, Available from: http://www.swc-fc.gc.ca/pubs/pubspr/0662653327/200102_0662653327_e.pdf (Accessed: 10 March 2008).

Devaus, D.A. (2001) *Research Design in Social Research*, SAGE, London,.

Dressel, P.L. (1988)'Gender, race, and class: beyond the feminization of poverty in later life', *Gerontologist*, 28, pp. 177-80.

Duncan, S. & Edwards, R. (1997) *Single Mothers in an International Context*, UCU Press, London.

Esping-Andersen, G. (1990) *The Three of Worlds of Welfare Capitalism*, Polity Press, Cambridge.

European Commission (2006a) *Joint report on social protection and social inclusion*, Office for Official Publications of the European Communities, Luxembourg.

European Commission (2006b) *Gender inequalities in the risks of poverty and social exclusion for disadvantaged groups in thirty European countries*, Office for Official Publications of the European Communities, Luxembourg.

Exley, S. (2008) Interviewing Elites (Lecture), *ESRC PhD Summer School on Evidence and Policy 7th-11th July 2008*, King's College, London (unpublished).

Feuerstein, M. T. (1997) 'The poverty factor: a special problem for women', *Planned Parenthood Challenges*, (1-2), pp. 3-9.

First Welfare Society (KWS) Records (2007), Jeddah (unpublished).

First Welfare Society (KWS) Records (2008), Jeddah (unpublished).

Frankfort-Nachmias, C. & Nachmias, D. (1992) *Research Methods in the Social Sciences*, Edward Arnold, London.

Fukuda-Parr, S. (1999) 'What does feminization of poverty mean? It isn't just a lack of income', *Feminist Economics*, 5. 2, pp. 99-103.

Fuwa, N. (2000) 'The Poverty and Heterogeneity Among Female-Headed Households Revisited: The Case of Panama', *World Development*, 28, pp. 1515-1542.

Galeb, J. & Maimari, R. (2003) Micro Finance Projects in Lebanon, in Assaf, G. *et al.*, (eds) *Poverty and Social Development in Lebanon*, Lebanese Centre for Policy Studies (LCPS), Beirut.

General Organization for Social Insurance (GOSI) (2000), Social Insurance Law [Online], Available from: http://www.gosi.com.sa/_SocialInsurance.php, (Accessed: 19 May 2009).

Gimenez, M.E. (1989) 'The feminization of poverty: myth or reality?', *International Journal of Health Services*, 19, pp. 45-61.

Gonyea, J.G. (1994) 'The paradox of the advantaged elder and the feminization of poverty', *Social Work*, 39, pp. 35-41.

Gordon, D. & Townsend, P. (2000) (eds) *Breadline Europe: the Measurement of Poverty*, The Policy Press, Bristol.

Griffin, F.N. (1994) 'The health care system: factoring in the ethnicity, cultural and health care needs of women and children of color', *ABNF Journal*, 5. 5, pp.130-133.

Gubrium, J.F. & Holstein, J.A. (1998) 'Narrative Practice and the Coherence of Personal Stories', *The Sociological Quarterly*, 39, pp. 163-187.

Hamaam, M. (2004) Dialectic of Poverty and Development in the Islamic World, *Conference on the Problem of Poverty in the Islamic World*, International Institution for Muslim Unity (IIMU), Malaysia, (In Arabic).

Hamdan, K. (2003) The Phenomenon of Poverty in Lebonan: Limits; Determinants and Economic policies of the Reconstruction Era in ASSAF, G. *et. al.*, (eds) *Poverty and Social Development in Lebanon*, Lebanese Centre for Policy Studies (LCPS), Beirut.

Hossain, M. (2003) 'Review: Women's Human Rights and Islam, A Study of Three Attempts at Accommodation, Jonas Svensson', *Journal of Islamic Studies*, 14, pp. 101-103.

Hoynes, H. W. (1995) *Does Welfare Play a Role in Female Headship Decision?*, Paper no 1078-95, [Online], Institution for Research on Poverty Discussion, Available from: http://www.irp.wisc.edu/publications/dps/pdfs/dp107895.pdf (Accessed: January 2009).

HRDF, (2009) Human Resources Development Fund - The Guide Book. The Guide Book, [Online], Available from: http://www.hrs.ualberta.ca/Learning/Funding/HRDF.aspx. (Accessed: 5 April 2009).

Ibn-Mandhour (d.c. 1311 CE) *Lisan al-Arab*, Dar El Maaref, Cairo (In Arabic).

Iqbal, M. (ed.) (2002) *Islamic Economic Institutions and the Elimination of Poverty*, The Islamic Foundation, Leicester.

IRW (2008) *Definitions of Poverty* [Online], Available from: http://www.islamic-relief.com/InDepth/downloads/Islamic%20Relief%20-%20Definitions%20of%20Poverty%20-%20Jan08.pdf. (Accessed: 20 June 2007).

Islam Online (2005) *Saudi poor people and the requirement justice* [Online], Available from: http://www.islamonline.net/Arabic/economics/2005/08/article06.shtml (Accessed: 7 July 2007).

Jordan, B. (1996) *A theory of poverty and social exclusion*, Polity Press/Blackwell, Cambridge.

Karofa, A. (2004) Poverty and Means for Solution, *Conference on the Problem of Poverty in the Islamic World,* International Institution for Muslim Unity (IIMU), Malaysia, (In Arabic).

Kenworthy, L.(1999) 'Do Social-Welfare Policies Reduce Poverty? A Cross-National Assessment', *Social Forces,* 77.

Kimenyi, M.S. & Mbaku, J.M. (1995) 'Female Headship, Feminization of Poverty', *Southern Economic Journal*, 21. 1, pp. 44-52.

King Abdul-Aziz University (2006) A survey of some Female-Headed Households. Jeddah (unpublished).

Krivenko, E.Y. (2009) *Women, Islam and International Law: Within the Context of the Convention on the Elimination of All Forms of Discrimination Against Women*, Martinus Nijhoff Publishers, Leiden/Boston.

Lewis, J. (ed) (1997) *Lone Mothers in European Welfare Regimes*, Jessica Kingsley Publisher, London.

Medeiros, M. & Costa, J. (2008a) 'Is There Feminisation of poverty in Latin America?', *World Development*, 36. 1, pp. 115-127.

Medeiros, M. & Costa, J. (2008b), 'What Do We Mean by "Feminisation of Poverty?"', Number 58, at International Poverty Centre IPC, United Nations Development Programme UNDP.

Meucci, S. (1992) 'Moral Context of Welfare Mothers: A Study of US Welfare in the 1980s', *Critical Social Policy*, 12, pp. 52-74.

Mhanna, K. (2003) 'Health policy and poverty reduction' in Assaf, G. *et al.,* (eds) *Poverty and Social Development in Lebanon,* Lebanese Centre for Policy Studies (LCPS), Beirut (in Arabic).

Miles, M.B., & Huberman, M. (2004) Qualitative Data Analysis: An Expanded Sourcebook. Sage Publications: Thousand Oaks, CA.

Ministry of Awqaf & Islamic Affairs (MAIA) (1992) Zakah. *Encyclopedia of Islamic Jurisprudence,* (23), The Ministry of Awqaf and Islamic Affairs (MAIA), Kuwait, (In Arabic).

Ministry of Economy and Planning (2004) *Census of Population in KSA 2004*, MEP, Riyadh.

Ministry of Economy and Planning (2005), *The Eighth Development Plan (1425/1426–1429/1430) A.H. (2005–2009) A.D*, MEP, Riyadh.

Ministry of Economy and Planning (2007) *Population and Housing Characteristics in the Kingdom of Saudi Arabia: Demographic Survey 2007/1428 H*, MEP, Riyadh.

Ministry of Finance (2009a) *Real Estate Development Fund (REDF)*, [Online], Available from: http://www.mof.gov.sa/Arabic/Pages/realstatedevelopment.aspx (Accessed: 13 March 2009).

Ministry of Finance (2009b) *Saudi Credit Bank (SCB)* [Online], Available from: http://www.scb.gov.sa/?lang=ar-SA (Accessed: 13 March 2009).

Ministry of Social Affairs (MSA) (2003) *Ministry of Social Affairs: The System and Legislations*, MSA, Riyadh.

Ministry of Social Affairs (MSA) (2005) *Annual Statistics Book 2004/2005*, MSA, Riyadh.

Ministry of Social Affairs (MSA) (2006) *Annual Statistics Book 2005/2006*, MSA, Riyadh.

Ministry of Social Affairs (MSA) (2007) *The New Agenda of Social Security System*, MSA, Riyadh.

Ministry of Social Affairs Records (2005), Jeddah (unpublished).

Ministry of Social Affairs Records (2006), Jeddah (unpublished).

Ministry of Social Affairs Records (2007), Jeddah (unpublished).

Ministry of Social Affairs Records (2008), Jeddah (unpublished).

Minkler, M. & Stone, R. (1985) 'The feminization of poverty and older women', *Gerontologist*, 25. 4, pp. 351-357.

Mutwali, M. (2007) 'The Efficiency of the Institutional Framework of Poverty Reduction in Egypt', *Poverty, Institutions and Development in the Arab World: The Eighth Annual Conference of the Arab Society for Economic Research (ASFER)*, ASFER, Cairo (In Arabic).

Mylad, A.-G. & Abu-Gararah, D. (2004) 'Financial System as One of the Reasons for the Spread of Poverty in the Islamic World', *Conference on the Problem of Poverty in the Islamic World,* International Institution for Muslim Unity (IIMU), Malaysia, (In Arabic).

Nahass, S. (2003) 'Macro-economic Policies and Financial Crisis in Lebanon and its Impact on Poverty' in ASSAF, G. *et al.* (eds) *Poverty and Social Development in Lebanon*, Lebanese Centre for Policy Studies (LCPS), Beirut.

Nassief, F. (1997) *Women's Rights and Obligations in the Light of the Qu'ran and Sunnah,* Maktabat Dar Jeddah, Jeddah (In Arabic).

National Charity Fund (Saudi Arabia) (2008) *Report on National Charity Fund: Aims and Programs*, NCF, Riyadh (unpublished).

National Poverty Reduction Strategy (Saudi Arabia) (2008*) Report on the National Poverty Reduction Strategy: Aims and Programs*, NPRS, Riyadh.

Northrop, E.M. (1990) 'The feminization of poverty: the demographic factor and the composition of economic growth', *Journal of Economic Issues*, 24. 1, pp. 145-160.

O'Grady-LeShane, R. (1990) 'Older Women and Poverty', *Social Work*, 35. 5, pp 422-424.

Orloff, A. (2002) 'Explanation of US Welfare Reform: Power, Gender, Race and the US Policy Legacy', *Critical Social Policy*, 22. 1, pp. 96-118.

Outhwaite, W. & Turner, S.P. (eds) (2007) *Social Science Methodology*, SAGE, London.

Patton, M.Q. (2002) *Qualitative Research and Evaluation Methods*, SAGE, London.

Pearce, D. (1978) 'The Feminization of Poverty: Women, Work and Welfare', *Urban and Social Change Review*, 11, pp. 28-36.

Poverty Forum (2006) *International Forum on the Eradication of Poverty: 15-16 November 2006,* [Online], Available from: http://www.un.org/esa/socdev/poverty/PovertyForum/Documents/bg_6A.html, (Accessed: 16 January 2007).

Pressman, S. (2002) 'Explaining the Gender Poverty Gap in Developed and Transitional Economies', *Journal of Economic Issues JEI*, 36. 1, pp. 17- 40.

Pressman, S. (2003) 'Feminist Explanation for the Feminization of Poverty', *Journal of Economic Issues JEI*, 37. 2, pp. 353-361.

Punch, K.F. (2005) *Introduction to Social Research*, SAGE, London.

Quisumbing, A.R., Haddad, L. & Peña, C. (2001) 'Are women overrepresented among the poor? An analysis of poverty in 10 developing countries', *Journal of Development Economics*, 66, pp. 225-269.

Quraishi, A. & Vogel, F. (eds) (2008) *The Islamic Marriage Contract: Case Studies in Islamic Family Law*. Harvard University Press, Cambridge.

Ravallion, M. (1992) *Poverty Comparisons, A Guide to Concepts and Methods*, Living Standards Measurement Study, Working Paper 88, World Bank, Washington D.C.

Restrepo, H.E. & Rozental, M. (1994) 'The social impact of aging populations: some major issues', *Social Science & Medicine*, 39, pp. 1323-38.

Roberts, K. (2009) *Key Concepts in Sociology*, Palgrave Macmillan, New York.

Rogers, B.L. (1996) 'The implications of female household headship for food consumption and nutritional status in the Dominican Republic', *World Development*, 24, pp.113-128.

Rowntree, B. S. (1902) *Poverty: A Study of Town Life*, Macmillan, London.

Sabra, A. (2000) *Poverty and Charity in Medieval Islam: Mamluk Egypt, 1250-1517*, Cambridge University Press, Cambridge.

Sabra, A., Esim, S., Skalli, L.H. & Turkyilmaz, S. (2006) 'Poverty' in Joseph, S. (ed.) *The Encyclopedia of Women and Islamic Cultures*, Brill, Leiden.

Scottish Poverty Information Unit (2003): *Women, poverty and health, briefing sheet 18, July 2003* [Online], Available from: http://www.povertyinformation.org/fileuploads/Thu_2_pmbriefing_18.pdf. (Accessed: 20 May 2008).

Sheldon, S. (1968) 'Identity Salience and Role Performance: The Relevance of

Shorish-Shamley, Z. (n.d.) Women's Position, Role, and Rights in Islam [Online], Available from: http://www.wapha.org/islam.pdf. (Accessed: 20 September 2009).

Short, C. (2000) *Eliminating World Poverty: White Paper Presented to Parliament by Secretary of State for International Development* [Online]. Available from : http://www.dfid.gov.uk/pubs/files/whitepaper2000.pdf, (Accessed: 5 December 2006).

Singer, A. (2003) 'Charity's Legacies: A Reconsideration of Ottoman Imperial Endowment-Making' in Bonner, M., Ener, M. & Singer, A. (eds) *Poverty and Charity in Middle Eastern Contexts*, State University of New York Press, Albany.

Singer, A. (2008) *Charity in Islamic Societies*, Cambridge University Press, Cambridge.

Skalli, L. H. (2001) 'Women and Poverty in Morocco: The Many Faces of Social Exclusion, *Feminist Review*, 69, pp. 73-89.

Social Security Department (SSD) (2007), *Social Security System: New Updated Bill*, SSD, Riyadh.

Social Security Department Records (2004), Jeddah (unpublished).

Social Security Department Records (2005), Jeddah (unpublished).

Social Security Department Records (2006), Jeddah (unpublished).

Social Security Department Records (2007), Jeddah (unpublished).

Social Security Department Records (2008), Jeddah (unpublished).

Sonbol, A.E-A. (ed.) (1996) *Women, the family, and divorce laws in Islamic history*, Syracuse University Press, New York.

Spicker, P., Leguizamon, S.A. & Gordon, D. (2007) *Poverty: An International Glossary*, CROP International Studies in Poverty Research, London.

Symbolic Interaction Theory for Family Research', *Journal of Marriage and Family*, 30, pp. 558-564.

Thomas, D. (1990) 'Intra-Household Resource Allocation: An Inferential Approach', *Journal of Human Resources*, 25, pp. 635-664.

Tibi, B. (1983) 'The Renewed Role of Islam in the Political and Social development of Middle East', *Middle East Journal*, 37, pp.3-13.

Townsend, P (1979) *Poverty in the United Kingdom*, Penguin, Harmondsworth.

UN (1995) *The Copenhagen Declaration and Programme of Action: World Summit for Social Development 6-12 March 1995* [Online], United Nations Department of Publications, Available from: http://www.un-documents.net/aconf166-9.pdf. (Accessed: 6 June 2007).

UN (2005) *The millennium development goals in the Arab region 2005* [Online], United Nations, Available from: http://www.pogar.org/publications/other/escwa/mdg-arab-05e.pdf (Accessed: 20 December 2006).

UN- Department of Public Information (2006) *Forum at United Nations 15-16 November to discuss novel ways to reduce poverty* [Online], Available from: http://www.un.org/News/Press/docs//2006/dev2601.doc.htm. (Accessed: 22 January 2007).

UN-Department of Economic and Social Affairs (2006) *First United Nations decade for the eradication of poverty 1997-2006* [Online], Available from: http://www.un.org/esa/socdev/poverty/poverty.htm. (Accessed: 5 January 2007).

UNDP & MEP (2005) Kingdom of Saudi Arabia, Millennium Development Goals 1420H /2005G.

UNDP (1995), Human Development Report 1995 [Online], United Nations, Available from: http://hdr.undp.org/en/reports/global/hdr1995/ (Accessed: 22 August 2008).

UNDP (1997) *Human Development Report 1997: Human Development to Eradicate Poverty* [Online], United Nations, Available from: http://hdr.undp.org/en/reports/global/hdr1997/chapters/. (Accessed: 10 July 2008).

UNDP (2002) *Arab Human Development Report 2002: Creating Opportunities for Future Generations* [Online], United Nations, Available from: http://www.arab-hdr.org/publications/other/ahdr/ahdr2002e.pdf. (Accessed: 3 June 2007).

UNDP (2003) *Arab Human Development Report 2003: Building a Knowledge Society* [Online], United Nations, Available from: http://www.arab-hdr.org/publications/other/ahdr/ahdr2003e.pdf. (Accessed: 10 August 2007).

UNDP (2004) *Arab Human Development Report 2004: Towards Freedom in the Arab World* [Online], United Nations, Available from: http://www.arab-hdr.org/publications/other/ahdr/ahdr2004e.pdf. (Accessed: 5 October 2007).

UNDP (2005) *Arab Human Development Report 2005: Towards the Rise of Women in the Arab World* [online], United Nations, Available from: http://www.arab-hdr.org/publications/other/ahdr/ahdr2005e.pdf. (Accessed: 10 January 2008).

UNDP (2006), *Country Programme Document for Saudi Arabia 2007–2011* [Online], Available from: www.undp.org.sa/pages/Off_Doc_Agr/CPD_2007_2011.pdf. (Accessed: 16 July 2008).

UNDP (2008), *Human Development Report 2007/2008: Country Fact Sheet (Saudi Arabia)* [Online], United Nations, Available from:

http://hdrstats.undp.org/countries/country_fact_sheets/cty_fs_SAU.html (Accessed: 30 August 2008).

UNDP (2009) *Arab Human Development Report 2009: Challenges to Human Security in the Arab Countries* [online], United Nations, Available from: http://www.arab-hdr.org/publications/other/ahdr/ahdr2009e.pdf. (Accessed. 5 January 2010).

UN-ESCWA (1994) 'Poverty In the Arab World: Background Paper for the World Summit for Social Development' in ESCWA (ed.) *Poverty Eradication Series*.

UN-ESCWA (2001) *Female-Headed Households in Selected Conflict-Stricken ESCWA Areas: an Exploratory Survey for Formulating Poverty Alleviation Policies*, United Nations, New York.

UN-ESCWA (2003), *Poverty and ways of measurement in the ESCWA region*. [Online], United Nations, Available from: http://www.escwa.org.lb/information/publications/edit/upload/sdd-03-25-a.pdf. (Accessed: 14 June 2008).

Vartanian, T.P., & McNamara, J.M. (2002) 'Old women in poverty: the impact of midlife factors', *Journal of Marriage and Family*, 64. 2, pp. 532-548.

Vecchio, N. & Roy, K.C. (1998) *Poverty, Female-Headed Households, and Sustainable Economic Development*, Greenwood Press, London.

Whitehead, A. (2003) *Failing Women, Sustaining Poverty: Gender in Poverty Reduction Strategy Papers* (Report for the UK Gender and Development Network), Christian Aid.

World Bank (1990) *World Development Report 1990: Poverty*, World Bank, Washington DC.

World Bank (1996) *Poverty Assessments: A Progress Review*, World Bank, Washington DC.

World Bank Poverty Net (2007) [Online], Available from: http://www.povertynet.org/. (Accessed: 15 August 2007).

Wynn, L. (2008) 'Marriage Contracts and Women's Rights in Saudi Arabia: Mahr, Shurut, and Knowledge Distribution' in Quraishi, A. & Vogel, F. (eds) *The Islamic Marriage Contract: Case Studies in Islamic Family Law*, Harvard University Press, Cambridge.

APPENDICES

Appendix A: Plan and timetable of the stages of the field work

Appendix B: Interview questions for the female heads of households

Appendix C: Socio-cultural and demographic characteristics of FHHs (profile)

Appendix D: Interview schedule for the elite informants and decision-makers

Appendix E: Coding cases

Appendix F: List of elite informants and decision makers who were interviewed

Appendix G: List of consulted policy documents

Appendix A: Plan and timetable of the stages of the field work

stage	N	The elements and details of the field work (empirical study)	2007 12	2007 1	2	3	4	5	6	7	8	9	10	11	12	2009 1
The initial exploratory data	1	Collecting data/statistic/policies from governmental and civil bodies	*	*												
	2	Collecting and listing names of poor families who are receiving social support and benefits	*	*												
	3	Choosing and listing FHHs /classifying them into categories	*	*												
	4	Determining position and names for the individual interviews.	*	*												
	5	Exploring communities of poor families headed by women.	*	*												
	7	Collecting up-to-date local studies in the subject area	*	*												
Pilot study	1	Designing and conducting focus groups (1)				*	*									
	2	Developing the questions of the qualitative study.				*	*									
	3	Conducting in-depth interviews with 5 female headed households				*	*									
	4	Conducting individual interviews with officials, experts, academicians and decision makers.				*	*									
	5	Analysing the findings of women's interviews						*	*	*	*	*				
	6	Develop the questionnaire and interview questions for the main field work						*	*	*	*	*				
Main field study	1	Conducting the whole qualitative study (in-depth interviews with women).											*	*	*	*
	2	Completing the individual interviews (decision makers)											*	*	*	*
	3	Continuous official document analysis											*	*	*	*

Appendix B

Interview questions for female heads of households

1- Woman's experience of poverty

- How do you understand poverty (the situation that you and your family are in)?
- Are you poor? What do you miss being able to afford?
- What does it mean when you say you are poor/not poor?
- What does your current marital status mean? Would your life change if you had another marital status?
- What are the social, cultural and legal aspects and implications of poverty?
- Do you think that the social conditions and social circumstances that created your experiences (being divorced, widow, prisoner's wife or married.....and head of family) lead to a specific social attitude from society towards you and your family ? How do people regard you (employers, family, neighbours and state officials)? Are they treating you differently?
- How do poor women (widows, divorced, abandoned, prisoner's wives and those with husbands) deal with everyday life
- How do you feel and express your beliefs and behaviour within specific frames of meaning (according to your experiences): are you satisfied with your situation? Do you reveal your feelings? To whom?

2- Woman's experience with the family:

- How did you become the family's breadwinner? How do you understand this experience (responsibilities, commitments, obligations etc.)?
- Do you think there is a difference between your position as head of family compared with MHHs? Accordingly do you feel different?
- What sort of difficulties and barriers do you face (socially, culturally, economically, legally....)?
- What have you done or tried to do to deal with these difficulties?

- What type of support did / do you get? From whom?
- Do you think about working to increase the income of family? How? If not ....why ?
- Do any of the family members work? What sort of job ...? If not.....why?
- What is the main thing that has increased your suffering? What is the main thing that alleviates your problems?

3- Social policy and poor FHHs in Saudi Society

Women's experiences with welfare state organizations as represented by the social security department:
- What sort of support do you receive from the SSD?
- Is it compatible with every day requirements?
- What do you need or expect from the state in this context?

Women's experiences with the voluntary organizations represented by charities and women's associations:
- What sort of support do you receive from charities and women associations?
- Is this support compatible with your every day requirements?
- What do you need or expect from the voluntary organizations?

Appendix C

Socio–cultural and demographic characteristics of FHHs (Profile)

No. ☐

- Code of institutions: SSD / KWS / FWS/ CH
- Date of interview
- Time: from……to ……
- Place of interview
- Martial status of the family head: (AB – PR – MR- WID –DIV)
- Code of case (the file number)
- The current problem (the reason for coming to the institution)

1	Name	
2	Code	
3	Marital status	
4	Educational level	
5	Age	
	Job	
6	No. of children	
7	Gender of children	
8	Age of children	
9	Educational level of children	
10	Area of living in Jeddah (name of district)	
11	Type of house	
12	Ownership of house	
13	Does the family receive support from SSD?	
14	Does the family receive support from charities or women's associations?	
15	Contact number	
16	Note on the case: (race, ethnicity etc)	

Appendix D

Interview questions for the elite informants and decision makers

Followed general issues such as:

1- The issues of poverty in Saudi in general
2- The issues of female poverty in Saudi society: women and social support institutions - women and policy and regulations - the barriers and difficulties faced by women in general and poor women and FHHs in particular – visions for future solutions
3- FHHs and state – FHHs and religion – FHHs and culture
4- FHHs and the social welfare system: the reality and expectations.

Appendix E

Coding cases

Variables	Indicators	Code
Marital status	Widow	WID
	Divorced	DIV
	Prisoner's wife	PW
	Abandoned	AB
	Married	MR
Age categories	<40 (young age)	Y
	41- 60 (Middle age)	M
	61> (old age)	O
Institutions	Social Security Department	SSD
	Fyasalya Women's Society	FWS
	First Welfare Society (Alkyreah)	KWS
	Charitable residences	CH

Appendix F

List of elite informants and decision-makers who were interviewed

Table: 1 List of names of officials, administrators and decision- makers who were interviewed (December 2007-January 2008)

Name	Job / career position	Date of interview	Address
Ahmed A.	Public relations management information manager	27/12/2007 28/12/2007	MSA (Mecca province)
Nora A.	Manager	29/12/ 2007	OWSMR
Abduallah A	General manager	5,4,12/1/2008	SSD (Mecca province)
Fahed A.	Administrator		SSD (Mecca province)
Raeidah B.	Administrator	7/1/2008	EK
Dr. Muhamud A.	Manager	9/1/2008	JUO
Abul Mageed A.	Manager	10/1/2008	CCPF
Nesreen A.	Manager	26/12/2007	KWS
Alyaa A.	Administrator	26/12/2007	KWS
Tahany S.	Chief of Social Work dep.	Several times	KWS
Abeer A.	Chief of Social Work dep.	Several times	FWWS
Seham A.	Chief of Social Work dep.	Several times	BWS
Huda A.	Social worker	Several times	FWWS

Table 2: Informants who were interviewed during the fieldwork 17/10/2008- 30/1/2009

No	Name	Position	Place	date
1	Muhammed A.	Undersecretary of the Ministry of Social Affairs	Riyadh, Ministry of Social Affairs	1/2009
2	Saleh A.	Assistant Undersecretary of the Ministry of Social Affairs	Riyadh, Ministry of Social Affairs	1/2009
3	Dr. Abdulla Bin S. M.	General Secretary of National Poverty Reduction Strategy (NPRS) and National Charity Fund (NCF),	Riyadh, NPRS office	1/2009
4	Abduallah A.	Administrator and head of the SSD in Jeddah City	Jeddah, Social Security Department	11/2008
5	Awad A.	Undersecretary of the director of SSD in Jeddah city	Jeddah, Social Security Department	11/2008
6	Abdulrhaman A.	Social researcher in SSD	Jeddah, Social Security Department	12/2008
7	Ahmad A	Public relations management information manager, Ministry of Social Affairs, Jeddah branch	Jeddah, branch of Ministry of Social Affairs	12/2008
8	Hashim A.	Social researcher in Ministry of Social Affairs, Jeddah branch	Jeddah, branch of Ministry of Social Affairs	12/2008
9	Fwaz S.	Mayor of Bugdadyah District, Home Office, Jeddah City.	Jeddah, Dar Al-Rahmah House	1/2009
10	Ihssan T.	Ex head of Ministry of Social Affairs office, branch of Jeddah City.	Jeddah, Dar Al-Rahmah House	1/2009

11	Muhammed A.	Manager of Jeddah Urban Observatory (JUC)	Jeddah, Jeddah Urban Observatory (JUC)	11/2008
12	Lyla G.	Director of Dar Al-Ramah (charitable housing)	Jeddah, Dar Al-Rahmah House	11/2008
13	Nessreen A.	Director of First Welfare Society	Jeddah, First Welfare Society	11/2008
14	Aynaa A.	Assistant to the director of First Welfare Society	First Welfare Society	12/2008
15	Hanna A.	Head of social work department, First Welfare Society	Al Fasylaya Women's Welfare Society	12/2008
16	Houda A.	Social worker in 'First Welfare Society'	Al Fasylaya Women's Welfare Society	11/2008
17	Naeimah B.	Social worker in 'First Welfare Society'	Al Fasylaya Women's Welfare Society	1/2009
18	Dr. Mishan A.	Dean of Distance Learning, University of Taibah, Saudi Arabia,	Taibah University (Madinah City)	11/2007 1/2009

Appendix G

List of consulted policy documents

- Al Bir Welfare Society (BWS)'s records (2007). Jeddah: BWS.
- Al Fasylaya Women's Welfare Society (FWS)'s records (2007). Jeddah: FWS.
- First Welfare Society (KWS)'s records (2007). Jeddah: KWS.
- Ministry of Social Affairs records (2005). Jeddah: MSA.
- Ministry of Social Affairs records (2006). Jeddah: MSA.
- Ministry of Social Affairs records (2007). Jeddah: MSA.
- Social Security Department [SSD] records (2005). Jeddah: SSD.

- Social Security Department [SSD] records (2006).Jeddah: SSD.
- Social Security Department [SSD] records (2007). Jeddah: SSD.
- Ministry of Labour [ML] (2006), Labour Law, Riyadh: ML.
- Ministry of Economy and Planning [MEP] (2005), The Eighth Development Plan (1425/1426 - 1429/1430) A. H (2005 -2009) A.D, Riyadh: MEP.
- Ministry of Social Affairs [MSA] (2003). *Ministry of Social Affairs: the system and legislations*, Riyadh: MSA.
- Public Pension Agency [PPA] (2003), Pension System, [Online], http://www.pension.gov.sa/wps/portal. (Accessed 19/5/2009).
- Social Security Department [SSD] (2007). Social Security System: new updated Bill. Riyadh: SSD.
- General Organisation of Social Insurance [GOSI] (2000), *Social Insurance Law*, [Online]. http://www.gosi.com.sa/_SocialInsurance.php. (Access19/5/2009).
- Ministry of Social Affairs [MSA] (2007). *The New Agenda of Social Security System*. Riyadh: MSA publications.
- Ministry of Social Affairs [MSA] (2008), *The Regulations of the Social Security System*. Riyadh: MSA.
- Ministry of Social Affairs [MSA] (2008), *Guide to the Social Security department*. Riyadh: MSA.
- The National Charity Fund [NCF] (2004), *Guide to programs of individuals' rehabilitation and Productive Family Projects*, Riyadh: MSA.
- The National Charity Fund [NCF] (2008), National Charity Fund: Aims and Programs, Riyadh: NCF.

MoreBooks!
publishing

i want morebooks!

Buy your books fast and straightforward online - at one of world's fastest growing online book stores! Environmentally sound due to Print-on-Demand technologies.

Buy your books online at
www.get-morebooks.com

Kaufen Sie Ihre Bücher schnell und unkompliziert online – auf einer der am schnellsten wachsenden Buchhandelsplattformen weltweit! Dank Print-On-Demand umwelt- und ressourcenschonend produziert.

Bücher schneller online kaufen
www.morebooks.de

VDM Verlagsservicegesellschaft mbH
Heinrich-Böcking-Str. 6-8   Telefon: +49 681 3720 174   info@vdm-vsg.de
D - 66121 Saarbrücken   Telefax: +49 681 3720 1749   www.vdm-vsg.de

Printed by
Schaltungsdienst Lange o.H.G., Berlin